Teacher's Manual for
Light to the Nations
The History of Christian Civilization

Catholic Schools Textbook Project, Ventura, California

Catholic Schools Textbook Project

April 2010

Dear Catholic Educator,

Thank you for undertaking the education of the next generation of American Catholics in a century filled with both perils and promise. Christ offers our youth a challenge and a hope no other religion or philosophy permits. We, their teachers and parents, cannot allow our children to be ignorant of the origins of the Faith or of the beliefs of other cultures in an increasingly challenging world. We must know our history and teach it to our children. They must know why we are different from our neighbors in the world, and why our neighbors have developed as they have. Teaching history is teaching God's providential care for his people and his promise to the rest of the world. We must teach our children hope!

But as teachers of long experience, our editors have learned that in the matter of teaching history, there is a clear paradox: *Less is more*. Students learn better and learn more when they are taught the facts of history through the stories of the past, the legends of heroes, the tales of noble causes, and the lives of saints and holy men and women. Long lists of facts—names, dates, products, and causes—fade in the memory, but the stories remain and form the character and the understanding of a child. We encourage teachers to tell the stories, to expect the questions, and to offer a skeleton of key dates. What came before what, or after what, is more important to the learning mind than memory of the exact dates involved. All history is really a true and interesting story.

May our books bring both story and facts to life for our students, and for their teachers.

Michael Van Hecke, President
Catholic Schools Textbook Project
P.O. Box 4638
Ventura, California 93007

Introduction
How to Use This Manual

How to Use *Light to the Nations*

In *Light to the Nations*, the authors have adopted a pedagogy different from that assumed by most modern textbooks. The conviction underlying this book is that history is, first and foremost, a story—an enjoyable story, a story filled with drama. We have written this book, therefore, as if we were writing a story—in this case, a story of the origins and development of that unique historical culture that has been called *Christendom*. Our hope is that students, approaching history as a story, will learn to love history and will, thus, retain more historical knowledge than is normally the case with the more customary textbook style.

The difficulty is that the story approach to history often includes more information than a teacher might expect most students to retain. To insist that students retain every detail, every date, would be to undermine a chief purpose of the book—to make the reading history a matter of joy. We want students to approach history in a leisurely fashion, to read it as they would read a story, not a record of dry facts. Of course, one hopes that students will leave each chapter with more than the required knowledge, but this is best left to capabilities of each student. Those historical facts every student should know are listed in the section, "What Students Should Know," in this teacher's guide. Beyond these basic facts, teachers should merely see that their students retain the chief outlines of the stories they will study in the book. (A teacher, however, should encourage students to stretch themselves beyond what they assume to be their own capabilities.)

How to Use *Light to the Nations* in the Classroom

We propose that the chief occupation of classroom sessions on the book be spent in having students recite, in their own words, what they remember from their assigned reading in the book. The teacher may call on different students to recount what they have read in the text or to tell what they know about the various characters they have encountered in their reading. This will help students to solidify what they have learned and give them the opportunity to practice their language skills. The teacher may, then, patiently correct any false impressions the students may have or any inaccuracies in their presentations. Such exercises should be seen as merely educational exercises without the threat of grading.

The teacher should help students grasp the major themes of each chapter. To help with this task, we have provided in the teacher's manual a "Chapter Goals" section that details the major themes of each chapter. Each chapter in the book has, as well, an activities section to help students deepen their knowledge of the time period each chapter covers.

We also recommend that teachers use the timeline provided in the teacher's manual as a reference to help students make their own timelines for each chapter. After students have completed their own timelines, the teacher may use the timeline we have provided to help students correct and fill out the timelines they have drawn up.

Light to the Nations provides a number of maps and illustrations to enhance a student's reading of history. A teacher may continue where the book leaves off, bringing into the classroom pictures illustrative of the time period being studied or by showing educational videos. The assignment of fictional works of historical events will also help students get a feel for the time period they are studying. Recordings of period music—such as of the troubadours and minnesingers, Gregorian and Byzantine chant, Spanish and Sephardic music, compositions of the masters of the 15th–18th centuries—help create for students the "mood" of historical epochs. Learning to sing simple chants or folk songs from these time periods will, perhaps, be even more effective. This teacher's manual provides a list of suggested works of historical fiction as well as available recordings of period music.

Another Way to Use *Light to the Nations* in the Classroom

Some teachers may find it helpful to supplement the above method of using *Light to the Nations* with readings of the text in the classroom. Hearing the text read aloud can be helpful to students who are more auditory than visual in the way they take in information.

Teachers could assign readings of portions of the text to various students, or read them aloud themselves. After such a reading, the teacher could engage the students in conversation about the information found in the text or discuss with students the meaning of the ideas presented in the text. Such classroom readings should be seen as a reinforcement, not a replacement, of the reading each student does on his or her own. By reading the text aloud, students, too, can learn to pronounce unfamiliar words and, especially, foreign names and words correctly. (This teacher's manual provides a pronunciation key for foreign names and places.)

Along with the *Light to the Nations* text, we provide an audio recording on compact disc of a reading of the text. A teacher may wish to use the recording in the classroom as a supplement to, or in lieu of, having students read the text aloud in the classroom. A portion of the recording may be played (with students following along in the text), followed by a classroom discussion of the text.

Light to the Nations and Common Core Standards

The unique pedagogical style of *Light to the Nations* makes it a very effective tool to help teachers help students master the goals of the Common Core Standards Initiative in English language arts and social studies. In particular, the Initiative calls on history/social studies teachers to use "their content area expertise to help students meet the particular challenges of reading, writing, speaking, listening, and language." *Light to the Nations* is especially suited to these challenges.

In its literary and story approach to the narration of history, *Light to the Nations* helps students exercise themselves in the interpretation of narrative texts that rely more on description, literary coloring, analogy, and particular example than on a simple listing of facts. Students achieve the subtlety of mind necessary to understanding and interpreting complex texts and ideas. The wealth of detail used in the story mode of exposition gives students the opportunity to sift central ideas from more incidental facts.

Morever, since *Light to the Nations* does not rely solely on story, it gives students the experience of other literary styles that figure in the varied disciplines of knowledge. The text offers exercises that stimulate the critical sense in students. The short answer and essay form sought in student responses helps students develop the ability to express ideas in a complete and coherent fashion. Further, the story mode inspires a student's interest in the text. This interest, in turn, encourages the student to comprehend writing that may be somewhat more challenging than what he or she may be used to.

The Common Core Standards Initiative says its recommendations "are not meant to replace content standards . . . but rather to supplement them." The Common Core Standards, thus, have not dictated the *subject matter* of, or the events covered in, *Light to the Nations*. It is a text, however, well suited to the spirit and goals of the standards.

(The Catholic Schools Textbook Project is developing supplemental material to facilitate the impletation of the Common Core Standards criteria for grades 5-8. Please check the page "Teachers' Corner" at http://catholictextbookproject.com, for upcoming announcements on when these materials will be available.)

Contents of This Teacher's Manual

Scope and Sequence
Provides a general outline of the text and the contents of each chapter.

Chapter Goals
Develops the major themes for each chapter.

What Students Should Know
Presents the minimal knowledge of persons, places, events, and dates students should retain. We have provided, for the teacher's convenience, a brief review for each important fact.

Some Key Terms at a Glance
Puts in one place the various historical terms, persons, events, and vocabulary, with their definitions, highlighted in each chapter.

Chapter Checkpoint
Provides, for the teacher's convenience, the answers for each question presented in the "Chapter Checkpoint" section at the end of each chapter.

Chapter Activities
Gives suggestions for doing each activity, where necessary, plus explanations and reference material, where applicable.

Chapter Quizzes and Tests
Suggests questions for quizzes for different sections of each chapter, as well as a chapter test. Since our approach in *Light to the Nations* is literary, our quizzes and tests ask mostly short answer or short essay questions. We think it is important that students develop the ability to express their thoughts in complete sentences.

Resources for Further Reading or Investigation
This section gives suggestions for further student reading on each period covered in the text. It provides, as well, sources of recordings of period music.

Timeline
The timeline presents in a linear manner the historical events recounted in this volume. We include some events not mentioned in the book. The timeline is meant to aid teachers in helping students make their own timelines.

Pronunciation Guide
The guide helps teachers to pronounce the foreign words and names found in the text. The teacher should help students pronounce such words correctly.

Scope and Sequence

For a free electronic file of all tests and quizzes included in the teacher manual, please contact sales@CatholicTextbookProject.com.

Introduction: History's Beginnings

What Is History?
    The meaning of A.D. and B.C.
    Pre-history and history

What Is Civilization?
    The Stone Age—Paleolithic and Neolithic
    Paleolithic discoveries
    The Neolithic Revolution
    The meaning of civilization

The First Civilizations
    Mesopotamia, Nile River Valley, Indus River, and Yellow River centers
    The contributions of the Mesopotamian, Egyptian, Greek, and Roman Civilizations
    Israel

Chapter 1: A Light to the Nations

Palestine at the Time of Jesus' Birth
    Herod the Great
    Israelite divisions: Samaritans, Sadducees, and Pharisees

The Life of Jesus
    The Infancy and Hidden Life
    Political developments in Palestine
    Jesus' public life
    John the Baptist
    The teachings of Jesus
    The Passion
    The Resurrection and Ascension of Jesus

Pentecost and the Jerusalem Church
    The Twelve Apostles
    The first martyr

The Life and Journeys of St. Paul
    Saul's conversion
    The teachings of St. Paul
    The martyrdom of Sts. Peter and Paul

Jesus' Gifts to Civilization

Chapter 2: Emperors and Madmen

Augustus Caesar and the Principate
    The principate described
    Pax Romana
    Augustus, patron of the arts
    Despair of the Roman world

The Reign of the Julians
    Tiberius
    Caligula
    Claudius
    Nero
    The first imperial persecution of the Church
    The year of the four emperors

The Flavians
    Vespasian
    Titus
    Domitian

The "Good Emperors"
  Nerva
  Trajan
  Hadrian
  Jewish rebellions
  Antoninus Pius
  Marcus Aurelius
  Commodus

The Fifty Years of the Fifty Emperors
  The Severii
  The Sassanids defeat Emperor Valerian
  The division of the empire under Valerian
  Gallienus' Edict of Toleration
  Invasion, epidemics, and economic problems

The Reform of Diocletian
  Diocletian's political reforms
  Diocletian's economic reforms
  The removal of the Roman capital to the East

Chapter 3: The Blood of the Martyrs

Imperial Persecutions
  Why Christians were persecuted
  The character of the persecutions
  Blood of the martyrs, seed of the Church

The Threat of Heresy
  What is *heresy*?
  The Gnostics
  Marcion
  Montanus

Christian Theologians Fight Heresy
  Justin
  Irenaeus
  Athenagoras of Alexandria
  Tertullian of Carthage

Founding Christian Schools

Origen, Theologian and Philosopher

The Last Persecutions
  The Decian persecution
  The "Long Peace"
  The Great Persecution

The Triumph of Constantine
  Galerius' Edict of Toleration
  The Battle of Milvian Bridge
  The Edict of Milan
  The founding of New Rome (Constantinople)

Chapter 4: The Christian Empire

Christian Controversies
  The Donatist controversy
  Arianism
  The Council of Nicaea
  The trials of Athanasius

The Gothic Threat
  Visigoths and Ostrogoths
  Wulfilas and Gothic Arianism
  The Emperor Valens defeated at Adrianople
  Theodosius the Great

The Search for God in the Desert
  St. Anthony
  Hermits and cenobites
  St. Basil of Caesarea

Three Saints Who Moved the Church
  St. Ambrose of Milan
  St. Jerome
  St. Augustine of Hippo
  Pelagianism

The German Threat
  Stilicho
  Alaric and the Visigoths
  The sack of Rome
  St. Augustine's *City of God*

The Popes Defend the West
  Pope St. Leo the Great

Chapter 5: Germanic Kingdoms in the West

The Germanic World
Language and social classes
Germanic law
Germanic religion

The Visigoths in the Iberian Peninsula
The Visigoths move into Gaul
The Visigoths move into the Iberian Peninsula
The Visigoths and Iberian Roman civilization
The family of Severianus
Leovigild, Hermenegild, and Ingunthis
The Arian Visigoths become Catholic

The Vandals in North Africa
The Vandals move from Iberia to North Africa
Genseric
Vandal cruelty

The First Catholic Germanic Kingdom
The Franks
The Merovings
The conversion of Clovis
The mayors of the palace
Pepin the Younger
Charles Martel

The Kingdom of the Ostrogoths
The last emperor
Odoacer
Theodoric the Ostrogoth
Amalasuntha and Amalric

Chapter 6: Founders of Christendom—A.D. 500–700

Justinian the Great
Theodora
The *Nika* Revolt
Hagia Sophia and Byzantine art
Justinian's legal reforms
The reconquest of North Africa
War in Spain and Mesopotamia
The Italian wars

Founders of the Christian West
St. Patrick of Ireland
Boethius
St. Benedict of Nursia
Pope St. Gregory the Great
St. Augustine of Canterbury
The conflict between Gaelic and Roman Christians

Chapter 7: The Rise of Islam—A.D. 624–800

Persia Threatens Byzantium
Dissatisfaction with Byzantine rule in Syria and Egypt
Chosroes II of Persia conquers Syria and Egypt
Emperor Heraclius defeats Chosroes
The True Cross

The Arabians
Arabian caravan routes
The Bedouins
Arabian religion

The Prophet Muhammad
Muhammad's early life
The beginnings of Islam
Flight to Medina
The Koran
Jihad
Muhammad's teachings
The character of Islam

The Prophet's Successors
Abu Bakr, the first caliph
Mullahs, imams, and caliphs
Caliph Omar

Islam Expands Beyond Arabia
The conquest of Syria and Palestine
The conquest of Persia
The conquest of Egypt and North Africa

The Struggle for the Caliphate
Caliph Othman and his assassination
Caliph Ali
Ali's struggle with the Umayyad Mu'awiya
The assassination of Ali
Shiites and Sunnis

Umayyad Caliphate
The development of Islamic civilization
New Islamic conquests
The development of Islamic sea power
The conquest of Spain

The Rise of the Abbasids
The Abbasids overthrow the Umayyads
The rise of Baghdad

Chapter 8: The Defense and Building of Christendom

Emperor Leo III
Leo saves Constantinople from Muslim conquest
The iconoclastic controversy

The Muslim Conquest of Spain
Emir Tarik
Don Pelayo, the Battle of Covadonga, and the beginnings of the reconquest

Charles Martel
Sts. Willibrord and Boniface and the conversion of Germany
The Battle of Tours

Muslim Al-Andalus
The culture of Muslim Spain
The peoples of Al-Andalus

Springtime of Learning in the British Isles
Gaelic and Roman monasticism in the British Isles
St. Bede the Venerable

The Carolingian Empire of the Franks
Pepin the Short becomes king
Charles the Great (Charlemagne)
Charles the Great's wars with the Saxons
Wars with the Lombards
The Iberian invasion
Charles the Great's legal and cultural reforms
Charles the Great crowned Roman emperor

Chapter 9: The Achievements of Feudalism—A.D. 800–1008

Age of Invasions
The Vikings
Saracens and Magyars

Charlemagne's Empire is Divided
Louis the Pious
The Partition of Aachen and war
The roots of feudalism

The Emergence of Feudalism
Feudal relationships: lord and vassal
Knighthood
Chivalry
The feudal manor

Medieval Farm Life
Lords, serfs, and freemen
Farm economy
Medieval inventions
The drive to the East

The Growth of Towns
Town government
Guilds
Markets and fairs

Chapter 10: The Medieval Reformation

Abuses in the Medieval Church
Bishops and abbots as vassals of secular lords
Lay investiture
Simony
The dark age of the papacy

Monastic reforms
Cluny
The Truce of God and the Peace of God

The Cistercians
The Norbertines
The Carthusians

Rebirth of the Empire
Otto I, the Great
Defeat of the Magyars at Lech
Otto bases his power on the Church
Hroswitha and Hildegard of Bingen
Otto conquers Italy, reforms the papacy
Otto II
Otto III, emperor and reformer
Pope Sylvester II

The Investiture Conflict
Emperor Henry III
The pope's new electors—the College of Cardinals
Pope St. Gregory VII
Pope Gregory's conflict with Emperor Henry IV over investiture
The Concordat of Worms

Emperor Frederick Barbarossa
The emperor's struggles with the papacy
Emperor Henry VI

Chapter 11: The New Nations: Spain, England, and France

Beginnings of the Reconquest
The population of Al-Andalus
Alfonso III and the settling of Castile
Spanish kingdoms of Castile, León, Navarre, and Aragon
Alfonso VI and the reconquest of Toledo
The invasion of the Almoravids
El Cid Campeador

Growth of the English Monarchy
The Norman Conquest of England
The reign of William the Conqueror
King William Rufus
King Henry I
The reign of Henry II and the beginning of the House of Plantagenet
Eleanor of Aquitaine
Troubadours, trouvères, and minnesingers
St. Thomas Becket
Richard the Lion-Heart
King John Lackland
Simon de Montfort and the *Magna Carta*
King Henry III and the first parliament
King Edward I "Longshanks"

The Growth of the French Monarchy
Hugh Capet and the founding of the Capetian Dynasty
Abbot Suger and the strengthening of the French monarchs
St. Bernard of Clairvaux
King Philip II "Augustus"
King St. Louis IX

Chapter 12: The Crusades

"God Wills It!"
Conquests of the Seljuk Turks
Pope Urban II calls a crusade
The Peasants' Crusade
The First Crusade and the conquest of Jerusalem

The Crusader Kingdoms of Outremer
The character of the crusader kingdoms
Templars and Hospitallers

The Second Crusade
The weaknesses of the crusader kingdoms
The Turkish conquest of Edessa
The failure of the crusade
Saladin and the Turkish conquest of Jerusalem

The Third Crusade
Richard the Lion-Heart and Philip Augustus take up the cross
The crusaders capture Acre
Richard the Lion-Heart defeats Saladin
Richard's failure to deliver Jerusalem and his treaty with Saladin

The Failure of the Fourth Crusade
    Pope Innocent III calls for a crusade
    Crusaders and Venetians conquer Christian Zara
    Crusaders and Venetians conquer Constantinople
    The establishment of the Latin empire in Constantinople
    The Schism of 1054

The Iberian Crusade
    The Almohads conquer Muslim Spain and attack Christian Spain
    Pope Innocent III calls for a crusade against the Almohads
    Christian victory at Las Navas de Tolosa

The Albigensian Crusade
    The Albigensian heresy
    Count Raymond VI of Toulouse and the murder of Peter of Castelnau
    Pope Innocent III's deposition of Raymond and his calls for a crusade against the Albigensians
    Simon IV de Montfort and the northern French conquest of Languedoc
    The medieval Inquisition

The Last Crusades in Outremer
    The failure of the Fifth Crusade
    The Sixth Crusade and the return of Jerusalem to Christian control
    The Turkish Khwarazmians conquer Jerusalem

The Crusades of St. Louis of France
    The Seventh Crusade
    The Eighth Crusade and the death of Louis IX in Tunis
    The fall of the last Christian kingdom in Palestine

Effects of the Crusades

Chapter 13: The Great Century

The Flowering of Medieval Creativity
    Romanesque and Gothic architecture
    The rise of universities

The Age of Innocent III
    Pope Innocent's goals
    The Fourth Lateran Council

Mendicant Friars and New Orders
    St. Francis of Assisi and the Friars Minor
    St. Dominic and the Order of Preachers

Struggles on Christendom's Borders
    The Mongol invasions
    Marco Polo
    King St. Ferdinand III and the reconquest of Cordoba, Jaén, and Seville

The Achievements of Scholasticism
    Aristotelianism in the universities
    St. Bonaventure
    St. Thomas Aquinas

Chapter 14: Decline and Decay of the Middle Ages

The Wounded Authority of the Church
    The struggle between King Philip the Fair and Pope Boniface VIII
    Pope Boniface VIII insulted at Anagni
    Dante Alighieri
    The "Babylonian Captivity" of the Church
    The papal court at Avignon
    Abuses in the Church
    John Wycliffe and the English Lollards
    St. Catherine of Sienna
    The pope returns to Rome
    Geoffrey Chaucer

The Great Schism
    The election of Pope Urban VI
    French cardinals elect an antipope at Avignon
    Christendom split between two claimants to the papal throne
    The Council of Pisa and the election of a third pope
    The Council of Constance and the end of the Great Schism
    John Hus and the Hussites

Problems in the Church stemming from the Great Schism
The Black Death

The Empire and France
End of the Hohenstaufen line of emperors and the weakening of the empire
The weakening of regal authority in France
Philip V of France and the establishment of the Valois line of kings

Chapter 15: Two Centuries of Conflict

The Kingdom of Rus
The founding of Novgorod and Kiev
St. Vladimir and the conversion of the Rus
The development of Kiev "the Golden"
The Golden Horde and the conquest of Kievan Russia
Novgorod and Alexander Nevski
The rise of Moscow

The Hundred Years' War
Disputes between the kings of France and England
England's Edward III claims the throne of France
English victories at Crécy and Poitiers
The Treaty of Calais
Charles V of France
Henry IV (House of Lancaster) overthrows Richard II (Plantagenet)
Henry V and the English victory at Agincourt
The Treaty of Troyes
Joan of Arc
French victories; England's loss of its French territories
The results of the Hundred Years' War

Civil War in England
The growth of Parliament's power
The Wars of the Roses
The revolt of Duke Richard of York against King Henry VI of the House of Lancaster
The assassination of Henry VI; Edward VI (House of York) becomes king
King Richard III
Henry Tudor defeats Richard III at Bosworth Field
Henry VII and the House of Tudor

The New Muslim Threat to Christendom
The rise of the Ottoman Turks
The Ottoman conquest of Nicomedia
The Ottoman conquest of Adrianople
The Ottoman conquest of Bulgaria
The Battle of Kosovo

Chapter 16: The Birth of a New World

The Middle Ages and the Renaissance

Renaissance Humanism
Humanism and the Christian Faith
Petrarch and classicism
Anti-Christian Humanism
Niccolò Machievelli
The effects of Humanism on politics, religion, morality, and economics

Centers of the Renaissance
The Medicis and Florence
Pope Nicholas V and the Renaissance in Rome

Renaissance Artists
Leonardo da Vinci
Michelangelo di Buonarroti
Raphael Santi

The Fall of Constantinople
The Ottoman conquest of the Balkans
The union Council of Florence
The Battle of Kosovo
The siege and fall of Constantinople to Sultan Mahomet II
The siege of Belgrade

Moscow: The "Third Rome"
    The conquests of Grand Prince Ivan III, "the Great"
    Ivan as tsar, the successor to the Byzantine emperor
    Russian Orthodox theologians call Moscow the "third Rome"

Gutenberg and the Printing Press

End of the Reconquest and Beyond
    Marriage of Isabel of Castile and Fernando of Aragon
    The reconquest of Granada
    Portugal reaches India
    Columbus and the discovery of America

Chapter 17: The Protestant Reformation

The State of the Church by the 16th Century
    St. Peter's Basilica and the Jubilee Indulgence
    Abuses in the Church
    The Fifth Lateran Council

Luther's Call for Reform
    Pope Leo X grants Albert of Brandenburg part of the St. Peter's indulgence funds
    The preaching of the indulgence in Germany
    Martin Luther and the Ninety-five Theses
    Luther's debate with Eck—Luther rejects the authority of the Church
    Luther's teachings
    Pope Leo X's excommunication of Luther
    Luther condemned by the Diet of Worms
    Luther taken to the Wartburg

The Radical Reformers
    Religious radicals in Wittenberg
    Ulrich Zwingli
    Anabaptists
    John Calvin

Charles the Emperor
    Charles V's wars with King Francis I of France
    The conquests of Suleiman the Magnificent
    The sack of Rome
    Suleiman's withdrawal after the siege of Vienna
    The Diet of Augsburg and the Augsburg Confession
    The formation of the Smalkaldic League
    The Peace of Nuremberg
    The beginning of Catholic reform—the calling of the Council of Trent
    The death of Martin Luther
    The Peace of Augsburg—*cuius regio, eius religio*
    The abdication and death of Charles V

The Reformation in England
    Catherine of Aragon betrothed, then married, to Henry VIII
    Henry seeks an annulment of his marriage to Catherine
    Pope Clement VII delays his decision on the annulment
    The Cranmer annulment of Henry's marriage to Catherine; Henry's union with Anne Boleyn
    Henry's excommunication and schism
    The Oath of Supremacy
    The martyrdoms of St. John Fisher, St. Thomas More, and others
    The dissolution of the monasteries
    The character of Henry's schism
    The Protestantization of the Church of England under King Edward VI
    The reign of Queen Mary I—the English Church reunited with Rome
    Elizabeth I—the Church of England again becomes Protestant
    Pope Pius V excommunicates Elizabeth
    Persecution of Catholics in England
    The execution of Mary, Queen of Scots
    The Spanish Armada

Chapter 18: Catholic Renewal and Religious War

The Council of Trent
    The sessions of the council
    The accomplishments of the council

The Age of Catholic Renewal: The "Counter-Reformation"
    The Holy Office
    The Index of Forbidden Books
    The reform of the liturgy
    St. Charles Borromeo

St. Ignatius de Loyola and the Jesuits
    St. Ignatius's early life and conversion
    Ignatius's life from his conversion to his arrival in Paris
    Ignatius gathers his first followers
    The formation and approval of the Society of Jesus
    The work of the Society
    St. Francis Xavier
    St. Peter Canisius

The Turks halted
    The Turkish conquest of Cyprus
    Selim II's planned invasion of Italy
    Pope Pius V calls for a Holy League against the Turks
    The Battle of Lepanto

Religious War in France
    The Huguenots
    The wars between Catholic and Huguenot forces in France
    St. Bartholomew's Day Massacre
    The last Valois
    Henry de Bourbon becomes King Henry IV of France
    Henry IV returns to the Catholic Church
    The Edict of Nantes

The Rise of Cardinal Richelieu
    Richelieu's life before becoming prime minister of France
    Richelieu's views on kingly authority and the rights of the Church
    War with the Huguenots and the Peace of Alais

The Thirty Years' War
    The dispute over the crown of Bohemia
    The Defenestration of Prague
    The Bohemian Revolt
    The defeat of the Bohemians; continuing war in northern Germany and the Palatinate
    Christian IV of Denmark's invasion of Germany
    Wallenstein's defeat of Mansfeld; Tilly's defeat of King Christian IV
    The Edict of Restitution
    King Gustavus II Adolphus of Sweden's invasion of Germany
    Swedish victories
    The death of Gustavus Adolphus at Lützen
    The imperial victory at Nördlingen
    Richelieu and France enter the war on the side of the Protestants
    The French war against Spain
    The Peace of Westphalia
    France's continuing war against Spain

Chapter 19: Europe Before the Flood

James I and the Divine Right of Kings
    The king's conflicts with Parliament
    The Puritans

King Charles I of England
    The king's conflicts with the Puritans
    The Petition of Right
    Charles dissolves Parliament
    Charles finds sources of revenue outside Parliament
    Charles and Archbishop Laud's religious reforms
    The revolt of the Scottish Covenanters
    The Short Parliament
    The Long Parliament gains further powers from the king
    The Grand Remonstrance
    The Great Rebellion
    The defeat and surrender of King Charles
    Charles I's trial and execution

The Protectorate
 Cromwell disbands the Rump and Barebone's Parliaments
 The Cromwell dictatorship
 Puritan laws
 Cromwell's destruction of Ireland
 The death of Cromwell
 The recall of the Long Parliament

The Restoration
 Parliament invites Charles II to return to England
 The coronation of Charles II as king of England and Ireland
 The conversion of James Stuart to the Catholic Church
 Charles II's struggles with Parliament
 The Declaration of Indulgence and the Test Act
 The Exclusion Act and the formation of the Whigs and Tories
 Charles II's conversion and death

The "Glorious Revolution"
 James II becomes king of England
 James II appoints Catholics as commanding military officers and grants religious freedom to Catholics and dissenters
 The birth of James's Catholic son, James Francis Edward Stuart
 The "Glorious Revolution" drives James II from England
 Parliament declares William of Orange and Mary Stuart king and queen
 The Declaration of Rights
 Early Jacobite revolts

The United Kingdom of Great Britain
 Queen Anne and the Articles of Union
 The growth of Parliament's powers under the Hanoverians: George I and George II
 British colonies in North America

The Age of the Sun King
 Louis XIV becomes king of France
 Cardinal Mazarin
 Louis XIV decides to rule France without a prime minister
 Bossuet and the French theory of the Divine Right of Kings
 Louis establishes an autocracy in France
 The arts in the age of Louis XIV; Versailles
 The founding of Louisiana

Louis XIV's Wars
 Louis XIV increases and reorganizes the French army
 The war to gain the Spanish Netherlands
 The war with Holland, the empire, Spain, and several German states
 The war of the League of Augsburg
 The war of the Spanish Succession
 The Peace of Utrecht—the Bourbons established in Spain
 The effects of Louis XIV's reign on French society

Aftermath of Louis XIV's reign
 The reign of Louis XV
 The War of the Polish Succession
 The worsening of social problems in France

Introduction: History's Beginnings

Chapter Overview

- History is the story of God's dealings with humanity. It tells the tale of God's gift giving to fallen mankind and of mankind's response.

- God speaks truth to mankind through the order, beauty, and grandeur of creation, but he also speaks to mankind in extraordinary ways. God gave his word and law through Moses and the prophets, but he spoke in a final and most wonderful way through the coming of Jesus Christ.

- The Incarnation of Jesus Christ was humanity's greatest moment of grace-filled change. It changed history and it changed humanity.

- The Incarnation measures all events that came after it and before it. The years before the birth of Jesus are called *Before Christ*, B.C. The years after the birth of Jesus are called *Anno Domini*, A.D., or "in the Year of the Lord."

- History is concerned with what men and women in different times and places have written about themselves and their societies. Without the written word, there is no history.

- Whatever happened in the years before people wrote about their deeds or the things that happened to them is called prehistory.

- During the Paleolithic (Old Stone Age) period of prehistory, human beings were nomadic hunters and gatherers, but they also began making tools and discovered art. Old Stone Age humans discovered the use of fire, among other discoveries. They worshipped the forces of nature, which they called gods.

- During the Neolithic (New Stone Age) period of prehistory, human beings began to engage in agriculture and domesticated animals. Farming allowed people to settle in villages, some of which eventually became walled cities. Civilization arose from city life.

- The first civilizations grew up along four great rivers: the Tigris and Euphrates (Mesopotamia); the Nile River (Egypt); the Indus River (India); and the Yellow River (northern China).

- The center of civilization along the Mediterranean Sea passed from Egypt to Assyria and Babylon, then to the Persians, then to the Greeks (under Alexander the Great and his successors), and then to Rome.

- The great civilizations gave mankind many benefits, but none of these benefits could finally satisfy the human heart. God did not reveal himself to the great civilizations but to the humble nation of Israel. God made a covenant with the people of Israel, gave them divine laws, and spoke to them through prophets. Finally, God himself became man in Jesus Christ. Jesus' life, sacrifice, and resurrection transformed the story of human life and death.

Chapter Goals

This introductory chapter is merely meant to be that—introductory. In a few pages it covers a vast number of years. It thus does not cover any particular age before the birth of Christ in any complete or detailed way. The purpose of this chapter is as follows:

1. to aid students in orienting the ages of Christendom in the context of broader history;

2. to give them an understanding of key ideas in the discipline of history;

3. to help them understand what *civilization* is and how it differs from other manifestations of human culture;

4. to give them the *feel* for what the history of Christendom is—the culmination of the ages and the unfolding of God's plan for all of human history.

The chapter opens with a discussion of how to reckon time in terms of B.C. and A.D. The teacher should make sure that students know how to count "down" the years before Christ and how to count them "up" from Christ to our own day. It might be helpful for the teacher to explain that designating time as we do is a custom that arose among Christians in medieval Europe and is not the only way to number years. (Muslims, for instance, reckon their years from Muhammad's Hegira—our 622. Thus, the year 2000 in our reckoning is the year 1378 in Muslim reckoning.) Christians so reckoned time in honor of Christ, whom they have seen as the culmination and center of all human existence. The fact that Christ was born a few years "Before Christ" represents a misreckoning on the part of those who determined the B.C./A.D. system.

To help students understand where the Christian ages (and their own time) stand in the long roll of years, it would be helpful to have them draw out a timeline—each section a length proportional to the time period it represents. Thus, the section of the timeline representing the period from 50,000 B.C. to the birth of Christ would be far longer than the section representing the years from the birth of Christ to, say, A.D. 2010. The timeline could be placed on a wall, and as students progress through *Light to the Nations*, they can add dates and events by writing them on small pieces of paper and affixing them to the timeline.

It is very important that students understand what *history* is—a written account of what human beings have done—and how it differs from pre-history. Pre-history is not, properly speaking, history. An imaginative exercise might help students understand this. For instance, the teacher could ask the students to imagine they are archaeologists of a future time who have discovered the students' classroom or a room in their house. How would the archaeologist determine what was done in such rooms? How would he discover for what purposes the various objects he discovers were used? What could he know about what actually happened in these rooms, what sort of people lived in them, what was happening in the larger community in which they lived? How would written accounts help him in what he seeks to know?

Students should come away from the chapter with a good understanding of what a civilization is and how it differs from other forms of human culture. We sometimes use "culture" to designate the fruits of civilization—as when we speak of fine art and music as "culture" or when we call a refined person "cultured." But every human society has a culture, consisting of its arts (both practical and otherwise), its customs, its political organization, and, ultimately, its philosophy of life or religion. Uncivilized culture, indeed, is not debased culture. Much beauty and goodness can be found amongst uncivilized peoples. Civilization merely allows for a more developed culture, providing its beneficiaries with more efficient ways of working and greater leisure to pursue the higher arts and delve more deeply into such things as philosophy, science, and religious thought.

Students should become proficient at using maps. It has been said that geography is the handmaid of history—for, after all, historical events happen in *places*. And the character of these places affects the humans who act in them and what they do. A good map book or a set of wall maps should accompany the reading of this text. For instance, *Light to the Nations* provides maps of the first four civilizations but does not show them in the context of the continents in which they lay. Students should be shown where, on a world map, Mesopotamia, the Nile River, Indus River, and Yellow River valleys lay. Students, too, should become familiar with the locations of the lands, bodies of water, and nations discussed throughout the text of *Light to the Nations*.

What Students Should Know

1. **What B.C. and A.D. are and how we reckon time using these designations.**

    B.C. signifies "Before Christ," while A.D. is taken from the Latin phrase, *Anno Domini*, "in the year of the Lord." The designation B.C. refers to all the years preceding what was thought to be the date of the birth of Jesus Christ; thus, we count down from the more distant ages to the time of Christ. The year 1500 B.C., for instance, is farther back in time than 150 B.C.—whereas A.D. 1500 is closer to our time than A.D. 150.

2. **The difference between history and prehistory.**

    History is concerned with what humans have written about their times and places. Without the written word, there is no history. Prehistory is an attempt—through archaeology and paleontology—to learn how humans lived and what they did in the ages prior to written accounts or in situations where humans did not write about themselves.

3. **The meaning of *Paleolithic* and *Neolithic*.**

    These designations refer to the divisions of the Stone Age. The Paleolithic (Old Stone Age) period was the time during which human beings lived nomadically, hunting and gathering wild foods. Paleolithic peoples learned to use tools and made art. During the Neolithic (or New Stone Age) human beings formed settled habitations, villages, and cities.

4. **Paleolithic discoveries and their character**

    Neolithic discoveries were not only *technical*, but *spiritual* as well. Old Stone Age people discovered how to use fire and made weapons and tools out of wood and stone. Yet, the fact that they decorated their tools, clothes, weapons, and homes with elaborate carvings and paintings showed that ancient peoples loved beauty. That these designs often expressed religious notions shows that Old Stone Age people had a religious sense.

5. **What the Neolithic Revolution was and what it allowed for**

    The Neolithic Revolution was the discovery of agriculture and animal husbandry. Since these arts provided them a stable source of food, people did not have to live a nomadic life in search of game or wild foods. They could settle down and form villages, some of which would grow into larger towns and, then, cities. The settled life, providing a more certain supply of food, allowed populations to grow and afforded people the leisure to make new discoveries. Ultimately, agriculture allowed for the development of civilization.

6. **What culture and civilization are**

    Culture is the expression of the life of a people or a tribe. It is their "personality," if you will. Elements of culture include shared customs, a common language, technologies, and a religion.

A civilization is a culture that builds and supports cities.

7. **The four earliest civilizations**

   The four earliest civilizations were in:

   a) Mesopotamia (the valley of the Tigris and Euphrates rivers)

   b) Egypt (the Nile River Valley)

   c) the Indus River Valley

   d) the Shang, on the Yellow River in China

8. **What past civilizations contributed to Christian civilization**

   Mesopotamia and Egypt contributed to civilization such things as mathematics, astronomy, and the technology by which people could raise great buildings and cities. The *Greeks* gave the world philosophy, a rational understanding of the human and natural order. The *Romans* gave the world universal law and justice. From *Israel* civilization received a divinely revealed law and, ultimately, Jesus Christ.

Questions for Review

1. What does A.D. mean?

   A.D. means *anno Domini,* "in the year of the Lord."

   What does B.C. mean?

   B.C. means "before Christ."

   Do we call the years following the birth of Christ A.D. or B.C.?

   The years following the birth of Christ are designated A.D.

   Of the two dates 200 B.C. or 25 B.C., which one indicates a year closer to our time? Which date is farther from our time?

   Of the two dates, 25 B.C. is closer to our time, while 200 B.C. is farther from our time.

2. What is prehistory?

   Prehistory refers to the ages of the human story for which we have no written records. Prehistory differs from history, for the latter is concerned with what we can know from written records of human beings, their deeds and their works.

   Why might a historian give us a clearer understanding of the past than either an archaeologist or paleontologist?

   An historian can give us a clearer understanding of an historical period because his account is based on written records that describe what happened in that period. Because archaeologists and paleontologists study artifacts, they can only guess what happened during the period they are studying.

Some Key Terms at a Glance

Incarnation: God's taking on the nature of man in the person of Jesus of Nazareth. From the Latin *in carne,* "in the flesh."

history: the study of what people did and what happened to them, based on written records of past ages

agriculture: the cultivation of crops and domestication of herd animals for human food and use

civilization: a culture that builds and supports cities

3. **What were the important discoveries of the Paleolithic period?**

   In the Paleolithic (Old Stone Age) period, people discovered how to use fire and made stone and wood weapons and tools. They also engaged in elaborate carving and painting on their tools and weapons.

   Of the Neolithic period?

   The chief discovery of the Neolithic period was agriculture, which allowed human beings to settle in one place and build permanent villages. With the development of the art of architecture (another Neolithic discovery) and the growth in population, many of these villages grew into towns, some of which developed into cities.

4. **How did agriculture make civilization possible?**

   Agriculture made civilization possible by enabling human beings to settle in permanent habitations, such as villages. Some villages developed into towns, and some towns became cities.

   What are the benefits of civilization?

   The benefits of civilization are rule of law, the common good, justice, and improvement of life.

5. **The first civilizations arose along four great rivers. Please name these rivers and the lands through which they run.**

   The rivers are:

   a) the Tigris and Euphrates, which formed Mesopotamia

   b) the Nile River, which runs through Egypt

   c) the Indus River, which runs through western India

   d) the Yellow River, which runs through China

6. **What human problems did God answer through the gift of Jesus' life and death?**

   The gift of Jesus' life and death answered the human problems of slavery to sin and how to be free from entrapment by slavery to the laws of nature. That is, Jesus gave mankind a way to become immortal.

Ideas in Action

1. **Imagine yourself as a prehistoric man or woman. You experience various natural forces pleasant things, such as rain, snow, spring breezes, sunlight, and moonlight. You also experience unpleasant and disastrous things, such as hurricanes, earthquakes, tornadoes, bitter cold, sweltering heat, and raging fire. Write an essay or story describing how you, living in prehistoric times, would imagine the gods or spirits, based on your experience of the natural world. What would these gods or spirits look like? How would they act? (Maybe describe certain deeds you imagine them to perform.) Would they be lovable or terrible?**

   The teacher may help students to make a list of various natural phenomena, such as those mentioned in the question. Students may then consider the effects of such natural phenomena on the natural world itself or on the human world. For instance, the sun's rays help seeds germinate and bring warmth, which both humans and beasts find pleasant. The sun brings life, because, without the sun, there would be no life but only eternal cold But the sun's rays can bring discomfort, too—at times, extreme discomfort, as when they cause sunburn; or they can cause destruction, as when they desiccate plants or cause fires. If we were to imagine the sun as a person, what sort of person would it be? Would it be male or female? The ancients often thought of the sun as a "he" because they thought of "him" as an active principle—a giver rather than a receiver of warmth and life. For this reason, perhaps, in romantic languages, the word for sun is in the masculine gender, while the moon, which passively receives light, is in the feminine gender. Would the sun, if we imagine it as a person, be kindly? If so, how would we explain the fact that, at times, it brings destruction? What kinds of stories could be created to explain these different aspects of the sun's "character"?

2. **Imagine you are an archaeologist in the distant future, uncovering the remains of the society of our day. You possess no written records of the time period. Imagine uncovering the remains of the room in which you are sitting—whether it is a classroom or a room in your home. You find remnants of furniture, such as school desks or chairs, couches, and so on. Perhaps you find some religious pictures or a crucifix, and maybe there are disintegrating books. You find cups and saucers and plates; you find televisions and computers, which, of course, no longer work. What could be learned about our society from such an archaeological dig? Would future archaeologists be able to understand the uses of everything they discover? How would they know to what uses the room was given? Would they think us a very religious people? Would they think that we are great lovers of beauty?**

This exercise requires some imagination to help students step back and look at the world in which they live and evaluate it. The teacher could use the exercise as a means of helping students reflect on themselves as part of history. History is not simply what happened in the past; we are living today what will be history to people of tomorrow. How will they evaluate us? If we wish a fair and charitable evaluation of ourselves and our time, what does that teach us about how we should look at other historical periods? There are good and bad aspects to our time—and sometimes we are blind to both the good and the bad. Could this be true, too, for people in other times—did they always understand the moral or practical character of their time? Do we fully understand the moral or practical character of our own?

One of the most important habits of mind we need when studying history is the ability to place ourselves in the time period, and not simply judge it with the benefit of hindsight. Certainly we can evaluate whether what people did in other times was *objectively* good or bad, wise or foolish; but was the character of their actions was always clear to them? Are ours always clear to us? Could they always know what might result from the decisions they made any more than we can know whether what we choose to do will always turn out the way we want it to?

Sample Quiz for Pages 1–4

Please answer the following in complete sentences.

1. What do A.D. and B.C. stand for?
2. Why do we divide history into A.D. and B.C.?
3. Calculate the year for each of the following. (For instance, three years after 6 B.C. was 3 B.C.)
    a) 2,000 years after 5000 B.C.
    b) 300 years before 30 B.C.
    c) 1,900 years after 200 B.C.
    d) 150 years before A.D. 30
4. What is the name for a scientist who studies evidence of the human past (such as tools and ruins of buildings)?
5. What is prehistory?

Answer key to Sample Quiz I

Students' answers, of course, should only approximate the following.

1. A.D. stand for the Latin words *Anno Domini,* "in the year of the Lord." B.C. stands for *"before Christ."*
2. We divide history into A.D. and B.C. to indicate *that the Incarnation of Christ fundamentally changed history* and so is *the central event of history.*
3. a) 3000 B.C.
    b) 330 B.C.
    c) A.D. 1700
    d) 120 B.C.
4. A *paleontologist* is a scientist who studies evidence of the human past (such as tools and other artifacts.)
5. Prehistory is *the period of human life on Earth before the invention of writing.*

Sample Quiz for Pages 4–13

Please answer the following in complete sentences.

1. How did human life in the Neolithic period differ from what it was in the Paleolithic period?
2. What was the most important Paleolithic discovery?
3. Mesopotamia is the land between what two rivers?
4. Name one thing our civilization has received from the Egyptian and Mesopotamian civilizations. What was the chief contribution of Greece to our civilization?

Answer key to Sample Quiz I

Students' answers, of course, should only approximate the following.

1. While human beings in the Paleolithic *lived nomadically, hunting and gathering wild foods.* Neolithic people *discovered agriculture* and *formed settled habitations.*
2. *How to make fire* was perhaps the most important Paleolithic discovery.
3. Mesopotamia was the land between the *Tigris and Euphrates* rivers.
4. Mesopotamia and Egypt gave our civilization (possible answers):
    a) mathematics
    b) astronomy
    c) architecture

    Greece gave us *a rational way of understanding the world,* or *philosophy.*

For a free electronic file of all tests and quizzes included in the teacher manual, please contact sales@CatholicTextbookProject.com.

Sample Test

1. What Latin words does A.D. stand for? What do these Latin words mean? Why do we divide history by A.D. and B.C.?

2. Place the following dates in the order in which they occurred, going from the past to the present: 1935 B.C., A.D. 476, 4 B.C., 3674 B.C., A.D. 1517, A.D. 6.

3. How do both a paleontologist and an archaeologist differ from a historian?

4. Why is prehistory not the same thing as history?

5. Name three of the four earliest civilizations and along what rivers they arose.

6. Name one contribution our Christian civilization received from each of the following civilizations: Mesopotamia and Egypt; Greece; Rome; Israel.

Answer key to Sample Test

Students' answers, of course, should only approximate the following.

1. A.D. stands for *Anno Domini,* a Latin phrase meaning, *"In the year of the Lord."* We divide history between A.D. and B.C. to indicate *that the Incarnation of Christ fundamentally changed history* and so is *the central event of history.*

2. 3674 B.C.

   1935 B.C.

   4 B.C.

   A.D. 6

   A.D. 476

   A.D. 1517

3. Paleontologists and archaeologists differ from historians in that *they study such things as artifacts* to obtain evidence of the human past. A historian, however, *concentrates on the written records of the human past.*

4. Since prehistory refers to *the period of human history before the existence of written records,* it differs from history, *which relies on written records.*

5. *Possible answers*:

   a) Egypt, along the Nile River

   b) Mesopotamia, between the Tigris and Euphrates Rivers

   c) Indus civilization, along the Indus River

   d) The Yellow River civilization, along the Yellow River

6. *Possible answers*:

   a) *Egypt and Mesopotamia:* mathematics, astronomy, architecture

   b) *Greece:* philosophy, the rational understanding of the human and natural order

   c) *Rome:* universal law and justice

   d) *Israel:* the Law of God, his commandments

Chapter 1: A Light to the Nations

Chapter Overview

- Christian history begins with the birth of Jesus. His parents, Mary and Joseph, raised him in Nazareth of Galilee. This period of Jesus' life is known as the Infancy and Hidden Life.

- The second period of Jesus' life is known as the Public Life. After being baptized by John, Jesus journeyed through Galilee and Judea teaching, healing the sick, casting out demons, and bringing the message of hope and forgiveness. Jesus taught that love of God and neighbor is our proper response to God's forgiveness and love for us.

- At last, in the Passion and Death, the Jewish leaders plotted against Jesus, paying Judas Iscariot, one of the disciples, to betray him. On the Thursday before the Passover, Jesus instituted the sacrament of the Eucharist in a last supper with his disciples. That night, Jesus was arrested and brought before the Roman authority, Pontius Pilate; the Jewish leaders accused him of blasphemy of God and treason to Rome. Pilate condemned Jesus to death by crucifixion. Jesus endured this terrible torture and died on the cross.

- When the third day had dawned after his death, Jesus rose and was seen by several of his disciples and followers. His followers saw him ascend to Heaven on the fortieth day after his Resurrection.

- Jesus' followers experienced a renewal of their fervor 50 days after his death. On the feast of Pentecost, the Holy Spirit filled them with new life and zeal to carry Jesus' good news of forgiveness to all the world.

- The Twelve Apostles remained in Jerusalem after Pentecost, organizing the first community of believers in Jesus. Peter, the chief of the apostles, convinced his fellow Christians, who had all been Jewish, to admit Gentiles into the Church of the believers.

- Although he at first persecuted Jesus' followers, St. Paul was converted by a miraculous vision of the Lord and became the chief apostle and missionary to the people of the Roman world. His letters (epistles) to the churches he founded are now part of the Christian Scriptures. Paul and Peter together suffered martyrdom in Rome in the reign of the Emperor Nero.

Chapter Goals

Since *Light to the Nations* tells the story of Christian civilization, we begin with the life of Jesus Christ, who is the fount or source of that civilization. The section on the life of Christ, a reprise of the Gospels, should not be approached, at least primarily, as a devotional exercise or as theology but as an historical account of the life of Jesus. Students, thus, should come away from the study of this chapter able to recount the basic historical events of the life of Jesus. They should come to an understanding, as well, of the wider historical and cultural character of Palestine at the time of Christ. In this connection, the teacher should help students understand the Gospels as historical documents that have related to us whatever we know about the life of Jesus. For, besides being sources of theological reflection and doctrine, the Gospels are as much historical documents as, say, Julius Caesar's *Gallic Wars*.

The same may be said for our retelling of events of the early Church as found in *Acts of the Apostles* and the Epistles of St. Paul.

The teacher should help students to see the life of Jesus and the events surrounding the founding of the Church as a kind of climax or turning point in history. From very humble and unlikely beginnings came this thing we call the Church, the institution that would transform the world. Students should be led to see the wondrous fact that, arising from what the world of the time would have considered very insignificant people, the Jews, came a movement and society on account of which the world would never again be the same. The apostles were indeed unlikely protagonists of what would become a worldwide "revolutionary" movement.

Among the apostles, pride of place should be given to St. Peter, the chief of the Twelve and head of the Church, to whom was given the revelation that Gentiles were to be members of the Church along with Jews. Next and as important is St. Paul, writer of most of the New Testament books, the subject of most of the *Acts of the Apostles*, whose teachings gave Christian doctrine its basic form.

Finally, students should understand that the Christian faith is more than merely personal religion. Its effect has been, certainly, to change the hearts and minds of men and women, but it has also formed and molded whole societies and cultures. It has made our civilization, the society of Christendom.

What Students Should Know

1. **The Palestinian world into which Jesus was born**

   At the time of Jesus' birth, Palestine—Judea, Samaria, and Galilee—were under the rule of the Roman Empire. The Romans had placed these regions under the rule of King Herod. Herod, though a convert to Judaism, was a cruel and tyrannical ruler.

2. **The major Jewish religious groups of Jesus' time and their character**

   The Jewish people were divided into three religious groups—two of which could properly be called "Jewish," but one of which the Jews themselves would have seen as outside Judaism.

   a) *The Sadducees* (meaning "the Righteous"): Drawn from the Jewish aristocracy, the Sadducees were the group from whom the high priest was chosen. The Sadducees were not strict in interpreting the Law and did not believe in an afterlife. They accepted only the Torah, the first five books of the Old Testament, as inspired scripture.

   b) *The Pharisees* (meaning "the Separated"): These worked among the common Jewish people and concerned themselves with questions of practical justice. The study of the Law and the Torah was the center of their lives, though they accepted the other books of scripture as inspired. They believed in an afterlife.

   c) *The Samaritans*: These were descended from Israelites whose kingdom had been destroyed by the Assyrians five centuries before Christ. Because they worshipped God at a holy place on Mount Gerizim and not in Jerusalem, they were not accepted by the Jews. Like the Sadducees, the Samaritans accepted only the Torah as inspired scripture.

3. **The four periods of Jesus' life**

   The four periods of Jesus' life are:

   a) *The Infancy and Hidden Life:* This period extends from Jesus' birth in about 4 B.C. to his entrance into his public life, when he was around 30 years old. Though the Gospels give us some information about this period, little is known about it.

   b) *The Public Life and Ministry:* This period, covering about three years, begins with Jesus' baptism in the River Jordan and extends to his triumphal entry into Jerusalem.

   c) *The Passion:* This period begins with Jesus' entry into Jerusalem and includes the Last Supper, Judas' betrayal, Jesus' trials before the Sanhedrin and Pontius Pilate, and the crucifixion.

   d) *The Resurrection and Ascension:* This period begins with Jesus' rising from the dead on the Sunday after his crucifixion and extends 40 days to his ascension into heaven.

4. **Identify the teachings of Jesus**

   a) That we are to love God with all our heart and soul, and love our neighbor as ourselves

   b) That we are to love even our enemies

   c) That we are to forgive those who sin against us

5. **What special claims Jesus made about himself**

   a) Jesus claimed the power to forgive sins.

   b) Jesus said he came to fulfill the Law of Moses—to reveal its true meaning.

   c) Jesus said he was the Messiah whom the Jews had been awaiting.

   d) Jesus called himself the "Son of the Father," the "Son of God"—that is, he claimed to be God.

6. **The significance of Pentecost**

   On Pentecost, a Jewish holy day, the disciples were filled with the Holy Spirit and, speaking in other languages than their own, began preaching of Christ to pilgrims who had come to Jerusalem for the holy day. This was the "birthday" of the Church.

7. *Suggested:* **memorization of the names of the Twelve Apostles**

   Since it is good to cultivate the faculty of memory, a teacher may decide to have students memorize the names of the apostles. Students should know that the place of Judas Iscariot was filled by St. Matthias.

   A teacher may also want students to memorize the names of the women who accompanied Jesus and played a part in the formation of the Church, though not as apostles: Mary, the Mother of God; Mary, the mother of James and John; Mary and Martha of Bethany, the sisters of Lazarus; and Mary of Magdala (Magdalene), the first to whom the risen Jesus appeared.

8. **St. Paul and his role in the early Church**

   Paul was originally called Saul. He was a Pharisee who, in his zeal for the Law of Moses, persecuted the Christians. Saul took part in the stoning of the first martyr, the deacon, St. Stephen, and was sent by the Jewish authorities to Damascus in Syria to punish the Christians living there. En route to Damascus, Jesus appeared to him and Saul, the persecutor, became a Christian.

   Paul became a great missionary, preaching the Gospel to Jews and Gentiles throughout the eastern Mediterranean; eventually, he travelled as far as Rome and, possibly, Spain. He called himself the Apostle to the Gentiles because he saw that his main mission was directed to them. Some Christians objected to Paul's preaching, for he taught that Gentiles do not have to become Jews in order to be baptized. Paul taught that salvation was a free gift of God, given by the grace of faith and transforming the human heart by hope and charity. Faith, hope, and charity, he taught, were necessary for salvation.

Of the 21 epistles in the New Testament, 14 were written by Paul. *Note: a teacher may have students memorize these epistles, or, perhaps, the names of all the books of the New Testament.*

Paul eventually went to Rome, where he was martyred, along with St. Peter, in the persecution of the Emperor Nero. Paul's teaching gave the basic form to Church teaching, especially regarding the workings of God's Grace on the soul.

9. **St. Peter and his role in the early Church**

    St. Simon Peter was one of Jesus' twelve disciples and served as their spokesman. After Pentecost he became the chief of the Twelve Apostles. His name, Peter, means "rock," and Jesus told him, "on this rock I will build my church." To Peter it was first revealed that Gentiles could become Christians without first becoming Jews. Peter eventually went to Rome, where he was martyred in the persecution of the Emperor Nero.

10. **What Jesus' gifts to civilization were**

    Jesus and his teachings allowed the people of the Roman Empire to see God and understand his love for them as their Heavenly Father. People began to see that they were not subject to the fearful old pagan religions and that a civilization could be built upon a new goal—union in love with God. This revelation allowed civilization to follow paths of thought and invention not possible before.

Questions for Review

1. **What written evidence do we have for Jesus' life?**

    The chief written evidence we have for Jesus' life are the four Gospels: Matthew, Mark, Luke, and John.

2. **What are the four periods of Jesus' life?**

    The four periods of Jesus' life are:

    a) The Infancy and Hidden Life

    b) The Public Ministry

    c) The Passion

    d) The Resurrection

    Which period or periods do we know most about? Which period do we know least about?

    We know most about the Public Ministry, Passion, and Resurrection. We know least about the Infancy and Hidden Life.

    Why?

    We know least about the Hidden Life because very little is recorded about it in the Gospels, which focus mostly on Christ's public ministry, passion, and resurrection.

3. **What does *Eucharist* mean?**

    Eucharist means "thanksgiving" in Greek.

    Why was, and is, weekly celebration of the Eucharist so important to Christians?

    The Eucharist was, and is, the common meal of Christians where they give thanks to God for all his gifts to them and where they receive the body and blood of Christ and so achieve union with him.

4. **Why do you think the Christian faith spread so quickly?**

    Possible answers to this question:

    a) The Christian faith spread so quickly because of the zeal of the apostles and the first Christians in spreading the Faith.

    b) The Christian Faith gave hope to people. The Faith spread because the religion of the Roman world gave people little hope, sunk as it was in the worship of nature which

Some Key Terms at a Glance

testament: a contract, the covenant between God and Mankind. The covenant of God with Israel recorded in the books of the Hebrew Scriptures is called the Old Testament. The covenant with all mankind made through the sacrifice of Christ on the cross and recorded in the books of the Christian Scriptures is called the New Testament.

Passover: (Hebrew *pesach*) the Jewish ceremonial meal and feast commemorating the escape and deliverance of the Hebrew people from the bondage of Egypt

Eucharist: so named from the Greek word for "thanksgiving." The central sacrament of the Christian Faith. In the Catholic Mass, the Church gives thanks for Christ's sacrifice and redemption of sinners by repeating the words of Our Lord and the consecration of the sacred bread and wine.

Messiah: (Hebrew *Mashiach*; Greek *Christos*) the "Anointed One," a king or royal person

scripture: the sacred writings of a religion. The Hebrew Scripture is what Christians call the Old Testament. It consisted of the first five books, called the Torah, that recounted the origins and Law of the Hebrew people, as well as books of Israel's history, books of the prophets' teachings, and literature such as the poetry of the Psalms.

Pentecost: a Jewish holy day of thanksgiving for the wheat harvest. It was held 50 days after Passover (from the Greek word *pentekoste*, meaning "fiftieth.")

apostle: (from Greek *apostolos*) one sent forth, a messenger

martyr: (from Greek *martyros*, "witness") a witness, later coming to mean someone who dies rather than deny his faith

---

could not show them the mercy and love of God.

c) The Christian faith revealed to people a merciful and loving Father in heaven.

5. **What is a martyr?**

A martyr is one who is a witness. A Christian martyr is one who dies rather than deny his faith.

Who was the first martyr?

The first martyr was St. Stephen, the deacon.

6. **Where were Peter and Paul martyred?**

Peter and Paul were martyred in Rome.

Ideas in Action

1. **Attend Mass. Read the accounts of the Last Supper in the Gospels. Then discuss as a class: How is the Mass like the Last Supper? How is it different? What are the major divisions of the Mass? Why do we read Scripture from the Old Testament and the New? What is going on in the consecration? What is said and what is done? How does the Communion of the congregation repeat the early Church's thanksgiving love-feast meal?**

The Mass is like the Last Supper in that it is a meal with real food and drink. Like Jesus, the priest offers bread and wine, and speaks over them the words that Jesus used: "This is my body," "this is my blood." Like Jesus, the priest then distributes the bread (and sometimes the cup) to all those present. The Mass is different from the Last Supper in that it no longer takes place as part of a larger supper, and it occurs in a church rather than an upper room.

The major divisions of the Mass are the *Liturgy of the Word* and the *Liturgy of the Eucharist.*

In the Mass, we read from the Old and New Testaments as an act of honoring Christ offered in the Eucharist and as instruction for those gathered so they can learn of the saving acts of God both before and after the coming of Christ. The Old Testament points to Christ; the New Testament gives us the full revelation of Christ.

In the consecration, the priest repeats the words of Christ over the bread and wine, turning them into the Body and Blood of Christ. In the Roman Rite of the Mass, after each consecration (first of the bread, then the cup), the priest elevates the species (the bread or the cup) so the congregation can adore it, and then genuflects. In the extraordinary form of the Roman Rite (the "Tridentine" Mass), the priest first genuflects after the consecration, then elevates the species, and then genuflects again. The various Eastern Rites have different customs.

Communion is like the early love feast, for in a spirit of thanksgiving we partake of Christ who unites all believers in himself.

2. **Read from one of St. Paul's epistles (for instance, Ephesians or Colossians), and discuss what he is saying. Why would he say these things to an audience of the ancient world? What is he saying to people who were pagans? What is he saying to Jewish Christians?**

Suggested passages include: Romans 6; Romans 8: 14-39; Romans 12; Romans 13; I Corinthians 10: 14-33; I Corinthians 13; Galatians 5; Philemon

3. **How does the Church in our day spread the Gospel? Do we have preachers like Sts. Peter and Paul? In what ways can Christians spread the Gospel among their friends and family?**

The Church spreads the Gospel through the preaching of the Word both in and outside of Mass and through religious education. The Church, as always, sends out missionaries to other countries to witness to Christ through preaching and acts of charity. Through the media, priests, bishops, and laymen spread the Gospel. Christians may spread the Gospel by the witness of their lives and through the corporal and spiritual acts of mercy.

Sample Quiz for Pages 17–32

Please answer the following in complete sentences.

1. Which religious group or groups in Palestine at the time of Jesus accepted only the Torah as the inspired word of God?
2. Which religious group or groups in Palestine at the time of Jesus believed in an afterlife? Which group or groups did not?
3. What are the four periods of Jesus' life?
4. Give two key teachings of Jesus.
5. Why did some of the Jewish leaders accuse of Jesus of blasphemy?

Answer key to Sample Quiz I

Students' answers, of course, should only approximate the following.

1. The religious groups that accepted only the Torah were *the Sadducees* and *the Samaritans*.
2. Only *the Pharisees* believed in an afterlife. *The Sadducees* and *the Samaritans* rejected a belief in an afterlife.
3. The four periods of Jesus' life were:
   a) the Infancy and Hidden Life
   b) the Public Life and Ministry
   c) the Passion
   d) the Resurrection and Ascension
4. *Possible answers:*
   a) That we are to love God with all our heart and soul, and love our neighbor as ourselves
   b) That we are to love even our enemies
   c) That we are to forgive those who sin against us
5. Jewish leaders accused Jesus of blasphemy *because he called himself the Messiah and the Son of God the Father.*

Sample Quiz for Pages 32–42

Please answer the following in complete sentences.

1. What happened on Pentecost? Why is this day so important to the history of the Church?
2. What was St. Paul before his conversion to the Christian faith?
3. What was St. Peter's role in the early Church?
4. Besides St. Peter, give the names of two of the Twelve Apostles.

Answer key to Sample Quiz I

Students' answers, of course, should only approximate the following.

1. On Pentecost, *the disciples were filled with Holy Spirit* and, *speaking in other languages than their own, began preaching of Christ* to pilgrims who had come to Jerusalem for the holy day. Pentecost is important for the history of the Church *because it is her "birthday."*
2. Before his conversion, St. Paul was *a Pharisee and persecutor of the Christians.*
3. St. Peter was *the spokesman and chief of the Twelve Apostles.*
4. *Possible answers:*

   Andrew, James, John, Philip, Bartholemew, Thomas (Didymus), Matthew (Levi, the tax collector), James the Less (the son of Alpheus), Jude (Lebbaeus, Thaddaeus), Simon the Canaaean (the Zealot), Judas Iscariot, and Matthias.

For a free electronic file of all tests and quizzes included in the teacher manual, please contact sales@CatholicTextbookProject.com.

Sample Test

1. What great power controlled Palestine at the time of Jesus?
2. Why was King Herod called "the Great"? Why was "the Terrible" a better description of him?
3. Who were the Samaritans? What separated them from the Jewish people?
4. Name two ways the Pharisees differed from the Sadducees?
5. Name the four periods of Jesus' life.
6. From what do we get our chief information about the life of Jesus?
7. Whom did Jesus claim to be?
8. Why was Jesus important to civilization?
9. What is Pentecost? Why was the Pentecost that occurred 10 days after Jesus' ascension important for Church history?
10. What was St. Paul's role in the early Church? What was St. Peter's role?
11. How did Sts. Peter and Paul die?

Answer key to Sample Test

Students' answers, of course, should only approximate the following.

1. The power that controlled Palestine at the time of Jesus was *the Roman Empire.*
2. King Herod was the called "the Great" *because he had a long reign and outlived all his rivals.* He was more properly called "the Terrible" *because he was a murderer and a ruler who terrorized his subjects.*
3. The Samaritans were *descendants of the Israelites whose kingdom had been destroyed by the Assyrians five centuries before Christ.* They were separated from the Jewish people *because they worshipped God at a holy place on Mount Gerizim and not in Jerusalem.*

   Possible answers:

   a) Unlike the Sadducees, who were drawn from the Jewish aristocracy, the Pharisees worked among the common Jewish people.

   b) While the Sadducees accepted only the Torah as inspired scripture, the Pharisees accepted other books as well.

   c) The Pharisees believed in an afterlife, and the Sadducees did not.

5. The four periods of Jesus' life were:

   a) the Infancy and Hidden Life

   b) the Public Life and Ministry

   c) the Passion

   d) the Resurrection and Ascension

6. We get our chief information about Jesus' life *from the four Gospels: Matthew, Mark, Luke, and John.*
7. Jesus claimed to be *the Messiah and the Son of God;* that is, he claimed to be God.
8. Jesus was important to civilization *because his teachings allowed the people of the Roman world to see God and understand his love for them as their Heavenly Father.* People began to see that

9. Pentecost was *a Jewish holy day.* The Pentecost that occurred ten days after Jesus ascended into heaven was important for the Church because *it was the Church's birthday.*

10. Paul was a great missionary who taught and defended the idea *that the Gentiles did not have to become Jews in order to become Christians. Paul wrote most of the epistles found in the New Testament.*

Peter was *the spokesman for Jesus' twelve disciples.* He became *the chief of the Twelve Apostles.*

11. *Paul was beheaded* during the persecution against the Christians under Emperor Nero. *Peter was martyred by being crucified upside down* during the same persecution.

CHAPTER 2: Emperors and Madmen

Chapter Overview

- When Caesar Augustus died in A.D. 14, he left the principate, which survived to rule the empire for five centuries.

- Augustus' successors were both good and bad as rulers of an empire. Four families commanded the empire in the first two centuries after Christ—Augustus' own Julian family, the Flavians, the family of the Good Emperors, and the Severii.

- Tiberius, the second of the Julians, reigned during the last years of Jesus' life. His heir, Caligula, was assassinated by his own guards. Claudius, Tiberius' nephew, proved a wise and successful ruler. But Claudius' adoptive grandson Nero carried the empire to civil war and ordered the first official persecution of Christians in Rome.

- The Flavian emperors Vespasian and Titus worked to restore the glory of Augustus' empire. They besieged and destroyed Jerusalem in A.D. 70–71.

- The so-called Good Emperors were Nerva, Trajan, Hadrian, Antoninus Pius, and Marcus Aurelius.

- Pressure from the growing Germanic tribes on the north and the renewed threat of the Persian Empire on the east forced the Roman Empire to increase the size of its armies. Taxation, to pay for the huge armies, began to impoverish the common people who paid these taxes.

- Military commanders declared themselves emperors. Fifty emperors in 50 years brought chaos to the empire.

- In A.D. 260, the emperor Valerian led an army to defend the eastern empire against the kings of Persia. He was captured by the Persians and held for ransom.

- Diocletian, a general of the Danube legions, took command of the empire in 290 and reorganized it under four commanders.

- Diocletian moved his capital to Nicomedia in Asia Minor for the eastern empire, and Maximian moved his capital to Milan in Italy for the western empire. Old Rome became only the symbolic capital.

- Diocletian's attempts at reforming the tax system only made the financial life of the empire worse. Common workers were forbidden to leave their trade or place of birth.

Chapter Goals

The Roman Empire provided a political and legal organization that allowed all the elements that went into the creation of European civilization to survive and develop. Greece could not provide a political organization that could preserve its civilization and allow it to survive and develop. The Jewish nation was local and parochial; its law and scriptures were considered as the possessions of one people, God's Chosen People—Israel. The Christian Church saw herself as embracing all peoples; but, without the peace and order provided by the Roman Empire, Christian missionaries like St. Paul could not have so easily spread the Christian Faith. The Roman Empire provided the framework within which the Christian Faith could spread and influence (and be influenced by) Mediterranean culture.

In the period of the Roman Empire we find the real beginnings of European civilization. The Romans provided law; the Greeks provided the culture, arts, and philosophy; and the Jews (through the Christian Church) provided what would eventually be the religion of what was then considered "the world." So important was the Roman Empire that it would continue to inspire the imaginations of both Eastern and Western Europeans for centuries to come. Indeed, the Roman emperor would in centuries to come be seen as the secular leader of Christendom.

Thus, an understanding of the Roman Empire is most important for a proper appraisal of European history. No matter how many nations they were divided into, Europeans for centuries to come would continue to embrace the ideal of that one, international power and authority that was the Roman Empire. That ideal, though greatly changed, is with us to this day.

What Students Should Know

1. **Who Augustus Caesar was and what he accomplished**

   Augustus was the first Roman emperor and the founder of the Roman Empire. His uncle, Gaius Julius Caesar, had been dictator of Rome. After Julius' assassination, Octavian joined with Marc Antony and Marcus Lepidus to form the First Triumvirate to rule the Roman Republic. This government, however, did not last long. First Octavian and Antony overthrew Lepidus, and then Octavian eliminated Antony. Octavian (named Augustus by the Senate) then set up a new form of government, called the *principate*, over the Roman state

   Augustus' rule brought the Mediterranean lands a long period of peace, called the *Pax Romana*. Citizenship in the Roman state gradually extended to all the leading families outside Italy, Roman law brought a uniform legal system to all the imperial lands, and trade and manufacturing united all the corners of the empire.

2. **What the principate was**

   The principate was the remaking of the Roman government by Augustus. Called the *princeps* ("first citizen") and emperor ("supreme commander"), Augustus ruled the empire with the support and consent of the Senate. In reality, however, Augustus had sole power; the Senate merely did his bidding. Emperor and Senate ruled the empire through officials (a bureaucracy) and the army. The principate remained the basic form of the Roman government for about 270 years.

3. **Who the Julians were and what they accomplished**

   The Julians were the first ruling family of the Roman Empire. They derived their name, the "Julians," from the fact that they were "descended" from Julius Caesar; that is, Augustus, as the adopted son of Julius Caesar took on the family name, Julius, as well as Caesar. These names were passed on to Tiberius, Augustus' adopted son, and likewise to the remaining emperors of the Julian line.

   It was under the Julian emperor, Tiberius, that Jesus preached, was crucified, and rose from the dead, and the Church was founded. The Julian emperor, Claudius, added Britain to the Roman Empire and was a wise ruler. The last Julian,

Nero, however, became a cruel ruler. During his reign a great fire destroyed Rome—an event Nero blamed on the Christians. Nero became the first emperor to persecute the Church. Facing a revolt by his own Praetorian Guards, Nero committed suicide.

4. **Who the Flavians were and what they accomplished**

The Flavians were the Emperor Flavius Vespasian and his two sons, who themselves became emperors—Titus and Domitian. They reigned from A.D. 70–96. Vespasian worked to restore the old Roman virtues of frugality, self-control, and simplicity and to restore the army. Among the many public works of Vespasian was the Colosseum of Rome. Vespasian and his son, Titus, faced a Jewish rebellion in Palestine, and Titus destroyed Jerusalem and its temple in A.D. 71. Domitian tried to restore the old Roman religion and encouraged the arts and sciences. In the later years of his rule, however, he became a cruel ruler and was assassinated.

5. **Who the Good Emperors were and what they accomplished**

The Good Emperors were five emperors, reigning from A.D. 96–180, who brought the Roman Empire to its height of power, prosperity, and glory.

The Emperor Trajan restored the morale of the Roman legions and led them in conquests that brought the empire to its greatest territorial extent. Trajan was able to defend the imperial territories from the Persians and the European barbarians.

The Emperor Hadrian was a patron of architecture and the arts and a lawgiver who instituted humane laws. Though he abandoned some of the territories conquered by Trajan, Hadrian strengthened the defenses of the empire, building fortifications and walls, such as the wall separating Britain from the wild lands of what is now Scotland. Hadrian crushed the last Jewish rebellion in Palestine, led by Judah Bar Kochbar, in A.D. 132–135.

The reign of Emperor Antoninus Pius was a period of prosperity and peace. Antoninus Pius' legions pushed the Roman frontier farther into Germany and Dacia and built a wall to the north of Hadrian's wall in Britain.

The last Good Emperor, Marcus Aurelius, is known as the "Philosopher Emperor," who wrote a famous work of Stoic philosophy, called the *Meditations*. Under Marcus Aurelius, the Roman legions scored victories against the Persians (Parthia).

6. **How the empire declined after the death of Marcus Aurelius**

After the Good Emperors, the empire suffered under the reigns of generals who sought only power for themselves. Though under Septimius Severus and his sons (who reigned from 211–235), the empire continued to prosper and the legions held the borders against invaders, in the ensuing years, the empire suffered from wars waged between different generals who sought to seize the imperial throne for themselves. Between 218 and 268, fifty different men claimed the title of emperor, either at Rome or in other parts of the empire.

The empire suffered from attacks by German barbarians in the north and the Persians in the East. War and plague reduced the population, and money lost much of its value. The poor suffered from high prices and high taxes.

7. **Diocletian and his reform**

In 284, the Emperor Diocletian sought to save the empire by political and economic reforms. In this reform of the empire, Diocletian effectively ended Augustus' principate.

Diocletian divided the empire into eastern and western parts, each part ruled by an emperor, called an *Augustus*. Each Augustus had a *Caesar* as an assistant. Diocletian became Augustus of the East (and the chief Augustus in the empire), and moved his capital from Rome to Nicomedia in Asia Minor.

Diocletian increased the number of provinces in the empire from 50 to 100 so that none of them would be large enough to make serious trouble for the emperor.

Diocletian tried to ease the hardships of the poor by setting a limit above which prices and wages could not rise. But he also forbade people to change their jobs and to move from region to region. Maintaining a large army was very expensive and required high taxes. And Diocletian's taxes angered many people.

Questions for Review

1. **What is a "triumvirate"?**

   A triumvirate is the rule of three men.

   Who made up the Second Triumvirate?

   Octavian, Marc Antony, and Marcus Lepidus

2. **What was the principate?**

   The principate was the form of government established by Augustus to rule the empire. The two governing authorities in the principate were the *princeps*/emperor and the Senate.

   Who was the head of government in the principate?

   The head of government in the principate was the emperor.

3. **What was the Senate of Rome?**

   The Senate was the body of elected aristocrats or patricians who governed Rome.

   How did its role in governing the Roman state change after Augustus?

   Before Augustus, the Senate basically ruled Rome and the empire. Under Augustus, the Senate was supposed to govern the empire along with the emperor. In reality, the Senate simply did the emperor's bidding.

4. **Who were the good emperors and who were the bad?**

   This question does not require an exhaustive listing. The teacher might be content with only examples of good emperors and bad.

   Good emperors: Augustus, Tiberius, Claudius, Vespasian, Titus, Nerva, Trajan, Hadrian, Antoninus Pius, Severus, Diocletian

   Bad emperors: Caligula, Nero, Domitian, Commodus

   Why are they now thought of as "good or bad"?

   In evaluating the answers to this question, the teacher should judge whether students have supported their answers with facts from the text.

   Possible answers may include:

   a) Good emperors were those who worked for the good of the empire and not just to gain power, while bad emperors sought only to increase their own power.

   b) Good emperors brought prosperity to the empire, while bad emperors brought poverty.

   c) Good emperors extended the boundaries of the empire, while bad emperors weakened the empire's ability to defend itself.

5. **What were some of the signs that the Roman Empire was breaking apart?**

   a) civil war between generals

   b) invasions from barbarians in the north and the Persians in the east

   c) plague

   d) imperial money lost its value

   e) high taxes and prices that hurt the common people

Some Key Terms at a Glance

Senate: the body of elected aristocrats or patricians that governed Rome. After Augustus, the Senate lost its powers to the emperors.

principate: the new organization of government begun by Augustus, giving real power to the emperor or *princeps* ("first citizen")

emperor: "commander in chief," "supreme commander"; title of a commander of several legions, given by the Senate first to Augustus and then held by all his successors

Augustus: title given by the Roman Senate to Octavian, nephew of Julius Caesar and founder of the principate

legion: the name of a division of the Roman army, numbering about five thousand soldiers. Several legions would be combined into an army commanded by an *imperator* or "general."

Caesar: family name of Gaius Julius Caesar. The name was taken as a title by all succeeding emperors.

Pax Romana: the "Roman Peace," a long period of relative peace in the Mediterranean world, lasting from 27 B.C. to A.D. 180

---

6. **How did Diocletian change the government of the empire?**

   Diocletian brought an end to the principate. He divided the empire into eastern and western parts, each part ruled by an emperor, called an Augustus. Each Augustus had a "Caesar" as an assistant.

7. **Why was Diocletian unsuccessful in reforming the empire?**

   Diocletian could not ease the hardships suffered by the poor. Though he strengthened the army, life in the empire only became harder because of the taxes and other burdens he placed on the citizens to support the army.

Ideas in Action

1. **Discuss what might have been some difficulties of ruling an empire like Rome. Why was the job too big for one man?**

   Some points to consider in relation to this activity:

   a) the territorial extent of the empire and the manpower necessary to keep the peace from Britain to Palestine

   b) the immense stretch of border on the north requiring defense, as well as the eastern boundary with Persia

   c) the very diverse ethnic makeup of the empire

2. **Research these questions: Why was assassination a fear for emperors after Augustus? Which emperors were in fact assassinated?**

   This activity will require independent research outside the classroom. The teacher could assign different periods of Roman history to different students or groups of students for investigation.

3. **Compile a class timeline display of the emperors and their dates. Find any portraits of the emperors that may exist.**

   Information for this activity can be found at a library, in encyclopedias, or on the Internet.

Sample Quiz for Pages 47–56

Please answer the following in complete sentences.

1. Who was Augustus' (Octavian's) famous uncle? Was this uncle the first Roman emperor? Please explain.
2. What was the name of the government set up by Octavian, Marc Antony, and Marcus Lepidus?
3. What is the name for the government set up by Augustus over the Roman Empire? What were Augustus' titles?
4. What is the name for the long period of peace Augustus brought to the Mediterranean lands?
5. Who was the Julian emperor who added Britain to the empire?
6. Which Julian emperor blamed the burning of Rome on the Christians?
7. Which of the emperors faced the Jewish rebellion and destroyed the temple in Jerusalem in A.D. 71?

For a free electronic file of all tests and quizzes included in the teacher manual, please contact sales@CatholicTextbookProject.com.

Answer key to Sample Quiz I

Students' answers, of course, should only approximate the following.

1. Augustus' famous uncle was *Julius Caesar*. Julius Caesar was *not the first emperor*, but was *dictator of Rome*.
2. The name of the government set up by Octavian, Marc Antony, and Marcus Lepidus was *the Second Triumvirate*.
3. The name of the government set up by Augustus was *the principate*. Augustus' titles were *princeps* ("first citizen") and *emperor* ("supreme commander.")
4. The name for the long period of peace Augustus brought to the Mediterranean world was the *Pax Romana* ("Roman Peace").
5. The emperor who added Britain to the empire was *Claudius*.
6. The emperor who blamed the fire of Rome on the Christians was *Nero*.
7. The emperor who faced the Jewish rebellion was *Vespasian*. (*Students may also mention Titus, who directed the war against Jerusalem but was not yet emperor.*)

Sample Quiz for Pages 57–65

Please answer the following in complete sentences.

1. What is the name given to the emperors who brought the Roman Empire to the height of its prosperity and power?
2. Which emperor built the first wall separating Britain from what is now Scotland?
3. Which emperor is better known for his work, the *Meditations*, than for what he did as emperor?
4. Which emperor brought the Roman Empire to its greatest territorial extent?
5. Name one of the evils that afflicted the empire beginning in the mid-third century.
6. Who was the emperor who ended Augustus' principate, setting up a new form of government to rule the empire?

Answer key to Sample Quiz II

Students' answers, of course, should only approximate the following.

1. The name given to the emperors who brought the Roman Empire to the height of its prosperity and power is *the Good Emperors*.
2. *Hadrian* was the emperor who built the wall separating Britain from Scotland.
3. *Marcus Aurelius* is the emperor better known for writing the *Meditations* than for what he did as emperor.
4. *Trajan* is the emperor who brought the Roman Empire to its greatest territorial extent.

For a free electronic file of all tests and quizzes included in the teacher manual, please contact sales@CatholicTextbookProject.com.

5. *Possible Answers:*
   a) wars waged between generals seeking to seize the imperial throne for themselves
   b) attacks by German barbarians in the north
   c) attacks by the Persians in the East
   d) war
   e) plague
   f) debased currency
   g) high prices for goods
   h) high taxes
6. The emperor who ended the principate was *Diocletian*.

Sample Test

1. What role did the Senate play in Augustus Caesar's principate? Did emperor and Senate actually share power in the Roman government?
2. What role did officials in the bureaucracy play in governing the empire during Augustus' reign?
3. Name two benefits the Roman Empire brought to the Mediterranean world?
4. What was the *Pax Romana*?
5. Under what emperor was Jesus Christ crucified?
6. Why did Emperor Nero persecute the Christians?
7. Why do we call the emperors from Trajan to Marcus Aurelius the "Good Emperors"?
8. List three evils that afflicted the Roman Empire after the time of Septimius Severus and his sons.
9. Describe what Diocletian did to reform the government of the empire.

Answer key to Sample Test

Students' answers, of course, should only approximate the following.

1. In the principate, *the Senate was supposed to advise the emperor and consent to laws. It was supposed to be co-ruler of the empire. In reality,* the Senate *simply did the emperor's bidding. The emperor was the sole power in the empire.*

2. The role of the bureaucracy was *to carry on the day-to-day governance* of the empire's vast territories.

3. *Possible answers:*
   a) citizenship in the Roman state
   b) a uniform legal system for all the imperial lands
   c) economic prosperity

4. The *Pax Romana* was *the long period of peace Augustus* brought to the Mediterranean world.

5. Jesus was crucified *under Tiberius.*

6. Nero persecuted the Christians *because he needed to find a scapegoat on which to blame the Great Fire that destroyed Rome.*

7. We call these emperors the "Good Emperors" *because they brought the Roman Empire to its height of power, prosperity, and glory.*

8. *Possible answers:*
   a) wars waged between generals seeking to seize the imperial throne for themselves
   b) attacks by German barbarians in the north
   c) attacks by the Persians in the East
   d) war
   e) plague
   f) debased currency
   g) high prices for goods
   h) high taxes

9. Diocletian *divided the empire* into eastern and western halves. *Each part of the empire had its own emperor, called an "Augustus," who was assisted by a "Caesar." Diocletian increased the number of provinces from 50 to 100* so that no one of them could cause serious trouble for the emperor.

CHAPTER 3: The Blood of the Martyrs

Chapter Overview

- Roman officials saw the Christians' refusal to acknowledge the emperor as a god and pay him worship as a possible source of revolt and civil disorder.

- Domitian, the first emperor to call himself a god during his own lifetime, ordered the persecution of Christians as atheists because they refused to worship the Roman gods and the emperor.

- Local persecutions of Christians occurred under the "Good Emperors," though the Emperor Trajan issued an edict so that no one could be condemned merely for being a Christian.

- The early Church was threatened not just by persecutions, but by heresy. Early heresies were Gnosticism, Marcionism, and Montanism.

- Christian theologians rose up to defend the Faith against heretics. These theologians included St. Justin Martyr, St. Irenaeus of Lyons, St. Athenagoras of Alexandria, and Tertullian of Carthage.

- Origen of Alexandria was an early Christian who tried to explain divine revelation in light of Greek philosophy. He became one of the most famous writers of his time, read by Christians and pagans alike.

- After a period of some 40 years of peace, the Emperor Diocletian initiated the most brutal persecution of Christians to that time.

- After seeing in a dream a strange sign and hearing the words, "In this, conquer," Constantine defeated his rival in battle and became Augustus of the Western Roman Empire. He and Licinius, the Augustus of the East, issued the Edict of Milan in 313, granting religious freedom to everyone in the empire, including the Christians.

- After becoming sole ruler of the empire, Constantine established his capital at Byzantium, calling it *Nova Roma*, "New Rome."

Chapter Goals

This chapter tells the story of how the Church grew from what appeared to be an insignificant Jewish sect to became a force that shook imperial counsels and, eventually, won the endorsement of one of the greatest of the Roman emperors. It is an amazing story. Persecuted, despised, and rent by divisions within its very ranks, the Church would, in the end, conquer the very social order that had sought to destroy it. And it did not do this by arms or political power, but by the example of brave endurance of suffering and of love.

In presenting this time period to students, the teacher should try to help them to comprehend what

cution lasted until 311, when Galerius issued his own Edict of Toleration, freeing Christian prisoners, allowing Christian assemblies, and removing penalties for refusing to sacrifice to the gods. This edict marked the end of the last imperial persecution against the Church.

12. **Who Constantine was and what he accomplished**

Constantine was the son of the Caesar of the West, Constantius. In 306, Roman troops in Britain proclaimed Constantine Caesar. In 312, he marched into Italy to establish himself as Augustus of the West against Maxentius, who was in Rome. Before engaging Maxentius in battle, Constantine saw in a vision or dream a Chi Rho in the sky and Greek words, saying, "In this sign you will conquer." He ordered the symbol painted on all his troops' shields. At the Battle of the Milvian Bridge in 312, Constantine defeated Maxentius and became Augustus of the West.

In 313, with Licinius, Constantine issued the Edict of Milan, which granted freedom of religion to all groups in the empire, making special mention of Christians.

In 324, Constantine became sole ruler of the empire. Wishing to move his capital to the East, Constantine chose the city of Byzantium, on the Bosporus. There he built a new city, calling it Nova Roma. Later generations named it Constantinople.

Though he was not baptized until his death day, Constantine was a Christian catechumen. He was thus the first Christian Roman emperor.

Questions for Review

1. **The emperors persecuted the Christians to make sure there would be fewer of them, but Tertullian said, "The blood of the martyrs is the seed of the church." Why did persecution increase the number of Christians?**

   Persecution increased the number of Christians because people were impressed by the courage shown by the Christians.

2. **When and under what emperor did the first imperial persecution occur?**

   The first empire-wide persecution ordered by an emperor began under the Emperor Decius in 250.

3. **What did Gnostics teach?**

   The Gnostics taught that the material world (including the human body) is evil and a prison for the pure spirit. The spirit must be liberated from the material world by divine power.

4. **What did Montanists teach?**

   Montanists taught that Greek philosophy was useless in understanding Christian revelation. They taught that Christians had to follow a severe ascetic life. Their founder, Montanus, claimed that his teachings had the same authority as Scripture and that he was a prophet of the Holy Spirit.

5. **Why did Diocletian persecute the Christians?**

   The occasion for the persecution under Diocletian was the accusation that Christians had used a magic spell to spoil a sacrifice at which the emperor had been present. Diocletian persecuted Christians because they would not obey him and follow the imperial religion and sacrifice to the gods.

   Why is his persecution called the Great Persecution?

   The persecution is called "great" it was the most brutal persecution in the history of the Church to that time.

6. **What sign did Constantine see before going into battle?**

   Constantine saw the Chi Rho.

Some Key Terms at a Glance

heresy: a teaching that emphasizes part of the received faith and ignores or denies the rest of the received tradition; a false teaching. (From Greek *hairesis*, a "choice," a "faction.")

Marcionism: heretical sect founded by Marcion that rejected the Old Testament and most of the New. Marcion taught that the God of the Old Testament was not the God of Love revealed in the New Testament.

Gnosticism: one of the most powerful heresies in the early Church. Gnostics claimed that there is a secret knowledge (Greek *gnosis*) necessary for salvation. Most Gnostics held the material world to be evil and a prison for the soul.

Montanism: heretical sect, founded by Montanus, which held that only severe asceticism and strict adherence to the divine law would save a soul

Edict of Milan: edict of toleration of all religions in the Roman Empire promulgated by Constantine and Licinius in 313. The Edict of Milan granted legal status to Christians.

What did it stand for?

The Chi Rho represented the first two letters in the Greek word *Christos* (Xp).

Ideas in Action

1. **The 20th century, it has been said, had more Christian martyrs than any other century since the birth of Christ. Do some research to discover in what countries and when in the 20th century persecution of Christians occurred. Why were Christians persecuted in these lands? Does persecution of Christians still occur in our time? If so, where, when, and why does it happen?**

   The teacher may want to assign to individual students or groups of students the study of particular persecutions according to where they occurred. In the groups, individual students could report on different aspects of the persecution.

2. **Prepare presentations or reports on individual martyrs.**

   Sources for information on martyrs include the *Catholic Encyclopedia* (available on the Internet) and Butler's *Lives of the Saints*.

3. **Discuss whether Christians suffer persecution in our own country. If so, describe the persecution Christians suffer in our country; how does it differ from the Roman persecutions? If not, why are Christians in our country not persecuted?**

   This exercise can help students reflect on the various forms persecution can take. Does it always entail torture, imprisonment, or death? Is persecution always an activity carried out by a government? Or can individuals and families or other small groups persecute?

Sample Quiz for Pages 69–76

Please answer the following in complete sentences.

1. Give one reason why Christians were persecuted in the Roman Empire.

2. What was it about the persecuted Christians that drew more people into the Church?

3. What we do we call a teaching that emphasizes part of the received Faith and ignores or denies the rest of the received tradition?

4. What early group taught that the material world is evil and only the spirit is good?

5. What teacher said the God of the Old Testament differed from the God of the New Testament?

6. What early Christian teacher wrote the work *Adversus Haereses* ("Against Heresies")?

7. What early Christian teacher defended the Church against the pagans and heretics but himself eventually left the Church to join a heretical sect?

Answer key to Sample Quiz I

Students' answers, of course, should only approximate the following.

1. *Possible answers:*

    a) Christians refused to offer sacrifice to the emperor or the pagan gods.

    b) Some Christians refused to serve in the Roman army.

    c) Authorities feared the Christian Faith could undermine legitimate authority and the social order.

2. People were drawn by the example of *the martyrs' courage* in facing torture and death for the sake of Christ.

3. We call such a teaching a *heresy*.

4. The group that taught that the material world is evil and only the spiritual world good was *the Gnostics*.

5. The teacher who taught that the God of the Old Testament differed from the God of the New Testament was *Marcion*.

6. The Christian teacher who wrote the *Adversus Haereses* was *St. Irenaeus of Lyons*.

7. The Christian teacher who eventually joined a heretical sect was *Tertullian*.

For a free electronic file of all tests and quizzes included in the teacher manual, please contact sales@CatholicTextbookProject.com.

Sample Quiz for Pages 76–85

Please answer the following in complete sentences.

1. Who was the early Christian writer who became an authority on the philosophy of Plato and whose works were widely read by Christians and pagans alike?
2. Who was the Roman emperor who ordered an empire-wide persecution of the Christians?
3. What was the "Long Peace"?
4. What emperor brought an end to the Long Peace?
5. What emperor ended the Great Persecution?
6. In what battle did Constantine defeat Maxentius and become Augustus of the West? When was this battle fought?
7. What was the law issued by Constantine granting freedom of worship to the Christians? When was it proclaimed?
8. What was the name Constantine gave to his new capital city in the East? What did later generations call it?

Answer key to Sample Quiz II

Students' answers, of course, should only approximate the following.

1. The Christian writer who was widely read by Christians and pagans alike was *Origen*.
2. The emperor who ordered an empire-wide persecution of the Christians was *Decius*.
3. The Long Peace was *a period of about 40 years after the Edict of Toleration in which Christians were not persecuted*.
4. *Emperor Diocletian* brought an end to the Long Peace.
5. *Emperor Galerius* ended the Great Persecution.
6. Constantine defeated Maxentius in *the Battle of the Milvian Bridge* in *312*.
7. The law that granted freedom of religion to the Christians was *the Edict of Milan*. It was proclaimed in *313*.
8. Constantine called his new capital *Nova Roma*. Later generations called it *Constantinople*.

For a free electronic file of all tests and quizzes included in the teacher manual, please contact sales@CatholicTextbookProject.com.

Sample Test

1. Give two reasons why Christians were persecuted in the Roman Empire.

2. Why did the persecutions draw more people into the Church? What else about the Christians impressed the people of the ancient Roman Empire?

3. What is a heresy? How did heresy help the Church?

4. Please identify the following:

    a) The Christian heretic who rewrote and edited the Old and New Testaments, removing most of the Hebrew books and the harsher moral passages from the New Testament

    b) The early Christian teacher who called himself the prophet of the Holy Spirit

    c) The early Christian teacher who wrote defenses of the Faith and tried to show that Greek philosophy is not opposed to the Christian Faith

    d) The author of *Adversus Haereses* ("Against Heresies"), in which he witnessed to the unique authority of the Bishop of Rome

    e) The Christian teacher who was perhaps the greatest Christian philosopher of the first three centuries of the Church's history. He directed the Christian school in Alexandria.

5. Why, beginning in the middle of the third century, did persecutions against Christians become empire-wide?

6. What was the last Roman persecution of the Christians called? Under what emperor did it occur?

7. What sign did Constantine see in the sky before the Battle of the Milvian Bridge in 312? What did the sign represent? What words did Constantine see along with the symbol?

8. What did the Edict of Milan do? By whom was it issued?

9. Where did Constantine establish the new capital for the empire? What did he name this capital? What name did later generations give it?

Answer key to Sample Test

Students' answers, of course, should only approximate the following.

1. *Possible answers:*

    a) Christians refused to offer sacrifice to the emperor or the pagan gods.

    b) Some Christians refused to serve in the Roman army.

    c) Authorities feared the Christian faith could undermine legitimate authority and the social order.

2. People were drawn by *the example of the martyrs' courage* in facing torture and death for the sake of Christ. As well as Christian courage, *the Christian spirit of mutual love and brotherly charity* impressed the pagans.

3. A heresy is *a false teaching, one that emphasizes part of the received faith and ignores or denies the rest of the received tradition.*

   Heresy gave the Church *the opportunity to define and clarify her teachings* and *so come to a deeper and better understanding* of divine revelation.

4. *Answers:*

   a) Marcion

   b) Montanus

   c) St. Justin Martyr

   d) St. Irenaeus of Lyons

   e) Origen

5. The persecutions became empire-wide because the empire was undergoing hardships by the middle of the third century and *the emperors insisted on citizen loyalty to the office of emperor and the religion of the empire.* To show their loyalty, citizens had to sacrifice to the emperors and the pagan gods—which the Christian refused to do.

6. The last Roman persecution of the Christians was called *the "Great Persecution."* It was initiated under *Emperor Diocletian.*

7. Constantine saw the *Chi Rho* in the sky before the Battle of the Milvian Bridge. The sign signified *the first two letters in the Greek name for Christ.* The words accompanying it were *"In this sign you will conquer."*

8. The Edict of Milan granted *freedom of religion to all groups in the empire, including Christians.* It was issued by *Constantine and Licinius.*

9. Constantine established the new imperial capital *in the East, on the site of Byzantium.* Constantine called it *New Rome.* Later generations called it *Constantinople.*

For a free electronic file of all tests and quizzes included in the teacher manual, please contact sales@CatholicTextbookProject.com.

CHAPTER 4: The Christian Empire

Chapter Overview

- The Emperor Constantine not only legalized the Christian Faith, but took a deep interest in it. Besides building great basilicas and establishing Christian laws, the emperor took a hand in governing the Church.

- With the end of persecutions, the Church suffered from dangerous heresies. These heresies were Donatism, Arianism, and Pelagianism.

- The Arian heresy denied that the Son of God is equal to the Father. The Ecumenical Council of Nicaea condemned the heresy in 325. Though Constantine approved of the decisions of Nicaea, the imperial family continued to favor the Arians. In the empire, while most ordinary citizens held the orthodox Faith proclaimed at Nicaea, the ruling classes embraced Arianism. So did some of the Germanic peoples who had been converted by an Arian missionary.

- Germanic peoples, many of whom had been allowed to settle within the borders of the empire and were recruited into the Roman legions, began to threaten the empire from both within and without in the years following Constantine's death.

- Constantine's successors divided the empire into East and West, as Diocletian had done. In 379, the Emperor Gratian appointed Theodosius as co-emperor. After Gratian's death, Theodosius united the entire empire under his rule.

- Theodosius was a strong emperor who was able to hold back the Germans for a time. In 392, he removed government support from the old Roman pagan religion, establishing the Christian Faith as the sole religion of the empire.

- Even before Constantine, men and women had fled to the Egyptian desert to live the ascetic life. Many lived as hermits, but others formed communities in which they lived a life of prayer and mutual support. Monasticism spread from Egypt to the entire Church, East and West.

- Three great saints distinguished themselves under Theodosius' reign: St. Ambrose, the archbishop of Milan and advisor to the emperor; St. Jerome, who translated the Greek and Hebrew Scriptures into Latin (called the Vulgate); and St. Augustine, whose work became the foundation of theology in the Western, Latin Church for centuries to come.

- St. Augustine battled the Pelagian heresy, which taught that all men were born free of Original Sin and so had no need of God's Grace to live a virtuous life and attain salvation. Augustine taught that without God's Grace, men cannot live virtuously and attain salvation. He clarified the definition of Original Sin.

- After Theodosius' death, the empire was divided between his two sons: Honorius, in the West, and Arcadius, in the East. Under the general, Stilicho, the West was able to hold back the Visigoths under their king, Alaric. But, despite Germanic threats to the empire from the north, east, and west, Honorius had Stilicho assassinated.

- Hearing of Stilicho's death, Alaric led the Visigoths into Italy and sacked Rome in 410. After Alaric's death, the Visigoths left Italy and invaded southern Gaul and Hispania, where they established their military rule.

- Other threats to the empire came from the Huns, who invaded Gaul and pushed into Italy. Pope St. Leo the Great convinced their leader, Attila, to spare Rome and to withdraw from Italy.

- A Germanic tribe, the Vandals, being pushed out of Hispania by the Visigoths, invaded North Africa, where they established a kingdom. The Vandal king, Genseric, led an invasion of Italy and looted Rome.

Chapter Goals

The Edict of Milan and Emperor Constantine's profession of belief in the Christian Faith not only freed the Church from persecution but gave it a new status in society. It is important to emphasize the fact that the Edict of Milan did not make the Christian Faith the official religion of the empire; it merely gave the Church legal status.

Yet, during the reign of Constantine, already government and church were becoming intimately intertwined. This is seen in Constantine's intervention in the Arian controversy—his calling of the first ecumenical council. It can also be seen in his successors' attempts to determine doctrinal questions for the Church. Constantine's empire was the first experiment in a social order in which Church and state are not seen as opponents but as cooperating for the common good of all. Constantine's experiment was characterized, however, by the tendency of the emperor to take upon himself the role of the final arbiter in all Church affairs, even doctrinal ones. Emperors and, later, kings in western and eastern Europe would for centuries embrace this sort of "caesaro-papism." After all, they argued, if the emperor is the head of the state, he is the head of everything in the state, including the Church.

But, while many churchmen simply accepted the emperor's claim to power over the Church, others saw the Church as independent of the state—and as standing above the state, at least, in some respects. St. Ambrose's demand that Emperor Theodosius do penance for the massacre in Thessalonica betrayed the conviction that the Church stands above the emperor in matters of morality. The disintegration of imperial power in the West gave the popes the opportunity to assume both a spiritual and temporal authority independent of the emperor. For this reason, in part, the western Church developed a lively sense of her independence of civil authority, while, in the East, where imperial power remained, caesaro-papism was more readily accepted.

With Constantine and continuing through Theodosius, who made the Christian Faith the official religion of the empire, we see the beginnings and first developments of what is called Christendom, the society formed and inspired by the Christian Faith. Though in previous chapters we have spoken of civil society and the Church within it, in this chapter we speak for the first time of Christendom itself.

What Students Should Know

1. **What the Donatist controversy was about**

    The Donatist controversy arose from the larger controversy over what to do about the *traditores* or those who had betrayed the Faith in the last imperial persecution under Diocletian. The Donatists of North Africa refused to receive the *traditores* back in to the Church. The Donatists eventually went into schism, had their own bishops, and remained an important feature of the North African Church for 100 years.

2. **Who Arius was and what he taught. How the Church responded to Arianism. What was the aftermath of the Council of Nicaea?**

Arius was a deacon of the Church of Alexandria. He taught the Son was divine, but not equal to (did not share the same nature with) the Father. The spread of Arianism and the controversy over it in the Church caused Constantine to call a council of Church leaders at Nicaea. The council—the first ecumenical council in the history of the Church—represented the entire Church. In 325, the council condemned Arius' teaching and proclaimed that the Son was "consubstantial" (of the same substance) as the Father. The council issued a creed which, modified by a later council, is nearly identical to the creed Catholics say in Mass to this day.

Though the Council of Nicaea supported the "orthodox" Faith against the Arians, some of Constantine's successors as emperor favored Arianism and persecuted orthodox believers. Generally, the ordinary citizens were orthodox, while the ruling and upper classes were Arian. Among those who suffered at the hands of the Arian emperors was St. Athanasius, archbishop of Alexandria, who was several times exiled because he would not tolerate Arianism.

Eventually, with the backing of orthodox emperors, the orthodox faith triumphed over Arianism in the empire. In 381, the Ecumenical Council of Constantinople reaffirmed the teachings of Nicaea and added another section to the creed, declaring the Holy Spirit to be God, equal to the Father and the Son. Arianism, however, did not utterly die out. In fact, it spread among several German tribes, particularly the Ostrogoths, Visigoths, and Vandals.

3. **Who Emperor Theodosius was and what his importance was**

Theodosius was a general from Hispania whom the Emperor Gratian made Augustus of the East in 379. After Gratian's death, Theodosius became the real power in the empire, though for most of the years of his reign, he ruled with co-emperors and Caesars. Theodosius was able to protect the empire from German invasions. He is especially remembered for making the Christian Faith the official religion of the empire. On November 8, 392, Theodosius removed government support from the pagan religions while continuing to support Christian churches and clergy.

4. **How monasticism developed**

The movement that became monasticism began in Egypt, where ascetics fled to the desert to live lives of prayer and penance as hermits. Because they lived singly and alone, they were called *monks*. Eventually, some monks began communities, where they built houses and churches and shared a common table. These foundations of "cenobites" or "table monks" were the first monasteries.

Monasticism spread from Egypt throughout the eastern empire in the years after Constantine legalized the Church. St. Basil the Great established monasteries in less isolated areas and wrote two sets of monastic rules for them. Monasticism eventually spread to the West, where it became central to Irish Church life. Irish monasticism spread to Britain and northern Europe in the sixth and seventh centuries.

5. **Who Sts. Ambrose, Jerome, and Augustine were, and why they were important**

Ambrose was archbishop of Milan in the late fourth century and one of the most influential churchmen of his time. A spellbinding preacher and a writer of hymns, Ambrose served as an advisor to emperors, and even induced the powerful Emperor Theodosius to do public penance for his slaughter of the citizens of Thessalonica. Through Ambrose's influence, Augustine became a Christian.

Jerome was a scholar and great commentator on the Scriptures. In 382, Pope Damasus commissioned him to produce a new and authoritative translation of the Greek and Hebrew Scriptures into Latin. Moving to Bethlehem, Jerome spent over 20 years on his translation, which we remember as the Latin Vulgate. For the next 1,000 years, Jerome's Vulgate served as the chief translation of the Scriptures for the Church in the West.

Augustine, though raised by a Christian mother, rejected the Faith as a young man and followed Manicheanism, a Persian philosophy that taught the material world is evil and only the spiritual world is good. Augustine became a professor of rhetoric and a public orator. Like many other young pagans of his time, he indulged in immorality. After moving to Milan in Italy, however, where he heard the preaching of St. Ambrose, Augustine converted and was baptized in 387. Returning to his home in North Africa, Augustine at first lived as a monk but, in 395 was consecrated bishop of the North African city of Hippo.

St. Augustine has been one of the most influential theologians in the history of the Catholic Church. He helped the Church deepen its understanding of how God's Grace works on the soul of man and developed the concept of Original Sin. He has been called the "Doctor of Grace." Perhaps Augustine's most famous work is the *City of God*, in the first part of which he argues that the Christian religion was not the cause of the sack of Rome in 410. In the second part of the work, Augustine presents the parallel history of the "two cities," the City of God and the earthly city which arose when Satan and the angels rebelled against God. Both cities exist side by side in this world; but ultimately, Augustine shows, the City of God will triumph over the earthly city.

6. What Pelagianism was

Pelagianism gets its name from the British monk, Pelagius, who preached that Christians had to embrace a life of asceticism and extreme self-denial. But Pelagius taught that Christians did not need God's Grace to follow virtue and avoid sin. All people, he said, are born free of sin and choose either to sin or live righteously. Pelagius taught that people only needed to imitate Christ's behavior to achieve salvation.

St. Augustine argued against Pelagius, insisting that people, born with Original Sin, could not become virtuous or attain eternal salvation apart from God's Grace. Salvation comes to mankind by the Grace of God, given through Christ.

7. Who the two Gothic peoples were. Of Alaric and the sack of Rome.

The two Gothic peoples were the Ostrogoths (East Goths) and the Visigoths (West Goths). The Goths were Germans, and their religion was Arian Christianity.

Alaric was king of the Visigoths. In the early 5th century, he led his people across the Danube, pushing the Romans back to Constantinople. In 410, Alaric led the Visigoths into Italy. The same year, they sacked Rome.

Alaric died in Italy. His people, the Visigoths, left Italy and conquered southern Gaul and, eventually, Hispania, where they established a kingdom.

8. The importance of the popes in the western empire in the fifth century

In the years after Alaric and the Visigoths sacked Rome, Italy fell into anarchy and chaos. With the emperor holed up in Ravenna, the only authority left that could exercise any effective authority

Some Key Terms at a Glance

Nicene Creed: the creed recited in Catholic churches today at Mass; not the statement of faith of the Council of Nicaea, but a later version embodying that statement and accepted by the Church for liturgical use

consubstantial: sharing "one substance," one essence; of the same nature; the word used in the creed of the Council of Nicaea to express the relation of God the Father and God the Son

ecumenical council: a gathering of bishops that represents the entire Church

Arianism: the heretical teaching of Arius of Alexandria that God the Son was a later creation of God the Father and not coeternal with the Father

Vulgate Bible: the Latin translation of the Scriptures made by St. Jerome

Pelagianism: the heretical teaching of Pelagius, a British monk, who said that human beings could bring on their salvation by their own merits and works, without grace

Donatists: a schismatic sect that said that lay Christians and clerics who had cooperated with the Roman persecutors could not be legitimate Christians or priests

schismatic: from Greek *schisma*, meaning "a division." A schismatic sets up a rival church, causing a division of a part of the Church from the whole.

orthodox: adhering to teaching, established especially by a religious group; in the Christian Faith, adhering to the teachings revealed to the Church by Christ

Manicheanism: a Persian philosophy that taught the material world is evil; only the spiritual world is good. Manicheans called for a severe self-control and piety.

---

in Rome was the pope. So it was that the popes undertook the administration of the city and of central Italy.

In 440, Leo I the Great became pope. In 452 he led the defense of Rome against Attila the Hun. Meeting Attila, Leo convinced him not to enter Rome but to accept a payment in gold instead. In 455, Leo attempted to dissuade Genseric the Vandal to spare Rome. Though he could not keep Genseric from pillaging the city, Leo convinced him to spare the lives of its citizens.

9. **Who the Vandals were and what they accomplished**

The Vandals were a German tribe. Like the Goths, they were Arians. They invaded Spain, but then moved into North Africa where they established their kingdom. They conquered Carthage in 439. Their conquests were violent and destructive, and Genseric, the Vandal king, showed no mercy to Catholics. The Vandals eventually took to the sea, and in 455 sacked Rome.

10. **Who the Huns were and what they accomplished**

The Huns were not Germanic but came from the Mongolian plains. They were excellent horsemen. Having followed the Goths into the plains of Dacia and Hungary, the Huns, under their leader Attila, invaded the Rhine Valley and crossed into Gaul. They raided and looted wherever they wished and they left destruction behind them wherever they went. From Gaul they invaded Italy and in 452 reached Rome. After Pope Leo convinced Attila not to destroy the city, he led his Huns out of Italy.

Questions for Review

1. **What were the errors of the Arian, Pelagian, and Manichean heresies?**

   The Arians taught that the Son was divine but not equal to the Father.

   The Pelagians taught that people could become virtuous and achieve salvation without the Grace of God. Christ served only as an example of virtue. The Pelagians denied Original Sin.

   The Manicheans taught that the material world is evil and only the spiritual world is good.

   Why would educated people tend to favor these heresies over the orthodox Catholic Faith?

   Manicheanism gave its adherents a sense of being above ordinary people.

   Arianism seemed more reasonable than the orthodox belief in the Trinity.

   Pelagianism did not require any supernatural act on the part of God to account for salvation, and so it could seem more reasonable than the Catholic belief in divine Grace.

2. **What key term did the Council of Nicaea define?**

   Homoousios was the key term defined by the Council of Nicaea.

   What does it mean?

   Homoousios means "consubstantial," "of one substance," or the "same kind of thing."

   Why would Arians object to this term?

   The Arians objected to this term because they said the Son of God was not the "same kind of thing" as, or consubstantial with, the Father, but of a lesser nature than the Father.

3. **How did the German tribes become Arian?**

   The German tribes became Arian through Wulfilas, an Arian who evangelized the Goths. Wulfilas translated the Gospels, as well as the major prayers and litanies of the Church, into Gothic.

4. **Why did the pope ask Jerome to translate the Scriptures into Latin?**

   The pope asked Jerome to translate the Scriptures into Latin because existing Latin translations were of very poor quality.

   In what languages were they originally written?

   The Scriptures were originally written in Hebrew and Greek.

5. **What event inspired Augustine to write the *City of God*?**

   The event that inspired Augustine to write the *City of God* was the sack of Rome in 410 by Alaric and his Visigoths.

   On what did some Romans blame the sack of the city?

   Some of the pagan Romans said that Rome was sacked because it had abandoned the ancient gods for the Christian Faith.

6. **How did Leo the Great save Rome?**

   Leo went out to meet Attila. The pope convinced the chief of the Huns not to enter Rome but to receive a payment in gold instead.

Ideas in Action

1. **Discuss as a class the meaning of Augustine's concept of the two cities. What in this world belongs to the City of God and what to the earthly city?**

   It is important to note, in relation to this question, that St. Augustine's distinction between the City of God and the earthly city is not the distinction between the sacred and the secular, or the spiritual and material. The City of God is the society of those (both angels and men) who are faithful to God, while the earthly city consists of those who oppose God. It would be wrong, therefore, to equate the earthly city with the state or with human institutions *per se*. Augustine speaks of the two cities as being "in this present world commingled, and as it were, entangled together."

2. **Memorize the Nicene Creed as said in Mass. Discuss it in class. What does each part of the Creed mean in the daily life of a Christian?**

3. **Find several translations of the Bible. Compare as to their easy-to-read language, their beauty of expression, their overall effect on the reader. Why is it important to have several translations of the Bible? Discuss why the Church needed a Latin translation of the Scriptures.**

   Translations that the teacher and class may wish to consult are the following: Douay-Rheims version; the Authorized Version (King James); the Confraternity translation; the Revised Standard Version (Catholic edition); the *Jerusalem Bible*; the *New American Bible*; the translation by Father Ronald Knox.

Sample Quiz for Pages 89–97

Please answer the following in complete sentences.

1. What was the name of the schismatic group that refused to receive back into the Church those Christians who had betrayed their faith in the persecution under Diocletian?

2. What was the name of the archdeacon of Alexandria who taught that the Son is not equal to the Father? What was the name given to his followers?

3. Which Church council defined that the Son is equal to the Father? What Church council defined that the Holy Spirit is equal to the Father and the Son?

4. Both of the councils in Question 3 are called "ecumenical councils." What is an ecumenical council?

5. What emperor made the Christian Faith the official religion of the empire?

6. Where did monasticism first begin? How did the original monks live?

Answer key to Sample Quiz I

Students' answers, of course, should only approximate the following.

1. The name of the group who refused to receive back those who had betrayed their faith in the persecution under Diocletian was *the Donatists*.

2. *Arius* taught that the Son is not equal to the Father. His followers were called *Arians*.

3. *The Council of Nicaea* defined that the Son is equal to the Father. *The Council of Constantinople* taught that the Holy Spirit is equal to the Father and the Son.

4. An ecumenical council is *a gathering of bishops that represents the entire Church.*

5. *Emperor Theodosius* made the Christian Faith the official religion of the empire.

6. Monasticism began first in *Egypt*. The first monks lived *lives of prayer and penance as hermits.*

Sample Quiz for Pages 98–109

Please answer the following in complete sentences.

1. Identify the following

    a) The bishop of Milan in Italy who convinced the Emperor Theodosius that he should do public penance

    b) The bishop of Hippo who developed the Church's teaching on Original Sin

    c) The monk whom Pope Damasus commissioned to prepare a new translation of the Bible into Latin

2. Who wrote the *City of God*? What event inspired this work?

3. What was the name of the British monk who taught that people can become virtuous without God's Grace?

4. What do the names Ostrogoth and Visigoth mean?

5. What Gothic people ended up establishing a kingdom in southern Gaul and Hispania?

6. What German people brutally conquered North Africa and established a kingdom there?

7. Who was the pope that convinced Attila the Hun to spare Rome?

Answer key to Sample Quiz II

Students' answers, of course, should only approximate the following.

1. *Answers:*

   a) St. Ambrose

   b) St. Augustine

   c) St. Jerome

2. *St. Augustine* wrote the *City of God. The sack of Rome in 410* by Alaric the Visigoth inspired this work.

3. *Pelagius* was the British monk who taught that people could become holy without God's Grace.

4. Ostrogoth means *"East Goth."* Visigoth means *"West Goth."*

5. *The Visigoths* ended up establishing a kingdom in southern Gaul and Hispania.

6. The German people that conquered North Africa was *the Vandals.*

7. The pope that convinced Attila the Hun to spare Rome was *St. Leo I "the Great."*

Sample Test

1. What is an ecumenical council?

2. What was the first ecumenical council, who called it, and when was it held? What teaching did the council condemn? What doctrine did the council itself teach?

3. Why did Arianism continue to thrive even after it was condemned by the first ecumenical council? Why did it finally die out in the Roman Empire? Where did the heresy go after it was finally rejected by the empire?

4. What did Emperor Theodosius do that was of great importance to the Catholic Church and Christendom?

5. Where did monasticism first develop? How did the earliest monks live? What are cenobites?

6. Please identify the following:

   a) The Christian monk who translated the Bible from Hebrew and Greek into Latin

   b) The archbishop who convinced the Emperor Theodosius to do public penance

   c) The author of the *City of God*

   d) The Visigothic leader who sacked Rome in 410

   e) The pope who in 452 convinced Attila the Hun to spare the city of Rome

   f) The Germanic people who conquered North Africa and sacked Rome in 455

7. Who was Pelagius? What did he teach? What doctrine did he deny?

8. What Church father opposed Pelagius' teaching? What did this Church father teach against Pelagius?

Answer key to Sample Test

Students' answers, of course, should only approximate the following.

1. An ecumenical council is *a gathering of bishops that represents the entire Church.*

2. The first ecumenical council, the *Council of Nicaea*, was called in *325* by the *Emperor Constantine*. The council condemned *the teaching that the Son is not equal to God the Father.* The council of Nicaea taught *that the Son is God, equal to the Father.*

3. Arianism flourished in the empire after *the Council of Nicaea because it was favored and supported by the emperors*, the sons of Constantine.
   Arianism finally died out in the empire *because of emperors who supported the orthodox Faith against the heresy.*
   After it was stamped out in the empire, Arianism survived *among German nations.*

4. Theodosius *made Christianity the official religion of the empire.*

5. Monasticism first developed *in Egypt*. The earliest monks *lived alone (or as hermits.)* Cenobites are *monks who live together in a community.*

6. *Answers:*
   a) St. Jerome
   b) St. Ambrose
   c) St. Augustine
   d) Alaric
   e) St. Leo I, the Great
   f) the Vandals

7. Pelagius was *a British monk* who *taught that people could lead a virtuous life without the aid of God's Grace.* He denied *the doctrine of Original Sin.*

8. *St. Augustine* opposed Pelagius' teaching. Augustine insisted that *people, born with Original Sin, could not achieve virtue or eternal salvation apart from God's Grace. Salvation comes to mankind by the Grace of God, given through Christ.*

CHAPTER 5: Germanic Kingdoms in the West

Chapter Overview

- Germanic peoples came from the region of the Baltic Sea and the plains and river valleys of Eastern Europe. During the late Roman period, they moved south and east into Western Europe and then began to cross the boundaries of the empire.

- The Roman emperors allowed some Germanic tribes to settle within the empire, using them as allies against other Germanic tribes. Eventually, Germanic tribes moved into the empire as conquerors and permanent rulers.

- Germanic nations had similar cultures, though they did not consider themselves one people. They spoke related languages; were divided by similar social classes; governed themselves by customary, not written, laws; and were warrior societies. Germanic nations held that courage was the highest virtue.

- Pagan Germans worshipped fierce gods who were thought to fight wars against giants and demons of the ice and cold. Brave warriors who died in battle were thought to be taken to the hall of these gods, called Valhalla. Many Germanic tribes were converted to Arianism.

- After sacking Rome in 410, the Visigoths withdrew from Italy and established a kingdom in southern Gaul and the Iberian Peninsula. Driven from southern Gaul by the Franks in 507, the Visigoths continued to rule Hispania for over two centuries. The Visigoths, who were Arian, ruled a much larger population of Romans, who were Catholic.

- A Visigothic king in Hispania, Leovigild, married Goswintha, a zealous Arian. Through her influence and to unify his kingdom, Leovigild tried to force Arianism on his Catholic subjects. But it did not work. Even his son, Hermenegild, who became Catholic through the influence of his wife, Ingunthis, refused to obey his father. After an unsuccessful rebellion, Hermenegild was martyred for refusing to receive communion from an Arian bishop.

- Leovigild's second son, Reccared, himself became Catholic; and with Bishop Leander of Seville, Recarred brought the Visigoths into the Catholic Church. He officially forbade Arianism in his realm.

- The Visigoths had driven another Germanic nation, the Vandals, out of the Iberian Peninsula. Led by their king, Genseric, the Vandals went to North Africa, where they set up a kingdom after plundering the Roman settlements and capturing Carthage. Genseric led his people in an invasion of Sicily and Italy, conquering Corsica and Sardinia, and in 455 looted and sacked Rome itself. The Arian Vandals persecuted the Christians in the conquered lands.

- Clovis, the Merovingian king of the Franks, conquered large sections of Gaul, seizing also the lands held by other Frankish kings. Though a pagan (along with the rest of his people), Clovis, through the influence of his Burgundian wife, Clotilde, became the first Germanic king to become Catholic.

- After Clovis' death, his kingdom was divided between his four sons. Over the next two centuries, the Merovingian kings became merely figureheads, their mayors of the palace carrying on the actual work of ruling. Finally, Pepin the Short, the Carolingian mayor of the palace, removed the last Merovingian rulers from power and was crowned king in 751.

- Theodoric, king of the Ostrogoths, overthrew Odoacer, the German king who had deposed the last Roman emperor in the West. Theodoric made himself king of Italy. He governed Italy and other lands he subsequently ruled wisely and well for most of his reign. Though an Arian, he treated Catholics with tolerance. But, at the end of his life, fearing a plot against him by the Eastern Roman emperor and the Catholic senators in Italy, he assassinated several senators. After Theodoric's death, his Ostrogothic kingdom fell into disunity.

Chapter Goals

An understanding of ancient German culture is important for a full understanding of medieval western Europe. Medieval western Europe inherited the classical culture of Greece and Rome, the imperial and legal traditions of the Roman Empire, and the Christian religion—but the Germanic peoples, their languages and culture, also formed a part of the medieval mix. Germanic peoples took on the ancient Mediterranean cultures and the Christian religion, but their culture modified the expression of these elements, forming a new Western European culture that was rich, varied, and productive of a new and energetic civilization.

What Students Should Know

1. **How the German nations entered the Roman Empire**

   The Germanic peoples came from the forests south of the Baltic Sea and the plains and river valleys of eastern Europe. During the later years of the Roman Empire, they moved with their families and herds into the Danube and Rhine valleys, and from there into western Europe—Gaul, Italy, and the Iberian Peninsula. Another wave of Germanic tribes moved down from the Baltic Sea region, through Dacia and Hungary, and into Roman lands.

   The imperial armies made use of some Germanic tribes as allies against other Germanic peoples. Eventually the Romans allowed several Germanic tribes to move their families as settlers and colonists into empty or underpopulated lands in Gaul or along the Danube River. Because of mistakes made by Roman commanders, the tribes finally moved into the empire of the West as conquerors, ruling over a much larger Romanized population.

2. **The character of German culture**

   The Germans had a warrior-hunter society. All freemen were supposed to learn the use of arms, and women sometimes joined men on the battle line.

   It was thought that German "kings" were descended from gods or demigods of an ancient heroic age. Tribal elders chose the kings from among those who fought and hunted best. If a king proved bad, cowardly, or unfit, the elders could replace him with another. A Germanic leader was surrounded by a band of comrades, who pledged loyalty to their leader while the leader, in turn, rewarded his followers with loyalty and a share of battle spoils.

3. **The character of German law**

   For the Germans, law meant age-old custom. Laws were not written down but memorized and passed along by bards or council elders.

   Under German law, those accused of a crime were considered guilty until proven innocent. To prove his innocence, one had to appeal to three kinds of "evidence": the *oath*, the *ordeal*, and the *combat*.

   In the *oath*, one called on a god or on Christ to support him for telling the truth or punish him for lying. In an *ordeal*, the oath taker underwent severe pain or torture to prove he was telling the truth. In the *combat*, one fought with a court-appointed opponent or one's accuser. It was believed God would grant the victory to the one who swore truthfully.

4. **The character of German religion**

   In the Germanic myths, the gods were ever at war with the giants of the ice and cold. The German gods demanded human sacrifice and rewarded recklessness in battle; men who were brave and fought well would be taken to Valhalla after death to feast with the gods.

   The Germans thought the world and mankind would end in a colossal battle between the gods and giants. The end of all things would be defeat. So it was that the Germans glorified courage in the face of certain defeat.

5. **The character of the Visigothic kingdom**

   After conquering southern Gaul, the Visigoths crossed into the Iberian Peninsula and conquered it. The Visigoths, under their Balting kings (the family of Alaric), ruled southern Gaul until the Franks drove them out. In Hispania, the Visigoths ruled from Toledo over a much larger Roman population. The Visigoths were Arian, with their own bishops and liturgy, while the Romans were Catholic. The Visigoths constantly fought among themselves and assassinated many of their elected kings. Despite their barbaric ways, however, the Visigoths worked to preserve the classical culture of Greece and Rome.

6. **The significance of the Third Council of Toledo and the character of Catholic Visigothic Spain**

   At the Third Council of Toledo (589), the Arian clergy and the Visigothic ruling class made the public announcement of their conversion to the Catholic Faith. King Reccared formally outlawed Arianism in his realm.

   After Reccared's death, the Visigothic kingdom was again torn by strife. It was the Catholic bishops who held the kingdom together by their wisdom and counsel. Monasteries helped civilize the society by preserving classical learning and offering free schooling. The Visigothic Church made Spain a beacon of learning and civilization in the early Middle Ages.

7. **Who Genseric was and what he accomplished**

   Genseric was the king of the Vandals under whose leadership they conquered North Africa. Genseric led the Vandals in a raid on Italy, in which they sacked Rome in 455. Genseric used his Arianism as an excuse to loot Catholic churches and confiscate Church lands.

8. **Who the Franks were, where they came from, and what they accomplished**

   The Franks were a pagan Germanic people who had lived for centuries in what is now Belgium and along the Rhine and Main Rivers in Germany.

   The Franks had been allies of the Roman legions. When Roman power collapsed in Gaul, the Franks pushed into that land.

9. **Who Clovis was and why he is important to history**

   Clovis was a Meroving king of the Franks who secured his power by eliminating all other members of his family and by conquest. He married Clotilde, the niece of the king of the Burgundians and a Catholic. Through her influence, Clovis decided to accept baptism. On Christmas Day 496, he was baptized by Bishop Remigius at Reims, thus becoming the first Germanic king to become Catholic.

10. **The character of the Merovingian Frankish kingdom**

As was the way with Germanic kings, Clovis divided his kingdom between his sons. These sons, and their descendents, warred among themselves to gain sole power over the Frankish kingdom. Eventually, the kingdom of the Franks was divided between two realms—Austrasia, in the east, and Neustria, in the west.

Frankish kings were served by chancellors, called "mayors of the palace," who increasingly took on themselves the task of ruling. Eventually, while the Merovings kept the title of king, the mayors of the palace increasingly took on themselves the real tasks of ruling.

11. **Who was the last Roman emperor in the West? Why is his name significant? How did he become emperor? What became of him?**

Romulus Augustulus was the last Roman emperor in the West. His name recalls the legendary founder of Rome—Romulus—and Augustus, the first Roman emperor. He became emperor in 475 when his father bribed the Roman Senate to name him emperor. Romulus and his father promised their German troops one-third of Italy if they agreed to Romulus' appointment as emperor. But when this promise was not fulfilled, the Goth Odoacer removed the boy emperor and gave him a villa at Naples and a fortune in gold. Odoacer, who sent the imperial regalia to Constantinople, became king of Italy.

12. **Who Theodoric was and what he accomplished**

Theodoric was the king of the Ostrogoths, who, at the invitation of Emperor Zeno in Constantinople, overthrew Odoacer and his kingdom. Theodoric ruled Italy as king in the place of Odoacer. For most of his reign, Theodoric was a wise and provident ruler. He repaired city walls, aqueducts, and public buildings. He allowed the Roman Italians to rule themselves by their own laws and customs, while Theodoric's Ostrogoths followed their own customs. Though an Arian, Theodoric tolerated Catholics and Jews. Toward the end of his life, however, Theodoric became afraid that the Emperor Justin in Constantinople was plotting against him. He accused his Roman subjects, especially members of the Senate, of plotting to assassinate him.

Some Key Terms at a Glance

Council of Toledo: held in 589; unified the Catholic and Arian churches of Spain

king: a Germanic title for the ruling chief of the people, either an hereditary office or elected by the principal nobles. A Germanic king ruled through custom and tribal connections.

Germanic law: age-old custom, traditional justice

Merovings: the line of the Frankish kings claiming descent from the legendary hero, Merovech

Carolingian: the line of Frankish kings descended from Charles Martel (Carolus Martellus)

Questions for Review

1. **Why were the German tribes able to sweep across the Roman Empire?**

   Several German tribes had become Roman allies, fighting with the Roman legions against other German tribes. The Roman government allowed these German allies to move into underpopulated regions of the empire in Gaul or along the Danube River. As the Roman power weakened or disappeared in some regions, the German tribes drove out what remained of imperial opposition and settled the imperial lands as conquerors and rulers.

2. **In what way were the Germanic kings different from the Roman emperors?**

   Unlike the Roman emperors, who were the heads of a state and lawmakers, German kings were leaders of war who were appointed based on their skill and prowess in war and the hunt. German kings were not lawmakers, for German tribal life was governed by custom, not written laws or edicts. While the Roman emperor had absolute power over the empire, the German kings relied on the advice and good favor of the tribal elders. The German king, too, relied on the fidelity of his warriors and was bound to them by oaths of loyalty. A Roman emperor's power and authority was thought to come from the law of the empire.

3. **What were the main differences in government between the Germanic nations and the Roman Empire?**

   The Roman Empire was a huge state that controlled vast and far-flung territories and ruled over peoples of various races and languages. The empire united these peoples by a common law. The Germanic nations, on the other hand, were many and disunited. Neither a common language nor law united them.

   After Constantine, the Roman Empire was increasingly united by a common religion—the Christian Faith. The German nations, on the other hand, were either pagans, worshipping many gods, or Arian Christians.

   The Roman Empire had a highly advanced civilization, with great cities, developed arts, splendid architecture, agriculture, and commerce. The Germanic nations, however, were warrior societies. Germanic culture centered on the hunt and war.

4. **Did the German nations have a written law?**

   Germanic nations had no written law but were ruled by age-old custom. Their "laws" were memorized and passed along by the bards or council elders.

   How did they decide questions of justice?

   In Germanic law, someone accused of a crime was considered guilty until proven innocent. He had to prove his innocence by combat, oath, or ordeal.

   What is trial by combat?

   In a trial by combat, the accused fought with a court-appointed opponent or his accuser. If the accused was innocent, it was thought he would be victorious.

   Trial by oath?

   In a trial by oath, the accused called on a god or Christ to support him in his claim of innocence.

   Trial by ordeal?

   In a trial by ordeal, the accused underwent severe pain or torture to prove he was telling the truth.

5. **After whom are the days of the week named?**

   The days of the week are named after the ancient German gods—the Sun, the Moon, Tiw, Wodin, Thor, and Freia.

6. **Which Germanic peoples actually sacked the city of Rome?**

   Both the Visigoths and the Vandals sacked Rome.

7. **What do the names "Visigoth" and "Ostrogoth" signify?**

   "Visigoth" signifies "western Goth." "Ostrogoth" signifies "eastern Goth."

8. **Who married the Frankish king, Clovis?**

   Clotilde married Clovis.

   How did she manage to convert him to the Catholic Faith?

   She told him that only if he agreed to serve the one, true God would he defeat his enemy, the Alamanni, in an impending battle. Clovis swore to Christ that if he gave him victory over the Alamanni, he would accept baptism. Clovis was victorious over the Alamanni and was baptized.

9. **What was a "mayor of the palace"?**

   A mayor of the palace was the chancellor or chief magistrate of the Meroving kings. The mayors increasingly took on themselves the task of ruling the kingdom.

   Which mayor of the palace became king of the Franks?

   Pepin the Short was the mayor of the palace who became king of the Franks.

10. **Who were the Merovings? The Carolingians?**

    The Merovings were the family of Clovis, the kings of the Franks. The Carolingians were the family of Pepin the Short, mayor of the Meroving palace. Eventually the Carolingians themselves became the kings of the Franks.

11. **How did Theodoric bring peace between the Arians and Catholics in his kingdom?**

    Theodoric brought peace between Arians and Catholics because, although he himself was Arian, he tolerated the Catholics over whom he ruled.

Ideas in Action

1. **Write a report on the Germanic gods (a good source is Roger Lancelyn Green's *The Saga of Asgard*). How are they similar to the Roman and Greek gods?**

   If students have not studied Greek and Roman mythology, the teacher may need to assign reading material on it or devote a class to discussing the major gods and myths of the Romans and Greeks. A good source for the teacher's reference is *Mythology* by Edith Hamilton.

2. **Discuss why Germanic peoples valued courage so much. Why should such an idea have sprung from a pagan people like the Germans? How is the Germanic ideal of courage acceptable to the Christian Faith? What is the value of suffering or defeat? Can one "lose" and still "win"?**

   In a society centered on war and the hunt, courage, of course, is of the utmost value. The Germans were certainly not alone in valuing courage, even to the extent they did. Respect for courage was characteristic of other peoples, such as the Celts. Germanic courage in the face of certain defeat is not far from Christian courage, since the Faith calls us to follow Christ and to practice virtue even when it goes against all worldly advantage. Jesus said, "he who loses his life for my sake will find it," and he called us to take up our cross and to drink of the cup of death, as he did. Yet, even when defeated for following Christ, we are victorious, for we gain heaven, and we help, through our sufferings, to advance the Kingdom of God. As St. Paul said, we "make up in our bodies that which is lacking in the sufferings of Christ."

3. **Make a map of the Germanic kingdoms that replaced the Western Roman Empire.**

   Since the boundaries of the German kingdoms differed from time to time, the teacher may wish to assign different time periods to various students or groups of students. For instance, a student or group of students would make a map of the Germanic kingdoms at the time of Odoacer, another of the kingdoms at the time of Theodoric or Clovis. Students will have to carry on research outside the classroom. One source is the *Penguin Atlas of Medieval History*.

4. **On a map of Europe, find the original homelands of the Germanic peoples. Where are the Scandinavian lands? Where are the steppes? Where is the Danube River?**

   This could work well as an in-class activity, utilizing a wall map.

Sample Quiz for Pages 115–124

Please answer the following in complete sentences.

1. What were the chief occupations of men and, sometimes, women in ancient Germanic society?
2. What sort of man did the ancient Germans want as king?
3. What was the chief way in which Germanic and Roman law differed?
4. What was it about Germanic religion that made the ancient Germans glorify courage even in the face of certain defeat?
5. What regions did the Visigoths conquer after they left Italy following the sack of Rome in 410?
6. What was the name of the council where the Arian clergy and the rulers of the Visigoths formally became Catholic?
7. Who was the Visigothic king who formally outlawed Arianism in his kingdom? In what year did he do this?

Answer key to Sample Quiz I

Students' answers, of course, should only approximate the following.

1. The chief occupations in ancient Germanic societies were *hunting* and *war*.
2. The ancient Germans wanted a man who was a *good hunter* and *fighter* as king.
3. Germanic law differed from Roman law in that *Roman law was a written law,* while *Germanic law was age-old custom.*
4. *The Germans believed that a great battle between the gods and the giants would end in the destruction of the world and all mankind. Because of this, Germans glorified courage even in the face of certain defeat.*
5. The Visigoths conquered *southern Gaul* and *Hispania* (or *the Iberian Peninsula.*)
6. The Arian clergy and the Visigothic rulers became Catholic at the *Third Council of Toledo.*
7. *Reccared* was the Visigothic king who formally outlawed Arianism in his kingdom in the year *589.*

Sample Quiz for Pages 125–133

Please answer the following in complete sentences.

1. Under what king did the Vandals conquer Roman North Africa?

2. Who was the first Germanic king to become Catholic? On what day, in what year, did he convert? What Roman territory did his people, the Franks, conquer?

3. What were the mayors of the palace? Why were they so important to the Frankish kingdom?

4. What was the name of the last Roman emperor in the West? In what year was he removed from power?

5. Who was the king of the Ostrogoths who conquered Italy for the Emperor Zeno and ruled that land wisely and well for many years as its king?

Answer key to Sample Quiz II

Students' answers, of course, should only approximate the following.

1. The Vandals conquered Roman North Africa under their king, *Genseric*.

2. The first Germanic king to become Catholic was *Clovis*, who converted on *Christmas Day, 496*. His people, the Franks, conquered the *Roman territory of Gaul*.

3. The mayors of the palace were *the chancellors, chief magistrates, or head ministers of the Frankish kings*. They became important to the Frankish kingdom because *they eventually took on all the tasks of ruling*.

4. The last Roman emperor in the West was *Romulus Augustulus*, who was removed from power in *476*.

5. This king of the Ostrogoths who conquered Italy was *Theodoric*.

Sample Test

1. Why did the Roman government allow German tribes to settle within the boundaries of the empire?

2. Name the part of the Roman empire each of the following German tribes conquered:

    a) Vandals

    b) Visigoths

    c) Franks

    d) Ostrogoths

3. What were the chief occupations of the ancient Germans? What qualities did Germans look for in their kings?

4. How did Germanic law differ from Roman law? If one were accused of a crime under German law, by what three ways could he prove his innocence?

5. What was the Germanic ideal of courage? What in their religion made the ancient Germans hold to this ideal?

6. Neither the Vandals, Visigoths, Ostrogoths, nor the Franks were originally Catholic. What religion was each of these people? Which ones became Catholic, and when?

7. Please identify the following:

    a) The king of the Ostrogoths who conquered Italy and set up a kingdom there.

For most of his reign he was a wise and just ruler.

b) The last Roman Emperor in the West

c) The king of Visigothic Spain who became Catholic and outlawed the Arian religion

d) The Vandal king who conquered Roman North Africa and sacked Rome

e) The ruling family of the Franks; the family of Clovis and his descendents

8. Who was the first Germanic king to become Catholic? Who influenced him to convert? When was he baptized?

9. What were the mayors of the palace? Why did they become so important to the Frankish kingdom?

Answer key to Sample Test

Students' answers, of course, should only approximate the following.

1. The Romans allowed Germans to settle within the boundaries of the empire *as a way of paying them for their services as military allies against other German tribes.*

2. Answers:

   a) North Africa

   b) Hispania (or Spain or the Iberian Peninsula)

   c) Gaul

   d) Italy

3. The chief occupations of the ancient Germans were *hunting* and *warfare.* Germans wanted their kings to be *brave* and *good fighters* and *hunters.*

4. *Roman law was written law* while *German law was age-old custom, not written down* but *memorized.*

   If one were accused of a crime under German law, he could prove his innocence by taking an *oath,* undergoing an *ordeal,* or engaging in *combat* with his accuser or a court-appointed champion.

5. The ancient Germans believed that *courage exercised in the face of certain defeat is the highest human virtue. This conviction arose from their religion, where it was believed the struggle between the gods and the giants would end in the inevitable destruction of the universe and mankind.*

6. *The Vandals, Visigoths, and Ostrogoths were Arian. The Franks were pagan. The Visigoths and the Franks became Catholic—the Franks in 496* and the *Visigoths in 589.*

7. Identify the following:

   a) Theodoric

   b) Romulus Augustulus

   c) Reccared

   d) Genseric

   e) the Merovings

8. The first Germanic king to become Catholic was *Clovis,* the king of the Franks. He embraced the Catholic Faith through the influence of his wife, *Clotilde.* He was baptized on *Christmas Day, 496.*

9. The mayors of the palace were *the chancellors, chief magistrates, or head ministers of the Frankish kings.* They became important to the Frankish kingdom *because they eventually took on all the tasks of the king.*

CHAPTER 6: Founders of Christendom— A.D. 500–700

Chapter Overview

- The Eastern Roman Emperor Justinian dreamed of making the Mediterranean world once again a Christian Empire. With his wife, Theodora, he established his power in Constantinople and then proceeded to conquer the western lands the Roman Empire had lost.

- Justinian's general Belisarius reconquered North Africa for the empire, ending the Vandal kingdom there. In the First and Second Gothic Wars, Justinian's generals in a 20-year struggle took back Italy for the empire, laying it waste in the process.

- Justinian's reform of Roman law, called the *Codex Justinianus* (Justinian Code), simplified a thousand years of legal practice. It became the model for medieval law and practice in all Europe, as well as for reforms of legal systems in the 19th century.

- As a youth, St. Patrick was carried off into slavery in Ireland. Though he eventually escaped back to his homeland in Britain, he later returned to Ireland as a missionary. After Patrick's time, monasteries sprang up all over Ireland. Irish monks carried the Gospel to their fellow Gaels in Scotland and northern England.

- A descendent of a noble Roman family, Boethius tried to preserve Roman and Greek culture by translating the works of Plato and Aristotle from Greek into Latin. He composed books on the subjects included in the seven liberal arts, which became the schoolbooks of future generations for hundreds of years. He wrote the *Consolation of Philosophy* while in prison. Boethius was executed by order of Theodoric the Ostrogoth.

- St. Benedict fled the immorality of Rome to live as a hermit in the region of Subiaco. Eventually, men gathered around him, for whom he wrote a rule of monastic life, called today the *Rule of St. Benedict*. The *Rule* was more moderate than other monastic rules of the time, and monasteries following it sprang up over all Italy and Western Europe.

- Since the territories around Rome had been ravaged by disease and war, Pope St. Gregory I, the "Great," was the only authority who could bring order to those lands. Thus he established the temporal authority of the papacy.

- Pope Gregory collected the liturgical prayers of the city of Rome into the *Missale Romanum*. Missionaries throughout Europe carried the Missal and made the Roman Rite of the liturgy the rite followed by the peoples of Western Europe.

- St. Augustine, sent by Pope Gregory to Britain, converted the pagan Saxon peoples there. Augustine established Saxon bishops throughout England.

- The conflict over the different customs of the Gaelic Christians of England and the new Saxon Church was resolved by the Synod of Whitby. The synod determined that the Gaelic liturgical and monastic traditions had to give way to the Roman traditions.

Chapter Goals

This chapter deals with the seeds of what would make up the culture of Western Christian Europe, or western Christendom. The Eastern Roman Empire would continue to exist for many hundreds of years after Justinian; but the form of government and culture exemplified by Byzantium would not serve as the paradigm for the new nations of the West. These nations would have their Germanic and Celtic cultures transformed by the Christian Faith and the Greek and Roman civilization preserved through the institutions of the Church.

Students should come away from this chapter knowing the means by which the barbarian West would be civilized—namely, monasticism and the central authority of the pope in Rome. The "Romanizing" of the Gaelic Church is one chapter in the story of how Western Europe was brought within the ambit of the papal authority, which would provide all the western peoples with a source of unity both for ecclesiastical and political life.

What Students Should Know

1. **What the goals of the Emperor Justinian were and how successful he was in achieving them**

   Justinian wanted to reunite the western and eastern Mediterranean world into a Christian empire under the authority of the emperor. To do this, he sought to re-conquer all the areas of the Western Empire that had been lost to the Germans. He was partly successful in this. His armies reconquered North Africa, part of Spain, and Italy. A 20-year war with the Ostrogoths in Italy, however, left that land desolate and the people of Italy angry with the imperial government.

   Another of Justinian's goals was the reform of the Roman law, to correct abuses that had crept into it and to make action in the law courts easier for the ordinary citizen. Under Justinian, famous lawyers drafted a new code, called the *Codex Justinianus* (the Justinian Code.) This code later became the basis for law in Europe, both in the Middle Ages and, later, in the 19th century.

2. **How classical Greek and Roman civilization was preserved in barbarian Western Europe**

   Though some lay Christians in the west directed their efforts specifically to preserving classical culture, it was the monks (whose specific intent was to save their souls) and the missionaries (who wanted to spread the Gospel) who became the effective preservers of classical civilization.

3. **The character of the Celtic or Gaelic social order**

   The Celts or Gaels is the name for peoples who inhabited Ireland, Scotland, Wales, and England (before the Saxon invasion.) The Gaelic social structure consisted of clans, which acknowledged one hereditary chief who, with his associates, led them in battle. The clan was divided by a rigid social structure. At the top were the king and the ruling military elite, who alone were allowed to learn the art of warfare. Next came the free farmers and craftsmen, who, with the elite, were full members of the clan. Slaves were outside the clan structure and possessed no rights in Gaelic society. A guild or caste of hereditary priests drawn from the aristocracy handled all the religious and legal affairs of the clan. These priests, the Druids, were believed to able to work magic. They practiced human sacrifice. The Druids were trained from birth to memorize long lists and stories and to repeat from memory anything they learned, no matter how long.

4. **Who St. Patrick was and what he accomplished**

Patrick, the son of a deacon, was born in Britain in the late 4th century. Made a slave in Ireland at age 16, he later escaped and returned home to Britain. There he had a vision that he should return to Ireland as a missionary. Over the next several years, he trained himself for his task. Consecrated as a bishop, he returned to Ireland. He made his first converts among the common people. By miraculous feats he performed to combat the Druids' magic, Patrick was finally able to convert the High King Leoghaire (Leary). By Patrick's death, monasteries had grown up all over Ireland.

5. **The significance of Irish monasteries and the part they played in spreading the Gospel**

In the Roman world, the center of church life was the bishop, who generally resided in a city, the seat of that division of the Church called the diocese. Irish Church structure was unique. Instead of a city and its bishop, the monastery and its abbot were the center of church life in Ireland. (Like St. Patrick, abbots, it seems, had the powers of a bishop.) Monasteries continued to foster learning and memorization, thus keeping up the traditions of the Druids in a Christian context. Monks, however, applied these skills to preserving the Latin Christian culture brought to Ireland from the European continent. Irish monks became missionaries and evangelized their fellow Gaels in Scotland and northern England.

6. **Boethius and his signficance**

Boethius was a senator of Rome who lived during the first quarter of the sixth century. Fearing his countrymen would forget the works of the Greek philosophers (particularly, Plato and Aristotle), Boethius began translating the works of Plato and Aristotle in Latin. He also composed summaries of ancient learning that became school textbooks in Western Europe for hundreds of years. In particular, Boethius' summaries were the means by which Europeans learned the seven liberal arts (grammar, logic, rhetoric, arithmetic, geometry, music, and astronomy.)

Perhaps Boethius' most important work was his *Consolation of Philosophy*, which he composed in prison and while facing a death sentence from King Theodoric, who had accused Boethius of plotting with the king's enemies.

7. **Who St. Benedict of Nursia was; his rule, and its importance to Western Europe**

Benedict came from a family of Nursia in Italy. A student in Rome, he fled the city because of its immorality and went to live as a hermit. His heroic life attracted others, and he established a number of small monasteries. He eventually moved his monastery to Monte Cassino, which he organized like a self-sustaining village. For this monastery he wrote his famous *Rule*.

The *Rule* divides the monk's day into periods of prayer, work, and sleep. It prescribes communal prayer seven times a day, based on recitation of the Psalms. The *Rule* commands physical labor as a balance to the monk's life of prayer and meditative reading. According to the *Rule*, hospitality to travelers and petitioners is a duty of monastic life. The *Rule* required as well that the monks care for the poor from the surplus of the monastery garden and the monks' labor. St. Benedict's watchword was *Ora et labora*— "Pray and work."

Benedict's *Rule*, being less harsh than earlier rules, created a monastic life that could appeal to a greater number of people. Benedictine monasteries, thus, spread throughout all of Europe. They became havens of safety and sanity in terrible times. They brought shelter to the poor, peace to the troubled and fearful, and increasing prosperity to the countryside around the monasteries.

8. **The accomplishments of Pope St. Gregory I the Great and why his pontificate was so significant**

As pope, Gregory I exercised both temporal and spiritual rule. He had to exercise a good degree of temporal power because Rome could not rely on the emperor in Constantinople and faced a powerful enemy (the Lombards.) Gregory reorganized the administration of Rome, governed estates, and restored farms to productivity. Gregory made decisions that emperors and governors usually made, because he had to—no one else was left to do it. After Gregory, popes took on more and more temporal power, becoming not just spiritual leaders but temporal lords as well.

Gregory collected the rites of the Roman Church into the *Missale Romanum,* which he sent to missionaries working in the German lands. In this way, the liturgy of the Roman Church (the Roman Rite) spread throughout Western Europe. Along with the missal, Gregory equipped missionaries with the *Rule* of St. Benedict, thus helping to spread Benedictine monasticism throughout the West. Among the missionaries commissioned by Pope Gregory was St. Augustine of Canterbury, who preached the Gospel to the Angles and Saxons in England.

9. **The difference between temporal and spiritual power**

Temporal power refers to power over things having to do with life in this world, as opposed to spiritual power, which has to do with eternal or spiritual things. Making laws for a city or state, owning property, such as a farm or a house, or managing a business are matters having to do with temporal power. Spiritual power has to do with things connected to administering the sacraments and teaching the Faith. The pope exercised temporal power when he made laws for the city of Rome or bought and sold farms and estates.

10. **Who St. Augustine of Canterbury was and what he accomplished**

Augustine was a monk, who, commissioned by Pope Gregory I, went to England in 597 to preach the Gospel to the pagan Angles and Saxons. Augustine convinced Ethelbert, the king of Kent, of the advantages of baptism, and the king's council of tribal elders agreed to accept the Christian Faith. Augustine established his see at Canterbury in Kent and appointed Paulinus as archbishop of York in the north of England. From these two churches a network of churches and missions spread steadily across England. A hundred years later, the Angles and Saxons were Catholic.

11. **What the Synod of Whitby was and why it was significant**

The Gaelic and Saxon churches in England had been rivals for many years after the death of St. Augustine of Canterbury. The Angles and Saxons despised the Gaelic Christians, and their churches had different monastic and liturgical practices. The Saxon Benedictine monasticism was quite different than the old Gaelic form of monastic life. Controversy between the two churches confused the pagan Saxons and slowed missionary work.

In 663, the Saxon King Oswy of Northumbria called a synod of bishops to meet at Whitby to decide whether the Church in Britain would follow Roman or Gaelic practices. Based mostly on political considerations, Oswy decided in favor of supporting the Roman practices and suppressing the Gaelic customs. From that time on, the Church in England came firmly under Roman authority and the British Isles became part of Western European civilization and not a separate Gaelic culture.

Questions for Review

1. **Why is the *Codex Justinianus* so important to history?**

   The *Codex Justinianus* is so important to history because it served as the model for medieval law and practice in all Europe. It was used as the foundation for reforms of legal systems in the 19th century.

2. **What was Justinian's great dream?**

   Justinian's great dream was to restore the Roman Empire by reuniting the western and eastern Mediterranean lands under his rule.

   In what ways was he successful?

   Justinian was successful in that his generals were able to reconquer the Vandal kingdom in North Africa and Italy from the Ostrogoths.

   In what ways did he fail to achieve his dream?

   Justinian, however, did not reconquer any other portions of the western Mediterranean, including Gaul. To keep Italy under his authority, he had to fight a 20-year war there which laid the land waste. He was thus unable to establish the empire firmly in the west.

Some Key Terms at a Glance

Byzantine: the name given to the civilization that came from the city of Byzantium, renamed Constantinople or *Nova Roma*; a term referring to the Eastern Roman Empire and its people

mosaic: a picture made from thousands of little tiles of glass or stone

Justinian Code: *Codex Justinianus*, a compilation of Roman law made during Justinian's reign

clan: a family and tribal organization in Gaelic-speaking countries

Servus Servorum Dei: "Servant of the Servants of God." Title chosen by St. Gregory for himself and now given to all the popes

Roman Rite: the liturgy officially accepted by the pope as the liturgy for Rome and the Western Church

Gregorian chant: the form of sacred music sung in the churches of the Roman Rite

seven liberal arts: the disciplines that are the foundation of all learning. They are grammar, logic (the art which teaches orderly thinking), rhetoric (the art of public speaking), arithmetic, geometry, astronomy, and music.

The Rule of St. Benedict: the constitution of Western monastic life, first drawn up by St. Benedict for his monks at Monte Cassino

temporal power: power over things having to do with life in this world, as opposed to **spiritual power**, which has to do with eternal or spiritual things

3. **What were Boethius' great contributions to the generations to come?**

   Boethius' contributions were summaries of ancient learning, particularly on the subjects of the seven liberal arts. These summaries became the textbooks for western Europe for hundreds of years. Boethius' other great contribution was his book, *The Consolation of Philosophy*.

4. **From what land did Patrick come?**

   He came from Britain.

   How did he first come to Ireland?

   Patrick was brought to Ireland as a slave.

   Why did he return there?

   He returned to Ireland after receiving a vision calling on him to spread the Gospel in that land.

5. **What things made the Irish Church different from the Roman Church?**

   The Irish and Roman Churches had different practices, such as how their monks wore the tonsure. Irish monks were more independent of their abbots than Benedictine monks. The Gaelic liturgy was more elaborate—and twice as long—as the Roman liturgy.

   Why is there today no separate Irish Church with different customs from the Roman Church?

   The practices of the Irish Church were suppressed in favor of the Roman practices by the Synod of Whitby in 663.

6. **What does the *Rule of St. Benedict* prescribe for the life of monks?**

   The *Rule* divides the monks' day into periods of prayer, work, and sleep. It calls for prayer (reciting the Psalms) seven times a day and enjoins physical labor as a balance to the life of prayer and meditative reading.

   What, according to the *Rule*, were monks to do to help people outside the monastery?

   According to the *Rule*, monks are to show hospitality to travelers and petitioners who arrive at the monastery. They are also to care for the poor from the surplus of the monastery farm.

7. **What is the difference between temporal and spiritual power?**

   Temporal power is power over the things having to do with this life, while spiritual power has to do with spiritual or eternal things.

   Give examples of temporal and spiritual power.

   Making laws for a state or managing a farm are examples of temporal power. The administration of the sacraments and teaching the Faith are examples of spiritual power.

8. **Pope Gregory the Great took on more temporal power than the popes had before him. What events forced him to take on so much temporal power?**

   When Gregory became pope, Rome was threatened by the Lombards. The Italian countryside was laid waste. Unable to receive any aid from the emperor in Constantinople, it fell to Gregory to feed the Roman people and defend Rome itself.

Ideas in Action

1. **Study a Byzantine icon. What makes it different from other kinds of religious pictures? Why do you think Byzantine artists have made icons in this way? Iconographers are said to "write" their icons, not paint or draw them. Why do you think this is?**

   The teacher should help students to see and understand the various characteristics of

Byzantine icons—their two-dimensional feel, their exaggeration of certain characteristics (like the forehead), their stylized treatment of clothing or hair, their seeming lack of any perspective, and their use of reverse perspective (where what is in the foreground appears smaller than what is in the background.)

All these characteristics might indicate that iconographers are not trying to portray visual reality but are using visual means to point to spiritual truths. The "unrealistic" techniques iconographers use would then serve to alert the viewer to the fact that he is not to be looking at the icon, but through it to a deeper meaning.

Writing is generally used to convey ideas, while painting or drawing gives us visual impressions. Since an iconographer works to convey spiritual realities to the mind, his activity would more properly be called writing rather than painting or drawing. For the iconographer, the visual image is merely a means to convey meaning—like words are.

2. **Describe how the life of a Benedictine monk differs from that of a layperson. What can laypeople learn from the Benedictine monastic life?**

The teacher can help students to see that the external characteristics of monastic life—the strictly ordered day, set times of prayer, manual labor for self-discipline—do not exist as ends in themselves but as means to inculcate in the monk the twofold love of God and neighbor.

It is important to note here, however, that this purpose of monastic life is identical to the purpose of the Christian life itself. All Christians are called to love God with all their heart, soul, and mind, and to love their neighbor as themselves. The monastic life is one way of reaching this goal—a means, however, stripped of all that is extraneous, leaving only the essentials of prayer, self-discipline, and acts of charity. By observing the monastic life, laymen can learn what is most essential to reaching holiness and, in the context in which they live, dedicate themselves more to prayer, self discipline, and charity. The monastic life provides an example we all can follow, albeit in accordance with each person's vocations.

3. **Where are the missionary lands of our day? Is it possible for every Catholic to be a missionary? If so, how?**

If the missionary lands are only in foreign lands (in the still un-Christianized regions of Asia and Africa, for instance), then it is not possible for every Catholic to be a missionary, except by supporting the missions through donations. But students should be directed to ask what being a missionary actually entails. Does it mean bringing the Gospel to those who have never heard it before? Or does it mean simply bringing the Gospel to others? Is being a missionary, perhaps, a rather wide category, embracing more than the foreign missions?

4. **Learn as a class to sing one Gregorian chant, perhaps the *Pater Noster* or the *Salve Regina*.**

Sample Quiz for Pages 139–151

Please answer the following in complete sentences.

1. What were Justinian's two goals as emperor?
2. With what people did Justinian's Roman army fight in Italy?
3. What was Hagia Sophia?
4. What was the name for the Gaelic hereditary caste or guild of priests who were believed to work magic?
5. From where did St. Patrick come to Ireland? Why, after escaping slavery in Ireland, did he decide to return there?
6. What was the center of Church life in Christian Ireland?
7. What was Boethius' most important work?

Answer key to Sample Quiz I

Students' answers, of course, should only approximate the following.

1. Justinian's two goals were:
   a) to reconquer the territories in the West formerly belonging to the empire
   b) to reform Roman law
2. Justinian's army fought the *Ostrogoths* in Italy.
3. Hagia Sophia was *the great church in Constantinople rebuilt by Justinian.*
4. The name for the hereditary caste of Gaelic priests was *Druids*.
5. St. Patrick originally came from *Britain*. He decided to return to Ireland because *he had received a vision from God calling him to return there as a missionary.*
6. The *monastery* was the center of Church life in Christian Ireland.
7. Boethius' most important work was the *Consolation of Philosophy*.

Sample Quiz for Pages 152–162

Please answer the following in complete sentences.

1. Name two things monks had to do according to the *Rule* of St. Benedict.
2. Give an example of the sorts of things temporal power is concerned with.
3. Why did Pope Gregory the Great exercise temporal power?
4. Who was the monk whom Pope Gregory the Great sent to convert the Saxons in Britain? Where did he establish his episcopal see?
5. What was the name of the synod where the Gaelic Christians of Britain were forced to adopt Roman customs?

Answer key to Sample Quiz II

Students' answers, of course, should only approximate the following.

1. *Possible answers:* The *Rule* of St. Benedict prescribes:

    a) communal prayer seven times a day

    b) physical labor

    c) meditative reading

    d) hospitality to travelers and petitioners

    e) care for the poor

2. *Possible answers:* Temporal power is concerned with:

    a) making laws for a state

    b) owning property

    c) managing a business

3. Pope Gregory exercised temporal power *because the emperor and his governors were unable to help the people of Rome against their enemies or in improving their economic condition.*

4. *St. Augustine of Canterbury* was the monk Pope Gregory sent to convert the Saxons in Britain. He established his episcopal see at *Canterbury*

5. Gaelic Christians in Britain were forced to adopt Roman customs at the *Synod of Whitby*.

Sample Test

1. What lands that had formerly been part of the Western Roman Empire did Justinian's generals actually conquer? Were the conquests entirely successful? Please explain.

2. Why did Emperor Justinian order a reform of Roman law? What was the name of the reformed law code? Why has this code been important to history?

3. What were the two ways Gaelic monasteries aided in the building of Christendom?

4. List the seven liberal arts. How did Boethius help preserve the study of the seven liberal arts for future generations in Western Europe?

5. What was it about St. Benedict's *Rule* that led to the spread of Benedictine monasteries all over Western Europe?

6. Please identify the following:

    a) Power over things having to do with this life

    b) Power over things having to do with eternal things

    c) The missionary Pope Gregory I sent to convert the Saxons in England

    d) The first English king to become Christian

    e) The synod which ordered Gaelic Christians to adopt Roman customs

7. How did the role of the pope begin to change because of Pope Gregory I?

Answer key to Sample Test

Students' answers, of course, should only approximate the following.

1. Justinian's generals were able to reconquer only the *Vandal kingdom in North Africa, parts of Spain, and Ostrogothic Italy.* Justinian's conquests were *not entirely successful;* for, though *he was able to conquer Italy*, it was *only after a long war that left the peninsula devastated.*

2. Justinian ordered a reform of Roman law *to correct abuses that had crept into the law code* and *to make it easier for citizens to take action in law courts*

    The name of the new code was the *Codex Justinianus* (or *the Justinian Code.*)

    The code has been important to history *because it became the basis for law in the Middle Ages and in the 19th century.*

3. Gaelic monasteries helped in building Christendom by:

    a) preserving classical Latin manuscripts

    b) sending out missionaries who spread the Christian faith in Scotland and northern England

4. The seven liberal arts are: *grammar, logic, rhetoric, arithmetic, geometry, music,* and *astronomy.*

    Boethius helped preserve the seven liberal arts by *writing summaries of the arts* that became the textbooks for the Middle Ages.

5. Benedict's *Rule* was less harsh than earlier rules; it was more balanced. It thus could appeal to a greater number of people.

6. Identify the following:

    a) temporal power

    b) spiritual power

    c) St. Augustine of Canterbury

    d) Ethelbert

    e) Synod of Whitby

7. Under Pope Gregory I the role of the papacy began to change *because Gregory had to take on more temporal power. The pope was thus becoming a temporal as well as a spiritual leader.*

CHAPTER 7: The Rise of Islam— A.D. 624–800

Chapter Overview

- Because the Byzantine Roman emperors taxed the people of the empire heavily and punished heretics, many in the empire became discontent with Byzantine rule.

- The Persians invaded the Byzantine Empire, sacking Jerusalem and going as far as Chalcedon in Asia Minor. After 10 years of war, the Emperor Heraclius forced the Persian king Chosroes to surrender in 628.

- Muhammad began his life in poverty but became a wealthy owner of caravans. In his late thirties, he began to have dreams in which he said he heard divine voices. Muhammad believed he was given a new revelation that he was to be the prophet of Allah. This new revelation he called *Islam*, meaning "submission."

- Muhammad's revelations were collected into the Islamic holy book, called the Koran.

- Angry at Muhammad for attacking the worship of their many gods and making converts to Islam, the elders of Mecca drove Muhammad from their city in 622. The "Prophet" fled to the neighboring city of Medina.

- Muhammad called for a *jihad* or "holy war" against Mecca. In 624, his followers conquered the Meccans at the Battle of Bedr. The conquered city agreed to accept Islam and put away its ancient gods.

- Islam is a simple religion, calling only for worship of *Allah* as the only god and acknowledgment of Muhammad as his prophet. Those who submit to God are called Muslims. In some ways, Islam was an improvement over the ancient pagan religions of Arabia. Islam preached a universal brotherhood of all believers in Allah, but it also had many cruel and barbaric elements. The Muslim heaven is a paradise of sensual delights.

- After Muhammad's death in 632, his followers struggled over who should be his *caliph* (successor). The struggle between Muhammad's followers and their successors was often bloody.

- Under Caliph Omar, Islam began its violent expansion beyond the borders of Arabia. Over the next 100 years, Muslim armies conquered Persia, Syria, Palestine, Egypt, North Africa, and the Iberian Peninsula.

- The assassination of Caliph Ali and his son Husayn was the origin of a political and religious movement called the *Shiat Ali*. Ever since, Islam has been split between the "legitimate, loyal," and "traditional" believers, called *Sunnis*, and "partisans," the *Shiites*, the descendents of Ali's followers.

- The Umayyad caliphs oversaw a flowering of Islamic culture, drawn from Greek and

78 Chapter 7 The Rise of Islam—A.D. 624–800

Christian traditions. This flowering was continued and intensified under the Abbasid caliphs, who built their beautiful capital, Baghdad, in Mesopotamia.

Chapter Goals

This chapter introduces what was to become the chief rival to Christendom throughout the Middle Ages and into early modern times—Islam. Students should take from the chapter a basic understanding of the Islamic religion, including the militant character by which it united the Arab world and threatened the very existence of the Christian world. Students, too, should get a taste of the drama of the events that turned what had for hundreds of years been major centers of Christendom into the predominately Muslim lands of today.

It might be interesting to point out that medieval Christians came to see Islam, not so much as some sort of pagan religion, but as a Christian heresy. Some have opined that Islam essentially is rebirth of Arianism, with Muhammad replacing Christ as the intermediary between a distant God and man.

What Students Should Know

1. **Why the Eastern Roman Empire was deeply divided after the death of Justinian**

   To pay for his wars to recover the old Roman lands in the West, Justinian had heavily taxed his provinces. Resentment against these taxes was great in places like Syria and Egypt, where the people did not see why they had to pay for the emperor's wars in Mesopotamia, Western Europe, or elsewhere.

   Peoples in the East were angry over the emperor's use of the army to strike at his political opponents and punish heretics and rioters in the cities. Many in Syria and Egypt in particular joined heretical sects in opposition to the orthodox Christian emperor. The peoples of the eastern part of the empire began to think of the emperor, not as their defender, but as their oppressor.

2. **The extent of Chosroes II's conquests and how the Roman Empire recovered the lands he conquered**

   Chosroes II, king of Persia, conquered Roman-held Mesopotamia, Syria, and Palestine (including Jerusalem). The Persians penetrated as far as Chalcedon in Asia Minor. The Emperor Heraclius led the imperial armies against Chosroes, decisively defeating the Persians in 628. Heraclius regained all the lands the Persians had taken from the empire. The Persians, the empire's greatest foe, had been defeated.

3. **The main events of the life of Muhammad**

   The main events of Muhammad's life are as follows:

   a) His years as a caravan driver and his marriage to Khadija

   b) His conversion to monotheism and his first revelations in the month of Ramadan, 610

   c) Muhammad spreading his message and making converts

   d) The Hegira in 622—Muhammad's flight from Mecca to Medina

   e) Muhammad's first *jihad*—the conquest of Mecca in 624

   f) Muhammad's establishment of his theocratic rule over Mecca and his *jihad* to conquer other parts of Arabia

   g) Death of Muhammad, 632

4. **The teachings of Muhammad**

   a) There is no god but Allah (God), and Muhammad is his prophet.

b) God is perfectly one, not a trinity of persons.

c) Muslim faithful are to act justly toward their fellows, to care for the poor, etc.

d) Muslims are to observe dietary laws (such as abstaining from pork, alcohol).

e) Muslims are forbidden to make images or pictures.

f) Heaven is a paradise of sensual pleasures.

5. **Define the following terms: Allah, Islam, Muslim, Koran, Hegira, *jihad***

   a) *Allah* is the Arabic word for God.

   b) *Islam* means "submission"—it is the name of Muhammad's religion.

   c) *Muslim* means "one who submits"—it is the name for followers of Islam.

   d) The *Koran* is the holy book of Islam. It contains Muhammad's messages. Every letter of the Koran is thought to be inspired.

   e) Hegira is the name given to Muhammad's flight from Mecca to Medina and marks the beginning of the Muslim count of years.

   e) *Jihad* means "struggle." Originally in Islam it meant an inner struggle a believer undergoes to submit fully to God's will, but it later came to mean a holy war against the infidel.

6. **How Islam elevated the Arab people; how it fell short**

   Islam elevated the Arab people by replacing a cruel paganism that practiced human sacrifice, infanticide, and legal robbery with a religion that worshipped only one God and preached brotherhood. Muhammad required Muslims to support the poor and attempted to better the condition of women by limiting polygamy and regulating divorce. Islam tried to limit the power masters had over their slaves and laid out the rights of slaves.

   However, Muhammad's original vision centering around submission to God was compromised by his adoption of the notion of *jihad* as holy war. He allowed his followers to plunder and exact cruelties on those whom they conquered. Muhammad allowed the poor tax to be used to support holy war. He did not abolish polygamy. Though he allowed a man to have only four wives at one time, he could have as many concubines as he could afford.

7. **How Islam and Christianity chiefly differ**

   a) Both Islam and the Christianity are monotheistic, but Islam rejects the doctrine of the Trinity.

   b) The Christian Faith holds that Jesus is the Son of God; Islam holds that Jesus is one of the great prophets, the greatest but for Muhammad.

   c) Unlike Christianity, Islam has no sacraments or ordained priesthood, and no official theology.

   d) Christians enter the Church through baptism; people become Muslims by stating, "I testify: There is no god but Allah, and Muhammad is his Prophet."

8. **What a caliph is; what a mullah, imam, and emir are**

   Caliph means "successor." The caliph was said to be the successor of Muhammad as the judge, ruler of the faithful, and supreme commander of the armies. The first caliph, Abu Bakr, recognized the authority of *mullahs*, men who had the authority to preach and conduct prayer. An *imam* has religious authority over a local mosque or a particular territory.

9. **The Battle of Yarmouk, when it occurred, by whom it was fought, and what was its result**

The Byzantine army of about 80,000 met the Arab Muslim force of about 25,000 on the banks of the Yarmouk River in what is now Jordan in the late summer of 636. The Arabs wiped out the Byzantine army in the East and, because of this, the way was open for the conquest of Palestine. By 637, the Arabs had taken Antioch and Jerusalem itself.

10. How the Arabs changed during the caliphate of Othman

Having come into contact with the luxuries of the East, the Arabs began to abandon their simple life of piety. While Caliph Omar, Othman's predecessor, had slept on a bed of rushes and had eaten the common food of his desert dwelling ancestors, Othman himself lived more luxuriously and sought to increase his wealth.

11. The origin of the division of Shiites and Sunnis in Islam

The origin of the two groups lay in the struggle between Caliph Ali, Muhammad's cousin and son-in-law, and the Umayyads, the family of the murdered Caliph Othman. After Ali's assassination in 661, his son, Hasan, handed the caliphate over to the Umayyad leader. In 680, Ali's second son and Muhammad's only living grandson, Husayn, was cut down by the Umayyads as he went to join a rebel force in Iraq. Husayn's death became a symbol of heroic opposition for the political movement that arose to restore Ali's line to the caliphate. This group called itself the *Shiat Ali*, the "Party of Ali," and its members were called Shiites. The division remains today between the Shiites (the "partisans") and the Sunnis (the "legitimate, loyal, traditional" ones). The Shiites hold several different beliefs than the Sunnis.

12. How Islamic culture changed under the Umayyads

Under the Umayyads, Arab masters sought out scholars and teachers from the lands they conquered. The Umayyads began to search out the works of pagan writers, particularly the classical Greek authors. These were translated into Arabic and collected into libraries. In this way, the Umayyads helped preserve the artistic and scientific traditions of Greek Christian civilization.

Some Key Terms at a Glance

Allah: Arabic for God

Kaaba: the shrine at the center of Mecca and Islam's holiest place

Hegira: Muhammad's flight from Mecca and the beginning of the Muslim count of years

Islam: "submission" to Allah and the name of the religion founded by Muhammad

Koran: or *Qur'an*, the scripture of Islam containing the record of Muhammad's prophecies and commands

Jihad: interior "struggle" to submit one's will to Allah as well as a holy war against the unbelievers

Five Pillars of Islam: the central tenets of the Islamic faith

caliph: "successor" to the Prophet Muhammad and the spiritual and military leader of Islam

emir: the Muslim governor of a province

Shiite and Sunni: the two major divisions of Islam. *Shiite* means "partisan," and *Sunni* means "legitimate, loyal, and traditional."

The Umayyads also oversaw the building of exquisitely beautiful mosques. The Umayyad caliphate thus oversaw a sort of renaissance of learning in the Muslim lands.

13. **What was accomplished under the Abbasids**

The Abbasid caliphs built a new city on the Tigris River to be their capital. This was Baghdad, a rationally planned, luxurious city, with domed buildings, underground cisterns and water sewers, and fountains. Baghdad became a great center of trade and commerce and continued the intellectual awakening begun in Damascus under the Umayyads. The Abbasid caliphs patronized poetry, philosophy, medicine, mathematics, and astronomy. Their law courts developed the system of Islamic law derived from the Koran, the *Sharia*.

Questions for Review

1. **Why did the Emperor Heraclius' army lose the Battle of Yarmouk?**

   The emperor's defeat at Yarmouk was caused, in part, by the fact that his army was made up mostly of untested raw recruits. The zeal of the Arabs, who thought they would obtain paradise in the battle, terrified the Byzantine soldiers and caused a rout.

   Why is this battle so important to history?

   The Battle of Yarmouk destroyed the power of the Eastern Roman Empire in the Middle East. It opened up the Christian lands of Syria and Palestine—and, later, Egypt and North Africa—to Muslim conquest.

2. **How did Muhammad first receive his "messages" from Allah?**

   Muhammad first received his messages from Allah when in trances.

3. **What is the name of Muhammad's religion?**

   Muhammad's religion is called *Islam*.

   What does that word mean in English?

   Islam means *submission*.

4. **How was the Koran written?**

   Muhammad's wife and followers wrote down the messages the Prophet received. The messages were collected after Muhammad's death and arranged in a collection, called the Koran.

   Why do Muslims believe it cannot be translated?

   Muslims believe every letter and every word of the Koran is inspired. Thus, only the Arabic original is the inspired word of Allah to them. Any translation would not be the inspired word.

5. **What are the two meanings of the word *jihad*?**

   Jihad originally signified the internal struggle a believer underwent to submit fully to God's will. It later came to mean a religious war against the infidel.

6. **Why is Islam called a simple religion?**

   Islam is called a simple religion because it teaches a simple monotheism (no complicated doctrine like the Trinity) and an uncomplicated morality. It has no sacraments, no priesthood, and no official theology.

7. **What is a caliph?**

   A caliph is the "successor" of Muhammad and, like him, functions as judge and ruler of the faithful or as supreme commander of the armies.

8. **Where does the name *Shiite* come from?**

   Shiite comes from the phrase, *Shiat Ali*, the "Party of Ali." The Shiites wanted to restore Ali's line to the office of caliph.

How do Shiites differ from other Muslims?

Shiites have several different beliefs from other Muslims.

9. **Who built Baghdad?**

The Abbasid Caliph Al-Saffah built Baghdad.

What city was it intended to rival?

Baghdad was intended to rival Constantinople.

Ideas in Action

1. **Discuss the five pillars of Islam. Which pillars might be acceptable to Christians and which might be unacceptable? Why?**

   a) *shehada*—acknowledgment that there is no god but God (Allah) and Muhammad is his prophet. (*Christians acknowledge only one God, but he is a God with Three Divine Persons—a notion Muslims consider polytheistic. A Christian of course could not acknowledge Muhammad as the prophet of God, since Muhammad taught things contrary to Christ and the Church.*)

   b) *salat*—prayer five times a day facing toward Mecca and the Kaaba. (*All religions have similarities. Prayer is enjoined by both the Christian Faith and Islam. But the mode of prayer differs. Since the objects of Muslim prayer—Mecca and the Kaaba—represent Islam, they are not, of course, the objects of Christian prayer.*)

   c) *sawn*—a fast from food and drink during the daylight hours for the whole month of Ramadan. (*Nothing in particular forbids a Christian to fast during the period called Ramadan any more than he or she is forbidden to fast at any other time of the year. To join in the Muslim fast, however, could lead to* indifferentism—*the notion that it does not matter to which religion one belongs.*)

   d) *zakal*—giving alms and paying the poor tax for the relief of the unfortunate. (*The Christian Faith, of course, enjoins acts of charity and almsgiving. Normally we think of this as voluntary and not a "tax." Support for the Church in the Middle Ages, however, was by way of a tax—the notion being that, since the Church contributes to the common good, it is not simply gratuitous, but a duty in justice to support the Church.*)

   e) *hajj*—making a pilgrimage to Mecca at least once in one's life. (*Pilgirmages have formed an important part of Catholic piety over the centuries; yet they have never been a matter of precept for everyone. Some Christians in the Middle Ages had to undertake pilgrimages for penance, but most others freely became pilgrims.*)

2. **Draw a map of the extent of Muslim expansion over the world since the founding of Islam. Color each conquered land a different color to show when the Muslims conquered it.**

   This activity can either be done as a class or as an individual or group homework assignment.

Sample Quiz for Pages 167–178

Please answer the following in complete sentences.

1. Identify the following:

    a) The emperor who reconquered Syria, Palestine, and Mesopotamia from Persia

    b) Muhammad's flight from Mecca to Medina

    c) A holy war against the infidel

2. What must someone confess in order to become Muslim?

3. What does *Islam* mean? What does *Muslim* mean?

4. What is the Koran? Why do Muslims believe it cannot be translated?

5. Name one way in which Islam and Christianity differ.

Answer key to Sample Quiz I

Students' answers, of course, should only approximate the following.

1. Answers:

    a) Emperor Heraclius

    b) *Hejra* or Hegira

    c) jihad

2. In order to become a Muslim, one must *confess there is no god but Allah (God) and Muhammad is his prophet.*

3. Islam means *"submission."* Muslim means *"one who submits."*

4. The Koran is *the holy book of Islam*. Muslims believe the Koran cannot be translated because *they say every word and letter of it is inspired by God.*

5. Possible answers:

    a) Both Islam and Christianity are monotheistic, but Islam rejects the doctrine of the Trinity.

    b) The Christian Faith holds that Jesus is the Son of God; Islam holds that Jesus is one of the great prophets, the greatest but for Muhammad.

    c) Unlike Christianity, Islam has no sacraments or ordained priesthood, and no official theology.

    d) Christians enter the Church through baptism; people become Muslims by stating, "I testify: There is no god but Allah, and Muhammad is his Prophet."

84 Chapter 7 The Rise of Islam—A.D. 624–800

Sample Quiz for Pages 178–189

Please answer the following in complete sentences.

1. What was a caliph? What is an imam?

2. At what battle did the Arabs destroy the Byzantine army of the East and so open up Syria and Palestine to Muslim conquest? What year did this battle occur?

3. What is the name of the Muslim group that arose from the followers of Ali. What does this name mean? What is the name of the other, larger Muslim group? What does this name mean?

4. What city did the Abbasid caliphs build near the Tigris River? Why is this city important to history?

Answer key to Sample Quiz II

Students' answers, of course, should only approximate the following.

1. A caliph was *a successor of Muhammad*. An imam *has religious authority over a local mosque or territory.*

2. The battle in which the Arabs destroyed the Byzantine army of the East was *the Battle of Yarmouk*, fought in *636*.

3. The Muslim group that arose from the followers of Ali is the *Shiites*. The name means *"partisan."* The other, larger Muslim group is the *Sunnis*, a name that means *"legitimate" or "loyal" or "traditional."*

4. The Abbasids built *Baghdad*. Baghdad became important *as a great center of trade* and was *the center of a great intellectual and artistic awakening.*

Sample Test

1. Give one reason people living in Syria, Palestine, and Egypt were dissatisfied with the rule of the Byzantine Empire after the death of Justinian.

2. Who was Heraclius? What great enemy did he defeat? Why can we say his reign ended in failure?

3. What is monotheism? How does Muhammad's monotheism differ from Christian monotheism?

4. What two things did Muhammad mean by *jihad*?

5. Identify the following:

    a) What the name *Muslim* means

    b) The city built by the Abbasid caliphs on the Tigris River in Mesopotamia

    c) The title for a Muslim leader who was said to be the successor of Muhammad as the judge, ruler of the faithful, and supreme commander of the armies

6. What do the following mean?

    a) *Allah*   c) mullah

    b) Islam   d) imam

7. What is the Koran? Why do Muslims believe it cannot be translated from Arabic into any other language?

8. In what year was the Battle of Yarmouk fought? Between whom was it fought? What were its results?

9. Who was Ali? What are those Muslims called who had as their goal the restoration of Ali's line to the caliphate? What is the name for those Muslims who, not belonging to Ali's party, consider themselves the "traditional" believers?

Answer key to Sample Test

Students' answers, of course, should only approximate the following.

1. *Possible Answers:*

    a) They resented the high taxes they had to pay to the imperial government.

    b) They were angry over the emperor's use of the army to strike at his political opponents and punish heretics and rioters in the cities.

2. Heraclius was *an Eastern Roman (or Byzantine) emperor*. The great enemy he defeated was *the Persians*. We can say his reign ended in failure because, not long after the defeat of Persians, *the Arab Muslims took all the territories Heraclius had regained from the Persians.*

3. Monotheism is *the belief in only one god.* Muhammad's idea of monotheism differs from the Christian idea in that *Christians believe in the Trinity—that there is one God in three divine Persons—while Muhammad taught that God is one, not a Trinity of persons.*

4. By *jihad* Muhammad meant:

    a) an inner struggle a believer undergoes to submit fully to God's will

    b) a holy war against the infidel (non-Muslims)

5. *Answers:*

    a) "one who submits"

    b) Baghdad

    c) caliph

6. *Answers:*

    a) Allah is the Arabic word for God.

    b) Islam means "submission."

    c) A mullah is a man who has the authority to preach and lead prayer in Islam.

    d) An imam is a man who has religious authority over a local mosque or particular territory.

7. The Koran is *the book containing the teachings of Muhammad*. Muslims believe it cannot be translated because *they think every word of the Koran was inspired by God*. So it is that only the Arabic version of the Koran is considered to be the word of God.

8. The Battle of Yarmouk was fought in the year *636* between the *Arab Muslims and the army of the East Roman or Byzantine Empire*. It resulted *in the complete destruction of the Byzantine army in the East* and *opened up Palestine and all of Syria to Muslim conquest.*

9. Ali was *Muhammad's cousin and the husband of his daughter*, Fatima. He was *a caliph*. Those Muslims who wanted to restore Ali's line to the caliphate are called *Shiites*. Those Muslims who consider themselves the "traditional" believers are the *Sunnis*.

CHAPTER 8: The Defense and Building of Christendom

Chapter Overview

- Caliph Suleiman sent an army of 100,000 under his brother Maslama to attack Constantinople. Leo, the governor of Anatolia, convinced Maslama to stop his advance. When the reigning emperor abdicated in his favor, Leo himself became emperor. Though Maslama laid siege to Constantinople, the Emperor Leo ultimately broke the siege, forcing the Muslim force to withdraw.

- Though Leo had saved the Church in Constantinople, he subsequently supported the heretical and unpopular cause of iconoclasm, ordering the destruction of holy pictures of the saints, Our Lady, and Christ.

- In 711, Muslim forces under Tarik defeated Christian forces at La Janda, near the southern tip of Iberia. The Muslim forces conquered most of the Iberian Peninsula, except for Asturias, where a small Christian kingdom continued its resistance to Islam. This resistance marked the beginning of the *reconquista*, the Christian reconquest of Spain, that would last almost 800 years.

- Though surrounded by heathens and Muslims, the Frankish kingdom had an able leader in Charles Martel. Charles sent missionaries to convert the pagan Germans to the east. St. Boniface established churches, monastic communities, and abbeys throughout southern Germany.

- In 732, an enormous Muslim force crossed into the Frankish lands. They were defeated by Charles Martel and his outnumbered army at the Battle of Tours.

- A rich and beautiful culture grew up in Al-Andalus, as Islamic Iberia was called. Though its peoples were often divided by strife, Al-Andalus became the envy of its less civilized and wealthy Christian neighbors.

- Monasteries in Britain and Ireland preserved the learning of the ancient world and the writings of the Church fathers. Notable among the scholars of these lands were St. Bede the Venerable and Alcuin, who founded a school in the court of the Emperor Charlemagne.

- After deposing the last Merovingian king, Pepin the Short, son of Charles Martel, was crowned king of the Franks by St. Boniface, as the pope's representative.

- Charles the Great (Charlemagne) succeeded his father Pepin as king of the Franks. Charles fought many wars, including a 32-year war against the Saxons, another against the Lombards in Italy, and a brief war against the Muslims in northern Spain. But Charles was not just a warrior; he was a great political reformer who brought peace, learning, and prosperity to his vast domains.

- Charles was also a protector of the Church. Pope Leo III crowned Charles emperor of the Romans on Christmas Day, 800. This marked the establishment of Christendom in the West.

Chapter Goals

The teacher should help students to see in what peril Christendom stood in the Dark Ages. The regions that were Christian in the 8th and 9th centuries were few in number, and most of them were barbaric (in comparison to Constantinople and the ancient urban centers of the eastern Mediterranean.) Even Rome was but a shadow of its former glory—a glory long since extinguished by barbarian invasion, conquest, and wasting war. The Eastern Roman Empire had lost most of its territory to the triumphant Muslim Arabs and was in a state of siege. The Muslims had conquered most of the Iberian Peninsula, where they established a high culture that cast in shadow the relatively primitive culture of the Christian German and Romano-Gaelic peoples.

The Christian realms not only faced the threat of Muslim conquest; on the eastern borders of Germany, pagan Saxons, Slavs, and Avars threatened the security and peace of the Christian lands. It was in this world of peril that Charles the Great established the first powerful state that the West had seen since the fall of the western Roman Empire. Charles's Frankish Roman Empire represented the promise of things to come—a culture unified by religion and led by a restored empire founded on the ideal of the Roman Empire. But Charles's reign was only a promise of this. As we shall see in the following chapter, his empire too all but fell to ruin during a 150-year period of invasions from barbarian pagan peoples (the Vikings and Magyars.)

What Students Should Know

1. **Why Emperor Leo III is to be remembered as the savior of Europe**

   In 717, Leo led the Byzantine forces in breaking a siege of Constantinople by Arab Muslims under the caliph's brother, Maslama. The Byzantine fleet defeated the Muslim fleet, while the Byzantine army defeated the Muslim army on the Asian side of the Bosporus. Maslama's army was cut off in Thrace, where it was destroyed by a force of Bulgarian Christians. If Constantinople had been taken by Maslama, Muslim forces would probably have defeated the pagan tribes of Eastern Europe, who would most likely have become Muslim. Gaul, the Germanies, and Italy might not have been able to stand up against Muslim invasions from the East and from Spain, and Christendom might have met an untimely end. By saving Constantinople, Leo may have saved all of Europe.

2. **What the iconoclast controversy was about, who instigated it, and how it finally ended**

   Though an able ruler in many ways, Emperor Leo III made the mistake of trying to eradicate the use of images in Christian worship. He became, thus, the first of the iconoclast ("icon-breaker") emperors. His attempts to remove all statues and images from churches was resisted by clergy, laymen, and monks, called iconodules ("those who serve images"), whom the emperor persecuted. Persecution of iconodules continued under Leo's successors. The Seventh Ecumenical Council, meeting at Nicaea, declared that the use of icons in worship or the act of honoring them is not idolatry as long as they are not worshipped as if they were divine. Images are only to be given honor for the sake of the persons they represent. Though Emperor Leo V resumed persecution of iconodules after the council, the Empress Theodora ordered the restoration of icons to the churches. On February 19, 842, the icons were solemnly carried into churches in what has been called the "Triumph of Orthodoxy."

3. **What happened at the Battle of La Janda or Guadalete, when it was fought, and what its result was**

   At the Battle of La Janda in 711, the Umayyad Emir Tarik defeated Roderick, the last king of the Visigoths in Spain. After the battle, the Muslims took the Visigothic capital, Toledo, and conquered the entire Iberian Peninsula, except for Asturias, a mountainous district in the northwest.

4. **What the *Reconquista* was, for what purpose it was fought, under whom it began, and what its first victory was and when**

   The *Reconquista* is the nearly 800-year reconquest of the Iberian Peninsula by Christian Spaniards and Portuguese. These fought to preserve their culture and their Catholic Faith, to organize society on Christian principles, and to drive Muslim rule from the formerly Christian-controlled lands of Iberia. The Reconquest began under the Visigothic leader, Don [the title for a noble in Spanish] Pelayo, who organized the small Christian kingdom of Asturias. In 718, at Covadonga, Don Pelayo and his Christian forces forced the Muslim army to retreat after a small skirmish. This was the first Christian victory in what would be a centuries-long war.

5. **Who Charles Martel was and what he accomplished for Christendom**

   Charles Martel was the Frankish mayor of the palace, serving under the Meroving king. He united the Frankish realms of Neustria and Austrasia under his rule and subdued the German Bavarians, Hessians, and Lombards. In 732, the Islamic Emir Abd-ar-Rahman invaded Gaul. Gathering the Frankish forces, Charles Martel met the Muslim forces at Tours and decisively defeated them. In this battle, Charles and the Franks halted the Muslim advance into Western Europe.

6. **Who St. Boniface was and what he accomplished**

   Boniface was an English Benedictine monk whom Charles Martel sent into Germany to missionize the pagan Germans and the heretical Christians of Bavaria. Boniface began his missionary labors among the pagan Frisians in 716. In 718, Pope Gregory II appointed Boniface a missionary to the pagan Germans. In 722, the pope consecrated Boniface a bishop. Boniface converted the pagan Hessians and restored Bavaria and Thuringia to orthodoxy. For his success, Boniface is known as the "Apostle of Germany." In 754 he was martyred at the hands of pagan Frisians.

7. **What Al-Andalus was and what kind of culture it had**

   Al-Andalus was the name for the Muslim-controlled lands of the Iberian Peninsula. It came under the rule of the Ummayad caliphs of Cordoba in Spain, but eventually divided into a number of warring Muslim states. It was a land boasting a high culture of art and learning, with poets and scholars, beautiful cities, just law courts, and booming commerce. Many different peoples lived in Al-Andalus—Christians, called *Mozarabes*; Jews; African Berbers; and Arabians, among others. Christians and Jews had to pay heavy taxes to continue to practice their religions.

8. **In what the "springtime of learning" in the British Isles consisted; who Bede the Venerable was**

   Monasteries, both Gaelic and Saxon, dedicated themselves to scholarship, sending for books from Gaul and Italy. They preserved classical

Latin texts, both those of pagan and Christian authors alike. Recopying these texts, the monks sent them to daughter houses scattered hundreds of miles around, and so helped to preserve classical learning.

Bede was a monk of Jarrow Abbey in Northumberland. He was a great scholar, writing on many subjects, including grammar, music, and natural science. He composed poems and hymns and wrote commentaries on the Scriptures. His most famous work is his *Ecclesiastical History of the English People*, in which he related the history of England from the conquest of Julius Caesar to his own time, the eighth century.

9. **How Pepin the Short became king of the Franks**

    Pepin the Short, like his grandfather Pepin and his father Charles Martel, was Frankish mayor of the palace. Pepin the Short's father and grandfather had not attempted to become king themselves, for, unlike the Merovings, they could not claim ancestry from a legendary hero. The last Meroving king, Childerich III, however, was an imbecile, and in part because of this, Pepin was able to convince the Frankish Great Council to elect him king. With the blessing of the pope and St. Boniface, the Frankish tribal assembly proclaimed Pepin king in 751.

10. **The role of the Carolingian kings in relation to the pope and the Church**

    Pepin the Short fought for the pope against the Lombards and subdued them. In return, the pope recognized Pepin as his protector. Charles the Great continued his father's relationship with the Church. In 774, Charles drove the Lombard king out of Italy and so saved the pope and the Patrimony of St. Peter from Lombard oppression. The pope recognized Charles as his protector.

11. **The accomplishments of Charles the Great**

    a) The conquest of the Lombards and the establishment of papal rule in central Italy

    b) The conquest and conversion of the pagan Saxons after a long series of wars that began around 770 and lasted until 804

    c) Bringing political order to the Frankish kingdom by dividing it into counties, each ruled by a *comes* (count), and the appointment of officials who traveled about the empire and reported on the state of things to the king

    d) Bringing the Anglo-Saxon renaissance in learning to the continent, establishing schools, and preserving the Latin classics

12. **How Charles the Great became Roman emperor and the significance of the event**

    As protector of the Church, Charles crossed the Alps and defeated the pope's enemies in 800, restoring Pope Leo III to the papal throne. On Christmas Day, 800, at the end of Mass in St. Peter's, while Charles remained kneeling before the altar, Pope Leo approached him and, placing a crown on the king's head, proclaimed him emperor of the Romans.

    Thus was established the Roman Empire in the West. The new empire was to be a close union of Church and state, the embodiment of Christendom, a society supported by workers, protected by its emperor and his lords, and guided by the pope and the bishops.

Questions for Review

1. **Why did Leo make an alliance with the sultan of the Muslims?**

    Leo made the alliance in order to save his troops (by marching them to Constantinople without their being attacked) and to buy time to build up the defenses of Constantinople.

Some Key Terms at a Glance

Golden Horn: the great natural harbor of Constantinople through which the city became rich and powerful

iconoclasm: "image-breaking," the rejection of the use of images depicting holy people and things as idolatry as well as the destruction of such images

Orthodox: "right teaching"; capitalized, the word *Orthodox* came to refer to the Eastern branch of Christianity

Al-Andalus: the Arabic name for Spain or Iberia

Emperor of the Romans: title given to Charlemagne by the pope on Christmas Day, 800

count: an official appointed by Charlemagne as the governor of a province or region (from Latin *comes*, meaning "companion")

How did Leo save Christendom?

Leo saved Christendom by breaking Maslama's siege of Constantinople and weakening the power of his army and navy

2. **What technological invention saved the Byzantine Christian fleet from the Muslim ships?**

The technological invention that saved the fleet was Greek fire.

3. **What happened at Covadonga?**

At Covadonga, Don Pelayo and the remnant of the free Christians on the Iberian Peninsula defeated a Muslim force.

Why was it important?

The battle was important because it lifted the morale of the Christians and inspired them to further resistance. It was the first battle in the nearly 800-year Christian Reconquest of the Iberian Peninsula.

4. **Who was the victor in the Battle of Tours in 732?**

Charles Martel and his Frankish forces were victorious at Tours.

Why was that battle important?

The victory at Tours halted the Muslim invasion of (or penetration into) northern Europe.

5. **Why did Pepin the Short ask to be crowned king of the Franks?**

As mayor of the palace, Pepin did all the work of the king without having the title of king. The reigning Meroving king, Childerich III, was an imbecile. These two considerations induced Pepin to seek the title of king from the Franks.

6. **How did the Irish and British monasteries help to preserve civilization?**

These monasteries helped preserve civilization by recopying manuscripts of ancient poets, philosophers, and Christian theologians.

7. **Why did Charlemagne start schools across Frankish lands?**

Charlemagne started schools because he saw that his clergy did not know enough Latin to understand the Scriptures. Thus he started schools in monasteries and cathedrals for the perfect learning of the Latin tongue.

8. **Why was the crowning of Charlemagne as Roman emperor so important to history?**

The empire that Charlemagne and Pope Leo III established represented a close relationship between Church and state. It was a pivotal moment in the development of the Christian society we call Christendom.

Ideas in Action

1. **Discuss why those who know the Ten Commandments might reject the use of images. Can images be used in worship if the Old Testament forbids anyone to make images or bow down before them?**

   The Old Testament forbids making an image of the invisible God. It does not forbid images in themselves but the worship of them. (For instance, God prescribed the making of cherubim images on the Ark of the Covenant.) The Incarnation made it possible to picture God in the person of Jesus Christ; in making statues and pictures of Christ, we do not make images of the invisible God, but of God incarnate in Christ. Since the saints are not to be worshipped as if they were divine, their images, too, are not to be worshipped. In honoring Christ through images, we do not "bow down before them" in the sense of paying them worship as if they were actually the one they represent.

   Do Catholics worship images?

   Catholics do not worship images but pay honor to the one (such as Christ or a saint) an image represents. If we bow before images, it is not to the image itself we bow but to the one it represents.

   How is reverence different from worship?

   Worship is paid to the one to whom it is due, on account of who he is. Reverence is respect shown to what belongs to the one worshipped simply because it belongs to him and not because of some divinity intrinsic to the object.

   Is iconoclasm still with us?

   Iconoclasm is a recurring phenomenon in Church history. The Protestant Reformation, for instance, inspired a number of image breakers. Some Catholics today think images (or too many of them) distract from worship, though few if any Catholics outright reject the use of images entirely.

2. **Like a medieval monk, copy a page from your Bible in your best handwriting (suggestions: the Twenty-third Psalm, the opening paragraphs of the Gospel of John, or some familiar passage). Decorate it with illustrations and ornaments. How is copying a text both a good exercise in memorization and a method of focusing on the text? Why would the old monasteries make copying a discipline of spiritual growth?**

   Note: In some Catholic versions (such as the Douay-Rheims), the Psalm 23 referred to here is Psalm 22.

3. **Find and copy out a Carolingian alphabet. Try to make the letters in the Carolingian form. Compare it to another style of making the letters, such as our own.**

   An example of an alphabet used in Carolingian times is *uncial*, used from the 3rd to the 8th in manuscripts, and afterwards more as a display face. Another alphabet, *Carolingian miniscule*, was developed during the time of Charlemagne and widely used until about 1200.

4. **Make a map of Charlemagne's empire. How much of Europe did it cover?**

   This activity can either be done as a class, working on one or a few posters, or as an individual or group homework assignment.

Chapter 8   The Defense and Building of Christendom

Sample Quiz for Pages 193–199

Please answer the following in complete sentences.

1. Why was Emperor Leo III's victory over the Muslims under Maslama important for the history of Europe?

2. What is an iconoclast? What emperor tried to force iconoclasm on the Church?

3. What is an iconodule? What is the name of the day the icons were solemnly carried into the churches following Empress Theodora's order that they be restored?

4. What happened at the Battle of La Janda (or Guadalete) in 711? What were its results?

5. What was the Reconquest? Under what king did it begin?

Answer key to Sample Quiz I

Students' answers, of course, should only approximate the following.

1. If Leo had not defeated Maslama, *the pagan tribes of Eastern Europe would probably have become Muslim instead of Christian. The western European Germanic kingdoms might not have been able to withstand attack from Spain and Eastern Europe.*

2. An iconoclast is *an image breaker. Leo III* tried to force iconoclasm on the Church.

3. An iconodule is *one who serves images* or *favors their use in worship*. The day the icons were solemnly restored to the churches is *the Triumph of Orthodoxy*.

4. At La Janda *the Muslims defeated the Visigoths*. Following the battle, *the Muslims were able to conquer nearly all of Spain*.

5. The Reconquest was *the nearly 800-year struggle to retake the Iberian Peninsula from the Muslims*. It began under *Don Pelayo*.

Sample Quiz for Pages 199–214

Please answer the following in complete sentences.

1. When was the Battle of Tours fought? Who led the Franks against the Muslims?

2. Who was the missionary and bishop, called the Apostle of Germany, who converted the pagan Hessians and restored Bavaria and Thuringia to orthodoxy?

3. What was the name for the Muslim-controlled part of the Iberian Peninsula?

4. Who was the monk of Jarrow Abbey and the author of the *Ecclesiastical History of the English People*?

5. Who was the first Carolingian king of the Franks? Why did he say he should be king?

6. When was Charles the Great, or Charlemagne, crowned emperor of the Romans? By whom was he crowned?

Answer key to Sample Quiz II

Students' answers, of course, should only approximate the following.

1. The Battle of Tours was fought in *732. Charles Martel* led the Franks against the Muslims.
2. *St. Boniface* is the bishop who converted the Hessians, restored the Bavarian Church, and is called the Apostle of Germany.
3. The Muslim-controlled part of the Iberian Peninsula was called *Al-Andalus.*
4. *St. Bede the Venerable* was the monk of Jarrow Abbey who wrote the *Ecclesiastical History of the English People.*
5. The first Carolingian king was *Pepin the Short.* He said he should have the title of king *because he was exercising the power of a king as mayor of the palace.*
6. Charles the Great was crowned emperor on *Christmas Day, 800,* by *Pope Leo III.*

Sample Test

1. How did Emperor Leo III and Charles Martel save Europe
2. What did the iconoclasts teach about the use of images in worship? What did the iconoclast emperor, Leo III, do to anger the iconodules? What did the Seventh Ecumenical Council finally decide about the use of icons in worship?
3. Identify the following:
   a) The battle where the Emir Tarik defeated the Visigoths, so opening the way for the conquest of nearly the entire Iberian Peninsula
   b) The Visigothic leader of the Christian resistance in Spain who founded a kingdom in Asturias
   c) The first battle of the Reconquest in which the Christians defeated the Muslims
   d) The year the Battle of Tours was fought
   e) The monk from England who converted the Hessians, reformed the Bavarian Church, and died a martyr. He is called the "Apostle of Germany."
   f) The monk of Jarrow Abbey in Northumberland, England, who wrote the *Eccesiastical History of the English People*
4. What was the Muslim part of Spain called? What religious groups lived there? What kind of culture did it have?
5. Why did it make sense that the mayor of the palace, Pepin the Short, should become king of the Franks in place of the last Meroving king, Childerich III? What is the name of the line of kings Pepin started?
6. List three of the accomplishments of Charlemagne.
7. What day and year did Pope Leo III crown Charlemagne as Roman emperor?
8. Why was the crowning of Charlemagne as Roman emperor so important?

Answer key to Sample Test

Students' answers, of course, should only approximate the following.

1. Leo III and Charles Martel both saved Europe *by saving Europe from Muslim invasions. Each defeated the Muslim invaders in a decisive battle.*

2. The iconoclasts taught *that using images in worship is idolatry* and so they said *religious images should be destroyed.* The iconoclast emperor, Leo III, *decreed that all images of saints and of Christ be removed from the churches and destroyed,* thus angering the iconodules. The Seventh Ecumenical Council declared *that the use of icons in worship or honoring them is not idolatry as long as they are not worshipped as if they were divine.*

3. *Answers:*
   a) Battle of La Janda (or Guadalete)
   b) Don Pelayo
   c) Covadonga
   d) 732
   e) St. Boniface
   f) Bede (the Venerable)

4. The Muslim part of Spain was called *Al-Andalus.* The religious groups that lived there were the *Muslims, Christians, and Jews.* Al-Andalus had *a high culture of art and learning,* with poets and scholars, beautiful cities, and just law courts, and booming commerce.

5. It made sense for Pepin the Short to become king in place of King Childerich III because, as mayor of the palace, *Pepin did the work of the king.* Childerich did none of the tasks of a king, though he held the title.

   The line of kings Pepin started is *the Carolingian line.*

6. *Possible answers:*
   a) the conquest of the Lombards and the establishment of papal rule in central Italy
   b) the conquest and conversion of the pagan Saxons after a long series of wars that began around 770 and lasted until 804
   c) bringing political order to the Frankish kingdom by dividing it into counties, each ruled by a *comes* (count) and the appointment of officials who traveled about the empire and reported on the state of things to the king
   d) bringing the Anglo-Saxon renaissance in learning to the continent, and the establishment of schools and preservation of the Latin classics

7. Charlemagne was crowned emperor on *Christmas Day, 800.*

8. The crowning of Charlemagne was important *because it embodied Christendom, a society characterized by a close union of Church and state.*

CHAPTER 9: The Achievements of Feudalism—A.D. 800–1008

Chapter Overview

- The Viking invasions from Scandinavia terrorized Europe from Spain to Russia during the ninth century. The Vikings, also called Northmen, pillaged and destroyed villages, cities, and monasteries, enslaving the inhabitants. The invasions set back the economy and agriculture of France, Italy, and Moorish Spain for decades. In Russia, England, and northern France (Normandy), Vikings set up permanent settlements.

- A barbarian people from the East, the Magyars, were fierce warriors and skilled horsemen. They settled the Hungarian plain, raiding Germany and northern Italy.

- Charlemagne's son, King Louis the Pious, divided the Frankish Empire between his three sons. Later, when another son, Charles, was born to the king, Louis cut out a domain for him from the lands he had already partitioned out to his other sons. This led Louis's three older sons to rebel against their father. Rebellions and rivalries between his sons lasted until the end of Louis's life.

- Because kings could not protect their subjects, the people began to seek aid from local lords. This was the beginning of feudalism, a customary network of local military leaders, who swore by oath to come to each other's defense.

- Under feudalism, men called vassals swore oaths of allegiance to lords, called lieges, promising to aid them in time of war. In return, the vassals received grants of land from their lords. Feudal lords were military men, called knights, who fought on horseback to defend their people.

- A feudal manor provided everything needed for daily life. Farmers on the manor were usually serfs—not slaves, but men bound to the soil they worked. Serfs were guaranteed the lifelong use of certain pieces of land, which their children could inherit. A serf could keep all his produce, except for what he owed in taxes to his lord or in tithes to the Church. Through hard work a serf could eventually buy his freedom.

- The code of chivalry laid out ideals for the behavior of knights, such as justice in war, fair play, protection of women and the poor, as well as behavior regulated by religious principles.

- During the medieval period, the veneration of Mary, the Mother of God, brought inner courage to the European peoples and inspired them with a new respect for women.

- Improvements in agricultural technology and techniques during the Middle Ages allowed for larger crop yields with less labor. This period has been called the "Second Agricultural Revolution." Among the important advances were the open field system, the moldboard plow, the breeding of the heavy farm horse, the horse stirrup, the padded horse collar, and the windmill.

- As the population of Western Europe grew, new lands were opened up for settlement in the East. Lords conquered lands held by pagan nations and invited peasants to settle them.

- The Middle Ages witnessed the growth of new towns and the renewal of old ones. Italian cities such as Venice, Genoa, and Pisa grew wealthy and powerful by carrying on trade between the eastern Mediterranean and North Africa, on the one hand, and the markets in Europe, on the other. In Lombardy and Tuscany, cities developed industrial specialties. In northern Europe, cities grew up around trade centers. Cities in the Low Countries thrived by manufacturing and trading in woolen cloth.

- Cities received charters that made them largely independent of local lords. Under these charters, cities established their own governments.

- In the cities, merchant and craft guilds developed as means of protecting, promoting, and regulating the economic activities of their members. The trade guilds were governed by master craftsmen, who were independent owners of their businesses under the guilds. These guilds included apprentices and journeymen who could, eventually, become masters themselves.

Chapter Goals

This chapter gives an overview of some important aspects of culture in the Middle Ages. It is important that the student understand the workings of feudalism and the manorial system, since these will provide him or her with the key to interpret much of the history related in subsequent chapters.

The summary nature of the chapter may make it appear that the Middle Ages was a pretty monolithic time, as far as culture goes. The teacher, therefore, should stress to students that medieval culture developed over a period of about 1,000 years and was as varied as that found in any other 1,000-year period. As subsequent chapters will show, the Middle Ages was a very dynamic era.

What Students Should Know

1. **Who the Vikings were, whence they came, what effect they had on Europe, and what lands they settled**

   Viking, meaning "sailor" or "traveler," was a name Northmen who left their homelands gave themselves. The Northmen were Germanic peoples (Swedes, Norwegians, Danes) who lived in Scandinavia. Their invasions into the regions of Europe south of Scandinavia and the British Isles had a devastating effect on the communities they raided. They destroyed villages, laid siege to cities, pillaged and plundered monasteries, enslaving the inhabitants of these places. They effectively halted the development of European civilization that had begun under Charlemagne. Their invasions helped weaken centralized government, which led to the development of feudalism.

   Though the Vikings were raiders, some settled in regions outside Scandinavia. Viking settlements included the region of northern France, called Normandy, and Novgorod and Kiev, in what is now Russia. In the latter places, the Vikings ruled over and mingled with a largely Slavic population.

2. **What other peoples invade Europe in the 9th and 10th centuries**

   Other invaders of Europe in this period were the Muslims from North Africa, whom the French called "Saracens." The Saracens conquered Sicily and Corsica, and established settlements on Sicily. From these points they raided southern

Gaul and the Italian peninsula, plundering Rome itself.

The Magyars, who came from the steppes of Asia, raided Italy and Germany during this period. They settled the Hungarian plain along the Danube.

3. **How the weakness of kings in the face of invasions led to the development of feudalism**

The inability of kings, like Charles the Fat, to protect their people from invasions meant that the people began to look elsewhere for protection. By necessity, the people turned to their local bishop, abbot, or count for leadership. This led to a decentralized form of government where local lords or strongmen agreed to protect the populace in return for land and service—in other words, it led to feudalism.

4. **The basic form of the feudal relationship**

Feudalism was based on a personal relationship between a lord (called a liege) and the one who served him (called a vassal). A liege lord would grant land as a *feod* or *fief* to one who swore an oath of loyalty to him. In return for the vassal's service, the liege lord granted him protection. Sometimes a lord would hand over his land to another, more powerful lord, and receive it back as a fief after swearing an oath of loyalty. If the vassal failed to keep his oath of loyalty, his liege could, in theory at least, take back the fief from the vassal.

The feudal order resembled a pyramid. At the top of the pyramid stood the king, the supreme liege lord. Under him as vassals were the great lords of the realm (the dukes). These dukes were, in turn, liege lords to other vassals (called counts or, in England, earls), and these vassals could be liege lords to yet other vassals. Feudalism, however, could get quite complicated, for one man could be the vassal of more than one lord—and kings at times were vassals of other lords. All lieges and vassals were members of the nobility.

5. **What knights were, how men became knights, what the code of chivalry entailed**

Knights were the soldiers of the Middle Ages. They fought on horseback. All male members of the nobility were knights, since the nobility was the class that had the task of defending society. Induction into the order of knighthood included religious rites, such as keeping vigil nightlong before a church or chapel altar, in which a young warrior pledged his use of arms to God or to Our Lady. In a ceremony in which he knelt before his lord, placing his hands in his lord's hands, the knight made an act of homage and swore an act of fealty to his lord, to render all due services to him and to be a friend of his lord's friends and an enemy of his enemies.

Chivalry was the code by which a knight was to conduct himself as a Christian warrior. It entailed the idea that a knight's actions were to be guided by religion, that warfare was to be governed by certain rules of conduct, that the knight was to engage in fair play, protect women and the poor, and to keep his word of honor. A knight's honor was held as sacred as his life.

6. **Why women came to be held as worthy of respect in the Middle Ages**

Devotion to the Blessed Virgin Mary and the honor shown her gradually began to elevate women in the eyes of medieval people. Because of this devotion, women were treated with new respect.

7. **What the medieval manor was and what life was like on the manor**

The manor was a farm and village belonging to a medieval lord. Both farmers and craftsmen lived on the manor. The manor consisted of a village, centered on a church, and located near the manor house, where the lord lived. The village often had, besides the farmers' houses, a mill, a blacksmith's shop, a common oven or bakery, and a harness-maker's shop. The manor, especially in the early Middle Ages, was designed to be self-sufficient.

8. **What serfs were, how they differed from slaves, and how they lived**

Serfs were men and women bound to the land on which they lived and worked. They were not slaves, since their lord could not sell them away from the manor nor could he put them to death without a legal trial. The lord could not turn his serfs off their land and they had a right to a portion of the manor's production. Serfs needed their lord's permission to leave the manor or to marry, and they were required to perform set tasks for the lord. Serfs, however, could accumulate property and buy land in their own right, and even purchase their freedom. As long as he performed his services to the lord, the serf had a right to portions of his lord's land, which he could pass down to his children. Part of a serf's crop went as payment to his lord, and another portion went to the support of the Church.

Improvements in agricultural techniques gradually improved the life of serfs. The influence of the Church, which insisted on justice and respect of traditional rights, gradually improved the lot of the serfs. Village councils representing the serfs decided on what crops to plant, what farming techniques to use, and how to divide the land.

9. **What medieval farming was like**

Medieval farms were divided into strips of land, some dedicated to the lord, others to the serfs. Beginning in the eighth century, farmers began to plant crops according to the "open-field" system in which the manor's farmland was divided into three great sections with only two sections in any one year planted with crops. The third section was left fallow or "open." This system helped maintain soil fertility.

10. **What inventions there were in the Middle Ages**

Medieval inventions brought about what has been called the Second Agricultural Revolution. These inventions included the moldboard plowshare, the breeding of heavy oxen and large horses for pulling plows, the horse stirrup, the iron horseshoe, and the padded horse collar.

Other medieval inventions included the windmill, which operated a pump to clear excess water into drainage ditches and for milling grain. Another important invention was the chimney.

11. **What the Drive to the East was and how it changed conditions in Europe**

The Drive to the East was the movement to settle lands east of Germany's eastern frontier, driving out pagan peoples and settling their lands with Germans. The newly opened eastern lands attracted settlers from the more settled regions of France and Germany—so much so that lords of manors in the older lands had to make life easier for their serfs to keep them from running away to the eastern lands. The Drive to the East increased the number of freer and more prosperous people in Europe.

12. **How towns developed**

The Middle Ages witnessed the growth of new towns and the renewal of old ones. Italian cities such as Venice, Genoa, and Pisa grew wealthy and powerful by carrying on trade between the eastern Mediterranean and North Africa, on the one hand, and the markets in Europe, on the other. In Lombardy and Tuscany, cities developed industrial specialties. In northern Europe, cities grew up around trade centers. Cities in the Low Countries thrived by manufacturing and trading in woolen cloth.

13. **How town government developed**

Cities received charters that made them largely independent of local lords. Under these charters, cities established their own governments.

14. **What guilds were and how they operated**

    In the cities, merchant and craft guilds developed as means of protecting, promoting, and regulating the economic activities of their members. The trade guilds were governed by master craftsmen, who were independent owners of their businesses under the guilds. Guilds sought to restrict competition, regulate prices, control how goods were manufactured and sold, and set quality standards for manufactured goods. These guilds included apprentices and journeymen who could, eventually, become masters themselves. To become a master, a worker had to demonstrate his skill by producing a masterpiece. Guilds also carried on religious observances and looked after the welfare of members and their families.

Questions for Review

1. **Why did the empire of Charlemagne break apart?**

    The empire broke apart, in part, because of invasions by Vikings, Magyars, and Saracens. Then the practice of Frankish kings dividing their domains among their sons weakened the kingdom and left it open to invaders.

2. **Where did the Vikings come from?**

    The Vikings came from Scandinavia—Norway, Sweden, and Denmark.

    Where did they settle in civilized Europe?

    Vikings settled in Northumbria, in England; in northern France (Normandy); in Russia (Novgorod and Kiev.)

3. **What sort of government is feudalism?**

    Feudalism is a system in which strong or powerful men of a region promise protection to people in the same region in return for land. The "lord" and his vassals swear loyalty to one another. Feudalism is based on personal loyalty.

    Why is it a local organization rather than a national one?

    Feudalism was local rather than national because it arose when the ability of central government to protect its people was breaking down.

Some Key Terms at a Glance

Vikings: wandering raiders from Scandinavia

feudalism: the system of local authority by which strong or powerful men were given control of a region by its inhabitants in return for protection and loyalty; a system dependent on oaths and loyalty for its continuation

vassal: one who swears an oath of loyalty and support to a lord

liege: one who takes an oath from another and gives him protection and gifts in return

fief: the land granted to a vassal in return for his service

knight: a man admitted to the fighting class as a mounted master of arms

manor: the house and farm of a landlord and the center of a medieval community

guild: an organization of merchants or craftsmen, formed to protect their craft or business

serf: a servant bound to the place of his birth and obligated to work for the landowner

What duties did a liege owe to a vassal?

A liege was duty-bound to aid and protect his vassal.

4. **What duties did a vassal owe to a liege?**

In return for his liege's protection and aid, the vassal swore an oath of loyalty to him and promised to serve as his warrior.

5. **What is chivalry?**

Chivalry is a code by which knights were to direct their behavior.

What are its ideals?

At the heart of feudalism was the ideal that a knight's actions were to be guided by religion, that warfare was to be governed by certain rules of conduct, that the knight was to engage in fair play, protect women and the poor, and to keep his word of honor.

6. **How did serfdom differ from slavery?**

Slaves in Roman society were considered the personal property of their masters. A master could sell his slave or even put him to death. Serfs were bound to the land on which they were born, but their lord could not sell them away from the land or put them to death without a trial.

What advantages did serfs have?

Being bound to the land, the serf could not be turned off the land to beg or starve. He was guaranteed the lifetime use of his land and could pass it on to his children. A serf could keep all of his produce over and above what he paid in fees to his lord and the Church. A serf could own property in his own name and buy his freedom.

7. **Why was the open-field system needed?**

The open field system was needed because food had to be produced locally and the land had to be kept fertile.

What advantages did it bring?

By allowing a field every year to lie fallow, the open field system helped preserve the fertility of fields.

8. **How did the increase in food production affect the population of Europe?**

The increase in food production led to an increased population in Europe.

9. **Why did the western European nations expand to the east?**

Western European nations expanded to the east to accommodate Europe's growing population.

How was that done?

Lands on the eastern frontier of Germany were conquered by lords, who established new estates in these unsettled or sparsely settled lands. To work these estates, the lords attracted workers from the more settled areas of the west.

Why did the new landowners not carry serfdom with them?

Serfdom did not characterize the new settlements because the lords needed to attract workers, and the promise of release from serfdom was a lure for many peasants.

10. **What were the functions of the medieval guilds?**

The guilds' purpose was to protect, promote, and regulate the economic activities of their members. Guilds also provided for the welfare of the families of their members and carried on religious observances.

What was an apprentice? A journeyman?

An apprentice was a young boy who lived and worked with a master craftsman to learn his trade.

A journeyman?

A journeyman was a man who had served his apprenticeship, earned wages, but had not yet raised the funds to purchase his own tools or rent a shop.

How might one become a master in a guild?

A journeyman could become a master in his guild if he demonstrated his skill before a jury of master craftsmen—usually by producing a "masterpiece."

Ideas in Action

1. **Read the Old English poem, "The Battle of Maldon." Dramatize the fight and the raid by Vikings on this Saxon English town. How did the defenders show heroism?**

   The teacher may wish to assign the task of rewriting the poem as a play to one or more students. The play may then be performed in class.

2. **Find a picture of a moldboard plow. What does it look like? How do you think it was discovered by its unknown inventor?**

   Pictures of moldboard plows, both ancient and modern, can readily be found by Internet image searches.

3. **Look carefully at a fireplace and chimney. What is the smoke shelf, and where is it? How is it operated today? Why was the chimney an improvement over an open hole in the roof?**

4. **Find out why a horse will tolerate an iron shoe nailed to its hoof. What does the shoe do for the horse? How does it keep the horse's hoof from damage?**

5. **What advantages and disadvantages did medieval people get for living in a city or a town?**

   Living in a city or town brought freedom to serfs who found a way to remain in town for the designated period without being discovered by their lords. Besides perhaps greater economic opportunities, living in towns often presented one with certain cultural opportunities that the country could not afford. At the same time, the poor sanitation in medieval towns rendered them disease-ridden; and people faced more temptations to vice in the populated city than in the country.

   Why did so many people not leave the country and go to the towns? What do you think was attractive about farm life? Is it still attractive? Why or why not?

   Many people probably did not leave the country because life on the manor offered a great amount of security. Peasants could not simply be turned off their land, and they could hand the land down to their children. As the Middle Ages progressed, the manorial duties placed on peasants grew less onerous and peasants became increasingly more like freemen than serfs.

Chapter 9 The Achievements of Feudalism—A.D. 800–1008

Sample Quiz for Pages 219–227

Please answer the following in complete sentences.

1. Where did the Northmen come from? What did their name "Viking" mean? Name an area settled by Vikings.

2. What did the French call the Muslims from North Africa?

3. In feudalism, what was the lord who granted a fief called? What was the one who served a lord called?

4. What was chivalry? What did it entail?

5. What was the act called by which a knight swore an act of fealty to his lord?

Answer key to Sample Quiz I

Students' answers, of course, should only approximate the following.

1. The Northmen came from *Scandinavia*. Their name "Viking" meant *"sailor" or "traveler."*

   Vikings settled (one of the following): *Normandy* (northern France), *Northumbria* (northern England), and *Russia* (Novgorod and Kiev).

2. The French called the Muslims from North Africa *"Saracens."*

3. A lord who granted a fief was called *a liege*. The man who served a lord was called *a vassal*.

4. Chivalry was *a code by which a knight, guided by religion, was to conduct himself*. According to the code of chivalry, a knight was to engage *in fair play, protect women and the poor, and to keep his word of honor*.

5. The act by which a knight swore fealty to his lord was called *the act of homage*.

Sample Quiz for Pages 228–238

Please answer the following in complete sentences.

1. What was a manor in the Middle Ages?

2. What was a serf?

3. What was the name for the system of farming in which farmland is divided into three great sections with only two sections in any one year planted with crops, and the third section left fallow?

4. Name two important medieval inventions.

5. *Please identify*:

   a) A young boy who entered the household of a master in a medieval guild to learn the master's trade

   b) The worker who worked for a master for wages

   c) What a worker had to produce before he could become a master craftsman

Answer key to Sample Quiz II

Students' answers, of course, should only approximate the following.

1. A manor was *a farm and village belonging to a medieval lord.*
2. A serf was *a man or woman bound to the land on which he or she worked.*
3. This farming system is called *the "open-field" system.*
4. *Possible answers:*
   a) moldboard plowshare
   b) breeding of heavy oxen and large horses for pulling plows
   c) horse stirrup
   d) iron horseshoe
   e) padded horse collar
   f) windmill
   g) chimney
5. *Answers:*
   a) an apprentice
   b) a journeyman
   c) a masterpiece

Sample Test

1. Describe one effect Viking, Magyar, and Saracen invasions had on Europe?
2. What is the name of the region of France settled by the Northmen? What was the name of the Northmen who settled what is now Russia?
3. Identify the following:
   a) A lord who granted land to another man in return for service
   b) The man who received land and protection from a liege in return for an oath of loyalty and service
   c) The land granted by a lord to a man in return for an oath of loyalty and service
   d) A lord who received land from the king; he was one of the great lords of the feudal realm
   e) A mounted soldier of the Middle Ages
   f) A farm and village belonging to a lord
4. Could the same man be a liege and a vassal? Please explain.
5. How did a serf differ from a slave? What rights did a serf have?
6. Name three important inventions developed during the Middle Ages.
7. List three things guilds did.
8. What in medieval religion led to an increased respect for women?

Answer key to Sample Test

Students' answers, of course, should only approximate the following.

1. *Possible answers*:

    a) The invasions of the Vikings, Magyars, and Saracens halted the development of civilization that had begun under Charlemagne.

    b) They further weakened the government of emperors and kings and helped bring about the development of feudalism.

2. The name of the region of France settled by the Northmen is *Normandy*. The Northmen who settled what is now Russia were *the Rus*.

3. *Answers*:

    a) a liege

    b) a vassal

    c) a *fief* or *feod*

    d) a duke

    e) a knight

    f) a manor

4. Yes, *the same man could be a liege and a vassal*. He was a vassal *if he received a fief from a liege*. He was a liege *if he gave land to another man in return for service*.

5. Serfs were men and women bound to the land on which they lived. They were not slaves, since their lord could not sell them away from the manor nor could he put them to death without a legal trial. Serfs could *accumulate property* and *buy land in their own right*, and even *purchase their freedom*. As long as he performed his services for the lord, the serf had *a right to portions of his lord's land*, which *he could pass down to his children*.

6. *Possible answers*:

    a) moldboard plowshare

    b) breeding of heavy oxen and large horses for pulling plows

    c) horse stirrup

    d) iron horseshoe

    e) padded horse collar

    f) windmill

    g) chimney

7. *Possible answers*:

    a) restrict competition

    b) regulate prices

    c) control how goods were manufactured and sold

    d) set quality standards for manufactured goods

    e) carry on religious observances

    f) look after the welfare of members and their families

8. *Devotion to the Blessed Virgin Mary* led to an increased respect for women in the Middle Ages.

CHAPTER 10: The Medieval Reformation

Chapter Overview

- The period from about 1000 to 1300 has been called the "Medieval Reformation." Reformers wanted to purify the lives of the clergy and to end abuses, such as simony and lay investiture.

- Reform of the Church began at the Benedictine monastery of Cluny, founded in 910. Daughter houses of Cluny spread all over Europe. Cluniac monks wanted to eliminate simony and encourage clerical celibacy. They also promoted measures to limit feudal warfare: the Peace of God and the Truce of God.

- Other reforming monastic orders inspired by Cluny were the Cistercians, Carthusians, and the Premonstratensians or Norbertines.

- Otto I, king of Germany, defeated the Magyars at the battle of Lechfeld in 955. Otto used the Church to unite his kingdom and appointed bishops. But he was careful to appoint only good, reform-minded men as bishops in the German Church.

- Otto I helped reform the papacy. The election of popes had been under the control of noble families in Rome, who did not appoint worthy men to head the Church. After Pope John XII crowned him emperor of the Romans, Otto undertook to reform the Roman Church. He appointed worthy men to the office of pope.

- Otto I had made the Roman Empire of the Germans a prosperous, united empire. His son, Otto II, was instrumental in converting the Slavic peoples to the Christian Faith.

- Emperor Otto III worked with Pope Sylvester II to reform the Church and society. Both Otto and Sylvester made the Churches in Poland and Hungary independent from the German Church and supported the crowning of Stephen I as king of Hungary.

- After the Ottos, the Church sought to gain greater independence from temporal rulers. In 1059, Pope Nicholas II established the College of Cardinals as a means of freeing the Church from lay control. Pope Gregory VII sought to free the Church entirely from the control of lay lords by fighting against simony and by forbidding the practice of lay investiture.

- Emperor Henry IV resisted Pope Gregory VII's attempts to end lay investiture. After the pope excommunicated the emperor twice, Henry marched into Italy and forced Gregory into exile in southern Italy, where he died.

- The Investiture Conflict ended in a compromise, called the Concordat of Worms. The concordat decreed that the emperor would give up investing bishops with the symbols of spiritual authority. He could continue to invest bishops with the symbols of temporal authority, but only after they had been elected by the Church. In

Germany, but not in the lands south of the Alps, the emperor or his representative would be present at the election of bishops.

- The emperors Frederick I ("Barbarossa") and Henry VI renewed conflict with the Church. In trying to control Italy, Frederick was opposed by the pope as well as by the northern Italian city-states.

Chapter Goals

This chapter demonstrates how the Church came out of a period of anarchy and decay to establish herself firmly as the leader of Christendom. Students should come from the chapter knowing the various stages of this reform of the Church:

1. the monastic reform movement;
2. the embrace of the reform by churchmen and temporal lords
3. the appointment of worthy men to hold the papacy
4. the establishment of the College of Cardinals
5. the Investiture Conflict, culminating in the Concordat of Worms and the triumph of the papacy over the empire.

The reestablishment of the Roman Empire in the West (or the Roman Empire of the Germans) under Otto I is another important development of the age. The empire played an important role as the Church's protector, and even helped in the reform of the Church. Yet, using the Church as the basis of imperial power in Germany, even good emperors, concerned for the good of the Church, continued appointing bishops and popes and practiced lay investiture. The Investiture Conflict opened up a period of struggle between the popes and the emperors that helped bring on the weakening of the empire's control of the Church.

What Students Should Know

1. **The effects of feudalism on the Church**

   Though it helped save Europe, feudalism often proved a grave danger to the good of the Church. Under feudalism, bishops and abbots came to control large tracts of land, and because of this, lords began treating churchmen like vassals. As lieges, bishops and abbots levied taxes and administered justice, and so became secular as well as spiritual lords. Because of the authority and power exercised by churchmen, secular lords tried to control their election—in order to have men in these offices that would benefit the secular power of the lord.

2. **What lay investiture was and what its problems were**

   Lay investiture was the practice by lay rulers of granting the symbols of spiritual authority to churchmen, such as bishops and abbots. Because a bishop or abbot received a benefice from the lord, the lord thought it his right to choose who should fill Church offices. The lord would then invest him with the symbols both of spiritual and temporal authority. So, even when the lord did not directly choose the candidate for Church office, the fact that he granted him the symbols of his authority assured that no one whom the lord opposed would be appointed bishop or abbot; and often lords did not choose worthy men to be bishops. Too, lay investiture of the symbols of spiritual authority made it appear that the bishop was receiving his spiritual authority from the lord, not the Church.

   Among the problems spawned by lay investiture was the practice of simony, the buying and selling of Church offices or privileges for money. Candidates for bishop or abbot might, and often did, pay the lord for granting them the office they sought.

The problems connected with lay investiture affected the entire Church, even the papacy in Rome.

3. **What Cluny was, how it differed from other Benedictine monasteries, and what effects it had on Church and society**

Cluny was a Benedictine monastery founded in France in 910. The monks at Cluny strove to return to the strict observance of St. Benedict's *Rule*. But departing from Benedict's ideal, Cluniac monks did less physical labor and dedicated themselves more to study. Unlike traditional Benedictine monasteries, each of which was autonomous, the abbeys at Cluny's sister houses were all under the authority of the abbot at Cluny. Each Cluniac monastery was, thus, a priory, not an abbey. Cluniac monasteries eventually spread throughout all Europe.

The abbey at Cluny worked for the reform of monasticism, of the Church as a whole, and of Christian society. Under Cluny's inspiration, councils of reform-minded bishops and abbots forbade, in what was called the Truce of God, armed conflict from Wednesday evening until Monday morning and during the entire week for some four months out of the year. Then there was the Cluniac-inspired Peace of God, which was an attempt to preserve certain groups from the horrors of war. Knights were not to harm clergy, monks and nuns, the poor, pilgrims, or even merchants.

Cluny inspired new monastic orders that were bent on reform. These were the Cistercians, the Norbertines (Premonstratensians), and the Carthusians.

4. **Who Otto I was and his importance**

Otto I was the son of Henry the Fowler, the duke of Saxony who had become king of Germany. Otto became king of Germany in 936. In 955, he led his army to victory over the Magyars at the Battle of Lech, thus stopping the Magyar invasions of Germany and forcing the Magyars to settle in what is now Hungary.

Otto worked to unite Germany under his authority. To do this, he needed to prune back the power of the great feudal lords. The way he accomplished this was by making the bishops independent of the temporal lords by granting them royal lands. Since the bishops could not hand their lands down to sons, they were more loyal to Otto than temporal lords would be. Otto also appointed men loyal to himself as bishops and abbots. He exercised control over the papacy in Rome. Otto, however, as a devotee of the Church reform movement, appointed worthy men as bishops.

The empire begun by Charlemagne was restored under Otto I. He brought northern Italy under his control and on February 2, 962, Pope John XII crowned him Roman emperor.

5. **What Emperor Otto III and Pope Sylvester II's ideals of Church and empire were**

Both Otto and Sylvester were devoted to Church reform. Both held to an ideal of Europe as a society united not by power but by the Christian Faith. In this spirit, Otto and Sylvester granted the Polish Church independence from the German Church. Otto treated the Polish ruler as "brother and co-ruler" instead of as a vassal. The emperor and pope helped make Hungary an independent kingdom.

6. **What the College of Cardinals is, when it was established, and why**

The College of Cardinals is the body of clergy who elect the pope. Pope Nicholas II's intention in establishing the college in 1059 was to make the election of a pope independent of lay lords, though the emperor still had the right to veto the election of a pope.

7. **What the Investiture Conflict was. What Pope Gregory VII demanded and why the emperor resisted him**

   The Investiture Conflict was a struggle between popes and emperors in the 11th and 12th centuries over whether the Church or lay lords would exercise authority over who would be appointed bishops. It began when Pope St. Gregory VII sent out legates to carry out a reform of the Church throughout Europe. In 1075, Gregory forbade lay investiture; Gregory thought that neither the emperor nor any lay lord had the right to invest bishops with either the symbols of temporal or spiritual authority. Only the Church should confer investiture. Emperor Henry IV, however, thought that as emperor he had the authority to reform the Church and to appoint bishops. If he did not possess this authority, Henry thought, it would spell the destruction of the empire, since he could not control who held Church offices.

8. **How the Investiture Conflict was resolved**

   The Investiture Conflict ended in a compromise treaty called the Concordat of Worms in 1122. The concordat was based on the notion that the Church would invest a candidate with the symbols of spiritual authority while the temporal lord would invest him with the symbols of the temporal authority. The concordat allowed the emperor to influence elections in Germany, but not in Italy.

9. **Who Frederick I Barbarossa was**

   Frederick was Roman emperor and king of Germany. During his reign, he was in almost continual war with the pope, even going so far as setting up anti-popes. Frederick tried to reestablish the imperial power over Italy. But the cities of northern Italy, in alliance with the papacy, resisted Frederick. Finally, the allies defeated the imperial army at Legnano in 1176. Frederick's son, Henry VI, who ruled Italy north and south of the papal states, sought, like his father, to establish his rule over the Church. But after Henry's short seven-year reign, struggles in Germany over who should succeed him gave the Church a breathing space it needed to continue Church reform without lay interference.

Some Key Terms at a Glance

Roman Empire of the Germans: the German kingdom raised by the pope to the imperial title once held by Charlemagne

benefice: lands and the wealth they produce, given as a grant by a secular lord to a member of the clergy; a fief

investiture: the granting of the symbols of spiritual and temporal authority to a bishop

lay investiture: the practice by lay rulers of granting the symbols of spiritual authority to churchmen, such as bishops and abbots

secular: having to do with worldly or temporal matters, not spiritual

simony: the buying and selling of Church offices or privileges for money

Cluniac reform: the beginning of the medieval reformation

College of Cardinals: the electors of a pope, established by Pope Nicholas II

antipope: one who claims to be pope while the true pope is ruling

Questions for Review

1. **What problems in the Church did the medieval reformation seek to correct?**

   The medieval reformation sought to end lay investiture, simony, as well as the power lay lords had over churchmen and the papacy itself.

2. **How was the Abbey of Cluny different from other abbeys and monasteries at the time it was founded?**

   The Abbey of Cluny differed from other abbeys and monasteries in that it founded daughter houses throughout Europe which were not independent abbeys but all under the authority of the abbot of Cluny. Other abbeys and monasteries of the time were independent foundations. At Cluny, monks dedicated less time than monks at other monasteries did to physical labor and, instead, dedicated themselves to study.

3. **What were the ways Cluny sought to reform Church and society?**

   Cluny tried to reform the spiritual life of the Church by demanding clerical celibacy, preaching against simony, and encouraging secular lords to protect the Church from corrupt clerics who practiced simony.

   The monks of Cluny worked to reform society by promoting the Truce of God and the Peace of God.

4. **What new orders besides Cluny came out of the medieval reform?**

   New orders that came out of the reform were the Cistercians, the Premonstratensians (Norbertines), and the Carthusians.

5. **Why did the Emperor Otto I give the bishops of Germany royal lands?**

   Since bishops were unmarried, they had no legitimate offspring who could inherit their possessions and thus claim that they owed their position to their birth, like the offspring of a lay lord could. In Germany, too, the king appointed bishops. Thinking that, because they had no legitimate offspring, churchmen would be more loyal to the crown than lay lords would, Otto granted churchmen royal lands, making of them a power to counteract the power of the lay lords.

6. **What was Otto III's great dream for the empire?**

   Otto dreamed of a sacred empire that would unite Europe, not by power, but by the Christian Faith.

7. **Why did Pope Nicholas II establish the College of Cardinals?**

   Pope Nicholas II established the College of Cardinals to prevent the election of an unworthy candidate as pope. He sought to remove lay lords from the election of the pope, placing it in the hands of the clergy.

8. **What was the Investiture Conflict?**

   The Investiture Conflict was a struggle between the popes and lay lords over who should have the right to confer investiture—the granting of the symbols of spiritual and temporal power to bishops and abbots.

   Why did kings and emperors want to have control of their bishops?

   Kings and emperors wanted control of their bishops because these churchmen held temporal as well as secular power. Kings and emperors wanted to make sure only men faithful to them were wielders of such power.

   Why did the pope want that right?

   The pope wanted the right to investiture because he wanted to make sure that only men who held the good of the Church as their first priority would be shepherds of the Church.

9. **What was the Concordat of Worms?**

The Concordat of Worms was a compromise agreement between the pope and the emperor that brought the Investiture Conflict to an end.

What problem did it solve and how?

The concordat solved the Investiture Conflict by acknowledging the Church's authority to grant a bishop or abbot the symbols of spiritual authority and by granting the emperor the right to confer the symbols of temporal authority.

Ideas in Action

1. **Make a map of medieval Germany. Show the empire and the several duchies that were part of it.**

   This can be a class or group project or be assigned to individual students.

2. **Why should it make so much difference who invests a bishop with the symbols of his office? Think about the appointment of a class president—who should give him his authority, the teacher or the parish minister? Consider the appointment of a new school principal—should the school board or the mayor appoint her? Why does it matter?**

   This activity is a good springboard for discussing the importance of symbols and how they are more than just "symbolic." In a very real way, the coronation of a monarch, the elevation of a pope, the swearing-in of a modern head of state are the ways authority is passed on to someone. They are outward signs of the reality of what is taking place—so much so, that if the wrong authority carries out the ceremony, over time people's notion of what is the source of the king, bishop, or president's authority will change, and the actual authority will eventually pass from those who rightly exercise it to those who do not.

3. **Report on one of the existing reform orders today: Cistercian, Carthusian, or Norbertine. What is its way of life, its dress (habit)? What makes it different from other orders?**

   This can be a project divided among several groups of students (each group taking a particular order) or assigned to individual students.

Sample Quiz for Pages 243–253

Please answer the following in complete sentences.

1. How was feudalism dangerous to the Church?
2. What was the name for the practice by which temporal lords granted churchmen the symbols of the spiritual and temporal authority?
3. What is simony?
4. What was the name of the French Benedictine monastery that led in the reform movement of the Church?
5. How was Otto I able to unite Germany more firmly under his control?
6. What was restored under Otto I?

Chapter 10   The Medieval Reformation   **111**

Answer key to Sample Quiz I

Students' answers, of course, should only approximate the following.

1. Feudalism was dangerous to the Church because, under the feudal system, *bishops and high churchmen became temporal as well as spiritual lords. They became vassals*, appointed by lay lords, *who often were more interested in having men who would be faithful to them than holy shepherds as bishops and abbots.*

2. The granting to churchmen by temporal lords of the symbols of temporal and spiritual power is called *lay investiture*.

3. Simony is *the buying and selling of Church offices or privileges.*

4. *Cluny* was the name of the French Benedictine monastery that led in the reform movement of the Church.

5. Otto I was able to unite Germany more firmly under his rule *by making bishops independent of lay lords by granting them lands and appointing those who should be bishops.*

6. *The western Roman Empire* was restored under Otto I.

Sample Quiz for Pages 253–262

Please answer the following in complete sentences.

1. **Name the German Roman emperor and the pope who wanted to use the Roman Empire of the Germans to unite Europe under the Christian Faith?**

2. **What is the name for the body of clergy that Pope Nicholas II established to elect the pope?**

3. **Who was the pope who fought Emperor Henry IV over the right of investiture of bishops?**

4. **What was the name of the treaty that ended the Investiture Conflict? When was it signed? By whom was it signed?**

5. **Who was the German Roman emperor who sought to regain control of Italy by conquering the independent cities of northern Italy but was defeated by them at Legnano in 1176?**

Answer key to Sample Quiz II

Students' answers, of course, should only approximate the following.

1. The pope and emperor who wanted to unite Europe under the empire were *Emperor Otto III and Pope Sylvester II*.

2. The name for the body of clergy that Nicholas II established is *the College of Cardinals*.

3. The pope who fought Henry IV over the right of investiture was *Pope Gregory VII*.

4. The treaty that ended the Investiture Conflict was the *Concordat of Worms*, signed in *1122*. It was signed *by the pope and the emperor*.

5. The emperor who tried to reestablish imperial authority over Italy but failed was *Frederick I Barbarossa*.

Sample Test

1. What was lay investiture? Why did it matter to the Church? How did it lead to simony?

2. With what monastery did the medieval reform movement begin? Name one way this monastery differed from other Benedictine monasteries of the time.

3. How did Otto I help the Church reform movement? Why did he give royal lands to bishops?

4. Identify the following:

    a) The Church sponsored measure that forbade armed conflict from Wednesday evening until Monday morning and during the entire week for some four months out of the year

    b) The battle where Otto I defeated the Magyars

    c) The emperor and pope who wanted Europe to be a society united not by power but the Christian Faith

    d) The emperor who tried to regain control of Italy but was defeated by the northern Italian cities at the Battle of Legnano in 1176

5. Why did Pope Nicholas II establish the College of Cardinals?

6. What was the Investiture Conflict? What did Pope Gregory VII demand in the conflict, and why did Emperor Henry IV resist him?

7. What solution did the Concordat of Worms of 1122 come up with to end the Investiture Conflict?

Answer key to Sample Test

Students' answers, of course, should only approximate the following.

1. Lay investiture was *the granting to a high churchman by a lay lord of the symbols of the churchman's spiritual and temporal authority.* Lay investiture mattered to the Church *because the practice made it appear that the bishop received his spiritual authority from the lay lord, not from the Church, and it gave the lay lord power to appoint bishops and abbots.* Lay investiture led to simony *because men paid money to lay lords to receive the office of bishop.*

2. The medieval reform movement began with *the monastery of Cluny* in France. Cluny differed from other Benedictine monasteries of the time because (*possible answers*):

    a) The monks there did less physical labor and more study.

    b) While traditionally each Benedictine monastery had been independent, Cluny founded other monasteries throughout Europe, all of which were under the authority of the abbot at Cluny.

3. Otto I aided the Church reform movement *by appointing worthy men as bishops.* He granted royal lands to the bishops *to reduce the power of the temporal lords.*

4. *Answers:*

    a) the Truce of God

    b) the Battle of Lech

    c) Emperor Otto III and Pope Sylvester II

    d) Frederick I "Barbarossa"

5. Pope Nicholas II established the College of Cardinals *to remove lay rulers from the papal election process and place it in the hands of the Church.*

6. The Investiture Conflict was *a controversy between the pope and emperor over whether the Church or lay lords would exercise authority over who would be appointed bishops. Pope Gregory VII demanded that the emperor give up entirely the right to invest bishops with the symbols both of temporal and spiritual authority.* Emperor Henry IV resisted this demand, *because it would mean he could not choose men who were faithful to him to be bishops.*

7. The Concordat of Worms resolved the Investiture Conflict *by granting the emperor the right to invest bishops-elect with the symbols of their temporal authority while recognizing the Church's right to invest bishops-elect with the symbols of spiritual authority to the Church.*

CHAPTER 11: The New Nations: Spain, England, and France

Chapter Overview

- The kingdom of Asturias was able to hold its own against the Muslim kingdoms of Al-Andalus and was able to expand. The rediscovery of the tomb of St. James the Apostle in Galicia gave Christian warriors the confidence that God fought on their side.

- King Alfonso III found settlers to repopulate lands along the frontier, southeast of Asturias. This region, for its many castles, became known as Castile.

- Alfonso VI made the Muslim kingdom of Toledo tributary to his kingdoms of León and Castile. Because of this, the Almoravids of North Africa invaded the Iberian Peninsula, defeating Alfonso in battle and overrunning all of Muslim Al-Andalus.

- One of Alfonso VI's Castilian vassals, Rodrigo Díaz—nicknamed *El Cid Campeador*—had several disagreements with the king and so was forced into exile. Though the Cid served Muslim lords in Al-Andalus, he remained faithful to Alfonso. In 1094, the Cid reconquered Valencia for King Alfonso VI.

- Both the Saxon Harold and William, duke of Normandy, claimed the throne of England after the death of its king, Edward the Confessor. William invaded England and, in 1066, defeated Harold at the Battle of Hastings. William the Conqueror became king of England, ruthlessly stamping out all opposition and establishing a government centralized under him as king. William put Norman reformist clerics in control of the English Church.

- William II made St. Anselm archbishop of Canterbury but sent him into exile when Anselm insisted on the rights of the Church. Anselm is one of the great theologians of the Middle Ages.

- King Henry I settled the crown's controversy with the Church by allowing for the free election of bishops but said bishops had to swear an oath of loyalty to the king.

- King Henry II ruled not only England, but the French lands of Normandy, Anjou, and Touraine. By his marriage to Eleanor of Aquitaine, he gained Aquitaine and other French territories.

- Eleanor of Aquitaine introduced a rich cultural life into the English court. In 1173 she encouraged her sons to rebel against their father, King Henry II, for which she was kept under house arrest until Henry's death. After his death, Eleanor reigned as regent while her son, King Richard the Lion-Heart, was on crusade.

- King Henry II appointed his close friend Thomas Becket as archbishop of Canterbury. Archbishop Thomas resisted the king, standing for the freedom of the Church. For this he was sent into exile and, finally, martyred.

- Henry II's sons, King Richard and King John, succeeded to the throne after their father. Richard spent much of his reign on crusade in the Holy Land and then in captivity to the duke of Austria. After Richard's death, John succeeded him. He quarreled with the Church and with his barons, who forced him to sign the Magna Carta in 1215. Under John's son, Henry III, England saw the beginning of Parliament.

- King Edward I ("Longshanks") completed the formation of England into a nation-state. Edward conquered Wales and invaded Scotland, where he met resistance under William Wallace. Scotland secured its freedom under King Robert I ("the Bruce"), who defeated Edward II at Bannockburn.

- The Capetian kings of France were weak. But beginning in the 12th century, the French king's power began to grow. Under Kings Louis VI and Louis VII, Abbot Suger established the beginnings of a royal court. Suger strengthened the French monarchy by his wise stewardship of the kingdom.

- St. Bernard, founder of the monastery of Clairvaux, was the leader of Christendom in the 12th century.

- King Philip Augustus was ruthless in strengthening the power of the crown. He became very popular, however, with most of his subjects.

- King Louis IX gave France an efficient administration and a supreme court of appeal, the *Parlement de Paris*, for the entire kingdom. Louis, who was later canonized, was pious, kind, honest, and dutiful.

Chapter Goals

This chapter deals with a very important aspect of European history—the development of the nation state. The model for government in both eastern and western Europe had been imperial, based on the Roman Empire—the government of many peoples and cultures under one, centralized rule. The Byzantine Empire was just such a polity, as was Charlemagne's empire. The empire established by Otto I, though it was to a great extent German, included Slavic peoples and Italy, and so was not national, but imperial. The only form of government most of Europe had known besides the imperial was tribal government.

The nation state, as it developed in England and France in particular, was the beginning of the form of government with which we are most familiar today. A big difference, however, is that, while today citizens think of themselves primarily as Frenchmen, Germans, Englishmen, Italians, etc., because of their nation states, this self-identification was not the prominent one in medieval Europe, and would not be for a long time to come. People still primarily identified themselves by the region from which they came, and then as French, or German, or English. The idea of the empire was still very much alive, encouraged by the Church which held to the ideal of a common, united society of Christian peoples, where one was neither "Jew nor Greek," Englishman or Frenchman or Spaniard, but all were united in Christ.

What Students Should Know

1. **Who King Alfonso VI was and what he accomplished**

   Alfonso VI was the king of León who united that kingdom with Castile and Navarre. By 1185, he had reconquered Toledo, the old Visigothic capital, from the Muslims. This conquest allowed Christians to push south of the Douro River in Portugal and to reconquer the cities of Segovia and Avila and other cities, making the Tagus River the southern boundary of Christian Spain. Alfonso faced an invasion by the North African Almoravids. Even though the Almoravids conquered him in a battle, Alfonso was able to keep them from overrunning Christian lands.

2. **When the Battle of Hastings was fought, between whom it was fought, why it was an important battle**

The Battle of Hastings was fought on October 13, 1066. It pitted the Saxon King Harold against William, duke of Normandy, who claimed the throne of England. Harold had been in the north of England fighting the Danes when he heard of Duke William's landing at Hastings. After a march of 15 days, Harold and his Saxons met William in battle. The Normans defeated the Saxons, and Harold was killed. William, called "the Conqueror," became king of England, ending Saxon rule over the island nation.

3. **The character of King William the Conqueror's government**

William was a harsh and unbending ruler. He claimed all land in England for himself, and then divided it amongst Norman nobles, the Church, its former holders, and himself. He kept tight control of his nobles and made sure they could not be powerful enough to resist him. William sent royal judges throughout England, establishing just royal courts. He worked to reform the Church according to the ideals of Cluny—but, he insisted, the Church in England was directly subject to the king, not the pope. No papal decrees could be published in England without the king's consent. William worked to make the king so powerful that neither secular nor lay lords could resist him.

4. **Who St. Anselm was and what he accomplished**

St. Anselm, an Italian, was an important medieval theologian; one of his most famous works is *Cur Deus Homo* ("Why did God become man?") A monk in Normandy and later abbot of Bec, Anselm was named archbishop of Canterbury by King William II Rufus in 1093. As archbishop, Anselm resisted attempts by William II and Henry I against the freedom of the Church—for which he went into exile. When Anselm threatened to excommunicate him, Henry I agreed to abandon lay investiture. Anselm died in 1109.

5. **Who Eleanor of Aquitaine was and what she accomplished**

Eleanor of Aquitaine was the daughter of William X, duke of Aquitaine in France, and the heir to vast French territories. William was a leading poet of medieval France and a patron of those poets called troubadours. Eleanor continued her father's patronage of poetry, first as the wife of King Louis VII of France (who had their marriage annulled) and later as the consort of King Henry II of England. She was an extremely capable woman who administered her French territories and, at times, served as regent for her husband and her sons in England. In 1173, she encouraged her sons to revolt against their father, Henry II, for which he placed her under house arrest until his death.

6. **Who Henry II was and what he accomplished**

Henry II was king of England and the founder of the Plantagenet Dynasty. As lord of several French fiefs, both in his own right and through his marriage to Eleanor of Aquitaine, Henry came to control more of France than the French king himself did. Henry worked to make England a united nation under the strong rule of the king. He made barons destroy castles they had built illegally and he increased the role of royal travelling judges. He helped establish what later became the grand jury system and trial by jury. Henry tried to weaken the power of Church courts and bring the Church in England more firmly under his control. This brought him into conflict with Thomas Becket, archbishop of Canterbury.

7. **What the controversy between Henry II and Archbishop St. Thomas Becket was about and how it ended**

   Henry II wanted to extend royal control more firmly over the kingdom of England. He hoped to break the power of the barons and increase the role of the travelling royal judges. In the Constitutions of Clarendon in 1164, he limited the jurisdiction of Church courts. The king forbade appeals to the pope and told bishops they could not excommunicate anyone without royal permission. Thomas Becket, who had been made archbishop by Henry II, resisted the Constitutions of Clarendon and finally had to flee to France. Having received the pope's support, Thomas returned to England and Canterbury with the king's permission. Thomas then excommunicated bishops who had gone along with the Constitutions of Clarendon. This ultimately resulted in Thomas's martyrdom on December 29, 1170. But, after Thomas's death, the people of England rose up and forced Henry to abandon much of what he had gained.

8. **What the troubadours, trouvères, and minnesingers were**

   The troubadours and trouvères were poets and singers of the Middle Ages who sang of the crusades and courtly love, including tales about King Arthur's court. The troubadours sang in the southern French dialect, while the trouvères used the northern French dialect. The minnesingers were German troubadours.

9. **What the *Magna Carta* was and when it was signed.**

   The Magna Carta was a document signed in 1215 by King John of England in which he recognized the barons' traditional rights. The Magna Carta expressed the medieval notion that kings do not stand above the laws and customs of their lands but are subject to them.

10. **What King Edward I's goals were and what he accomplished.**

    Edward I wanted to expand the powers of the king to free him from the rules of custom or law. He demanded obedience from his vassals and built up a large army to enforce that obedience. Edward conquered Wales and, for a time, Scotland. He called together representatives of the shires and towns along with the barons and representatives of the Church in what has been called the Model Parliament, because it became the model of all future parliaments. He forced the English people to think of themselves as a united people—a nation-state.

11. **What a nation-state is and what countries were developing into nation-states in the 11th and 12th centuries.**

    A nation-state is a grouping under one government of people sharing a common language and culture. France and England were developing into nation-states in the 11th and 12th centuries.

12. **Who Hugh Capet was and how much of France he and his immediate successors ruled.**

    Hugh Capet was the count of Paris whom the French nobles made king in 987. He and his immediate Capetian successors ruled only a small portion of France and exercised very little real control over their vassals.

13. **Who Suger was and what he accomplished**

    Suger was the abbot of Saint-Denis near Paris. During the reigns of three Capetian kings in the first half of the 12th century, he worked to bring the French nobles more firmly under the power of the king. Suger oversaw the building of the first Gothic church in Europe.

14. **Who St. Bernard of Clairvaux was and what he accomplished**

   Bernard was a monk of the Cistercian order who founded the monastery of Clairvaux in the early 12th century. Bernard was the leader of Christendom in his time, counseling cardinals, archbishops, bishops, abbots, popes, and temporal rulers. So influential was he that he was able to rouse Europe to undertake the Second Crusade.

15. **How the power of the French king increased under Philip Augustus and St. Louis IX**

   Philip Augustus was able to strengthen royal power by earning popularity among the French people by protecting them against the nobles. He forced King John of England to give up most of the lands he held in France. Under Philip's rule, northern French lords broke the power of the powerful lords of southern France. Philip also extended the power of the royal courts.

   Louis IX established the *Parlement de Paris* as a supreme court of appeal for all of France. He abolished feudal warfare and created a new governing system that ultimately would replace feudalism in France.

Questions for Review

1. **When was the tomb of St. James rediscovered, and by whom?**

   The tomb of St. James was rediscovered in 813 by Spanish Christians in Asturias in northern Spain who were fighting the Muslims.

   Why was the discovery of St. James's tomb important for Christians in Spain?

   The Spanish Christians took the discovery of the tomb as a sign that God fought on their side against Islam.

2. **What did El Cid accomplish?**

   El Cid reconquered Valencia from the Muslims and held it until his death.

   Is the retaking of Valencia sufficient reason to see him as a hero, or was his character the real reason to hold him up as an example and model for centuries?

   El Cid's character is the chief reason to remember him as an example—in particular, his loyalty to King Alfonso even after the king had exiled him from his home.

Some Key Terms at a Glance

monarch/king: kings were the feudal leaders of European nations, one among fellow noble equals. Monarchs assumed complete power over the nation-state and ruled alone.

Magna Carta: the document, signed by King John of England, expressing the medieval idea that kings do not stand above the laws and customs of their lands, but are subject to them

Parliament: the English representational assembly; begun as a council of barons, churchmen, and representatives of the shires and towns

nation-state: a grouping under one government of people sharing a common language and culture

Parlement de Paris: the supreme court of France

3. **What did William the Conqueror accomplish in England?**

   William conquered England and established Norman rule there. He was able to unite England under royal power more firmly than it ever had been before. He also carried on a reform of the English Church, though he insisted that it be subject to royal power and limited the pope's power over it. He set up courts that tried to unite French written law with Saxon customary law.

   How did his government differ from that of the Saxons?

   William kept some aspects of Saxon government, such as shires and sheriffs, but his government was more centralized. The nobles under William were weaker than they had been under the Saxons.

4. **Who was Eleanor of Aquitaine?**

   Eleanor was the daughter of William X, duke of Aquitaine. She was married to Louis VII of France, but their marriage was annulled. She then married King Henry II of England.

   What did she do in history (besides marry two powerful men) to make her so remembered and revered?

   Eleanor is remembered for her patronage of troubadour poetry, for her ability as ruler of her ancestral domains in France, and her service as regent in England. She was a worthy and able consort to King Henry II.

5. **How was St. Thomas of Canterbury martyred?**

   Four knights slew Thomas before the altar of the cathedral as he said Vespers.

   Why was he martyred?

   Thomas was martyred because he resisted King Henry II's attempts to bring the Church under the control of the king. The knights interpreted words rashly spoken by the king as expressing his desire to have them kill Thomas.

6. **How did St. Bernard of Clairvaux affect his own time?**

   St. Bernard was a great preacher, whose preaching gave religious direction to Western Europe. He helped to get Europeans to recognize the election of a pope, aroused European rulers to go on the Second Crusade, and was the counselor for churchmen, cardinals, and rulers.

7. **What did Louis IX accomplish as king?**

   Louis IX established the *Parlement de Paris* as a supreme court of appeal for all of France. He abolished feudal warfare and created a new governing system that ultimately would replace feudalism in France.

Ideas in Action

1. **Draw a picture from a photograph of a castle from Castile. What is the distinguishing mark of these castles? Against what enemy were they constructed? When?**

   This can be a class or group project or assigned to individual students.

2. **Discuss the Magna Carta in class. How is it different from what we moderns would expect in a constitution? What rights and powers did it give the people? The barons? The king? How does the Magna Carta limit government's powers to this day?**

   The Magna Carta was not a constitution as we understand constitutions today. Constitutions, like the U.S. Constitution, create governments and legal entities that did not exist previously. The Magna Carta simply spelled out existing customs by which the English ruled themselves. It thus gave no rights and powers to anyone but recognized rights and powers that already existed. It granted nothing to the "people" as such, since it concerned the rights and privileges of the nobility, not the common man. The idea of limited government as indicated by the Magna Carta, however, later became the basis for written constitutions, which spell out and delimit the extent of governmental powers.

3. William Wallace has achieved heroic stature in our time. His fight against Edward I is remembered as a crusade for freedom. Look up the history of Wallace and his campaign against the English. Who had the better right to the title of hero, Wallace or Edward Longshanks? What sort of freedom did Wallace fight for?

This can be a project divided among several groups of students or assigned to individual students.

Sample Quiz for Pages 267–278

Please answer the following in complete sentences.

1. What important city did Alfonso VI reconquer from the Muslims? What was the importance of this city before the Muslims conquered Spain in 711?
2. At what battle did William the Conqueror defeat the Saxon King Harold? In what year was this battle fought?
3. Who was the great medieval theologian (the author of *Cur Deus Homo?*) who became archbishop of Canterbury and resisted King William II Rufus and Henry I's attempts to control the Church in England?
4. Who was the queen of England who encouraged her sons to revolt against their father, Henry II?
5. Who was the English king who helped establish the grand jury system and trial by jury? What line of English kings did he establish?

Answer key to Sample Quiz I

Students' answers, of course, should only approximate the following.

1. Alfonso VI reconquered *Toledo*. It had been important before the conquest *because it was the capital of Visigothic Spain.*
2. William the Conqueror defeated Harold *at the Battle of Hastings* in *1066*.
3. *St. Anselm* was the theologian who resisted the kings' attempts to control the Church in England.
4. The queen of England who encouraged her sons to revolt against their father was *Eleanor of Aquitaine.*
5. The English king who helped established the grand jury system and trial by jury was *Henry II*. He established *the Plantagenet line* of English kings.

Sample Quiz for Pages 278–290

Please answer the following in complete sentences.

1. What was the name of the man whom King Henry II appointed archbishop of Canterbury but who resisted the king's attempts to control the Church?

2. What is the name of the document signed by King John of England in which he recognized the traditional rights of the English barons? When was it signed?

3. What groups in the kingdom of England did King Edward I call together to form the Model Parliament? Why is it called the "Model" Parliament?

4. Whom did the French nobles elect as king of France in 987?

5. Who was the abbot of Saint-Denis in Paris who, in the 12th century, helped strengthen the power of the French kings and oversaw the building of the first gothic-style church?

6. Who was the Cistercian monk who led Christendom in the early 12th century, was a counselor to kings and churchmen, and roused Europe to undertake the Second Crusade?

7. What was the *Parlement de Paris*? What French king established it?

Answer key to Sample Quiz II

Students' answers, of course, should only approximate the following.

1. The archbishop of Canterbury who resisted King Henry II's attempts to control the Church was *St. Thomas Becket*.

2. The name of the document signed by King John is the *Magna Carta*. It was signed in *1215*.

3. Edward I called together *representatives of the shires and towns along with the barons and representatives of the Church* to form the Model Parliament. It is called the Model Parliament *because it became the model for all future parliaments in England.*

4. The French nobles elected *Hugh Capet* as king of France in 987.

5. The abbot who helped strengthen the power of the French kings in the 12th century was *Suger*.

6. The Cistercian monk who led Christendom in the early 12th century was *St. Bernard of Clairvaux.*

7. The *Parlement de Paris* was *the supreme court of appeal in France*. It was established by *King Louis IX*, or St. Louis.

Sample Test

1. What did the conquest of Toledo by Alfonso VI allow the Christian kingdoms to do?

2. Identify the following:

   a) The battle where William the Conqueror defeated the Saxon King Harold

   b) The author of *Cur Deus Homo?*, who, as archbishop of Canterbury, fought the English kings William II Rufus and Henry I for the freedom of the Church

   c) The wife of King Henry II of England who patronized poets and was a capable ruler in her own right

   d) The monk who founded the abbey of Clairvaux and became the leader of Christendom in the early 12th century

   e) The abbot of Saint-Denis in Paris who oversaw the building of the first Gothic church in Europe

3. Give one reason why the English kings controlled so much territory in France. Which of the English kings lost most of his lands in France? To which French king did he lose them?

4. What did King Henry II demand of the Church when Thomas Becket was archbishop of Canterbury? What was Thomas's response? What finally happened to Thomas?

5. Though the Magna Carta only guaranteed the rights of England's barons, what important idea did it express?

6. What was the *Parlement de Paris?* By whom was it founded?

7. What is a nation state? What countries were developing into nation states in the 11th and 12th centuries?

Answer key to Sample Test

Students' answers, of course, should only approximate the following.

1. The conquest of Toledo allowed the Christian *kingdoms to push their borders further south and reconquer important cities from the Muslims.*

2. *Answers*:

   a) the Battle of Hastings

   b) St. Anselm

   c) Eleanor of Aquitaine

   d) St. Bernard of Clairvaux

   e) Suger

3. The English kings controlled so much territory in France because (possible answers):

   a) they were French lords as well as English kings

   b) King Henry II inherited lands in southern France by his marriage to Eleanor of Aquitaine

   King John of England lost most of his lands in France to *King Philip Augustus of France.*

4. King Henry II wanted *to limit the jurisdiction of Church courts and forbade any appeals to the pope. He told bishops they could not excommunicate anyone without royal permission.* Thomas refused to obey the king and *excommunicated*

bishops who went along with the king. Because of his resistance to the king, *Thomas suffered martyrdom.*

5. The Magna Carta expressed *the medieval notion that kings do not stand above the laws and customs of their lands but are subject to them.*

6. The *Parlement de Paris* was *the supreme court of appeal for all of France.* It was founded by *King Louis IX.*

7. A nation-state is *a grouping under one government of people sharing a common language and culture.* Nations that were developing into nation-states in the 11th and 12th centuries were *France and England.*

CHAPTER 12: The Crusades

Chapter Overview

- The Seljuk Turks conquered the Middle East, threatened the Eastern Empire, and forbade Christians from making pilgrimages to holy places in Jerusalem. The Eastern Roman emperor asked the pope for aid against this new threat.

- Pope Urban II called the First Crusade to recover the Holy Land for Christendom. Europeans, both lords and peasants, responded enthusiastically to the pope's call. The main host conquered Antioch and then Jerusalem in 1099. A feudal kingdom was established in Jerusalem, along with others in Antioch, Tripoli, and Edessa.

- These crusader kingdoms lasted for about 100 years. Two military religious orders, the Knights Templar and Knights Hospitaller, were established to protect the Holy Land.

- Quarrels among the crusader kingdoms allowed the reunited Turks to take Edessa. This inspired the unsuccessful Second Crusade in 1145. Under their great leader, Saladin, the Turks were able to overthrow most of the Christian kingdoms and take Jerusalem itself in 1187. Only three coastal cities in Palestine and Syria remained in Christian hands.

- This disaster led to the Third Crusade. Under the leadership of King Richard the Lion-Heart of England and King Philip of France, the crusaders took the coastal city of Acre in 1189. Philip then returned home, leaving Richard to face Saladin. Though he defeated the great Turkish leader in battle, Richard knew he could not hold Jerusalem, even if he succeeded in taking it. He thus signed a treaty in 1192 that opened Jerusalem to Christian pilgrims.

- The last four crusades to the Holy Land were not successful. The Fourth Crusade ended in the Latin conquest of Constantinople. The Fifth Crusade was an unsuccessful assault on Egypt. In the Sixth Crusade, the Emperor Frederick II won Jerusalem by negotiation, but it was again conquered by the Turks. The Seventh Crusade ended ingloriously on the northwest coast of Africa.

- In the late 12th century, the Muslim Almohads conquered Muslim Iberia and attacked the borderlands of the Christian kingdoms there. The kings of Castile, Aragon, and Navarre joined forces in a crusade to defeat the new Muslim threat. The crusaders crushed the Almohad power at Las Navas de Tolosa in 1212.

- Adherents of the dangerous Albigensian heresy had the protection of Raymond VI of Toulouse, the powerful lord of Languedoc in southern France. Pope Innocent III called a crusade against Raymond and his heretical subjects. Lords of northern France, however, joined the crusade—not for religious reasons, but to conquer and divide the rich lands of the south.

- To deal with the Albigensian threat that remained after the crusade against them, Pope Gregory IX established a tribunal called the Inquisition. It was an attempt to curtail violence and to reconcile the Albigenses to the Church.

Chapter Goals

The crusades are another chapter in the centuries-long struggle between Christendom and Islam. Students should see the peril the rise of the Turks posed for eastern Christendom and how the Christian people of the time would have seen the crusades—as a defensive war against "infidel" aggression. It is important to note that the crusades were not called against the Arab Muslims, who had been relatively tolerant of Christians, but against the Turks, who closed the holy places to Christians and threatened Christian lands with conquest.

The period of the crusades shows both the weaknesses and strengths of the medieval Christian order in western Europe. True zeal for religion was often mixed with self-interest and greed. It was these baser motivations that deflected the Fourth Crusade and the crusade against the Albigenses from their nobler trajectories. The crusades may have started with noble ideals but they were carried out by imperfect men.

What Students Should Know

1. **Background of the First Crusade**

   The Seljuk Turks overran and conquered the Arab Muslim lands. The Muslim Seljuks, under their leaders called sultans, were not as tolerant of other faiths as the Arabs had been. They forbade Christians to enter the holy places in Jerusalem and threatened Christian lands with conquest. Threatened by the Seljuks, the Eastern Roman emperor in Constantinople asked the pope for aid. Pope Urban II, at a Church council in Clermont in 1095, called on the princes of Europe to go to the aid of Constantinople.

2. **What the Peasants Crusade was and how it ended**

   Stirred by the preaching of Peter the Hermit, a virtually leaderless host of thousands of peasants set out for the Holy Land. This "Peasants Crusade" collected numbers as it moved eastward and left a trail of destruction in its wake. The Eastern Roman emperor ferried the peasants across the Bosporus into Turkish-held Asia Minor, where they were captured by the Turks and sold into slavery.

3. **What the First Crusade accomplished**

   Led by various lords, the crusaders marched to Constantinople and from there moved into Asia Minor. Passing through Asia Minor, the crusaders took Antioch in Syria and Edessa to the east. They then proceeded down the coast to Jerusalem. In July 1099, the crusaders captured Jerusalem. Following this victory, they established crusader kingdoms, the chief one being the Kingdom of Jerusalem. Europeans began immigrating to the newly conquered lands, which they called *Outremer* ("over-the-sea.")

4. **What the crusader kingdoms were like**

   The states of Outremer were based on feudalism. All but western "Latin" Christians were excluded from government. Not only Muslims, but native Palestinian Christians were treated as second-class citizens and forced to pay high taxes to support the Christian kingdoms.

   The Christian lands of Outremer were protected by two orders of warrior monks—the Knights Templar and the Knights Hospitaller. These were soldiers who took the threefold monastic vow of poverty, chastity, and obedience. Though these fighting monks formed their own states within the crusader states and were at odds with the king of Jerusalem and among themselves, they helped preserve the crusader states from Muslim conquest.

5. **What caused the Second Crusade, who promoted it and led it, and what were its results**

The fall of Edessa in 1144 was the immediate cause of the Second Crusade. St. Bernard of Clairvaux preached the crusade and Louis VII of France and Emperor Conrad III undertook it. Though Louis VII reached Antioch, an attempt to take Damascus failed. Both he and Conrad then returned home.

6. **What caused the Third Crusade, who promoted it and led it, and what were its results**

The capture of Jerusalem by the Egyptian sultan, Saladin, in 1187, led to the Third Crusade. Emperor Frederick Barbarossa, King Philip Augustus of France, and England's King Richard the Lion-Heart led the crusade. Frederick died, drowned in a river in Asia Minor. Richard and Philip took Acre in July 1191. After Philip returned to France, Richard continued the crusade. After defeating Saladin in battle, Richard thought to take Jerusalem. But determining that it was not possible to hold Jerusalem even if he should take it, Richard signed a truce with Saladin in 1192 in which Jerusalem remained in Muslim hands though Christians were allowed access to the holy places there.

7. **What the cause of the Fourth Crusade was and what were its results**

The failure of the Third Crusade moved Pope Innocent III to call for a new crusade. Knights from France and Germany took up the cross; but, unable to pay the entire amount of money they owed to the Venetians for transport to Egypt, the crusaders agreed to help Venice conquer the Christian city of Zara. After conquering Zara, the crusaders and Venetians, meeting the son of the deposed Eastern Roman emperor, sailed to Constantinople to drive out the usurper. In 1204, the crusaders and Venetians captured Constantinople, looting and pillaging it for three days.

After conquering Constantinople, the crusaders set up a French feudal state over the Eastern Roman Empire and imposed Latin Christianity on the Greeks, whose cities in Greece they looted, burned, and conquered. Pope Innocent III was at first appalled at the failure of the crusade, but he ended up accepting it as a way of reuniting the eastern Churches with the western, Catholic Church. Resentment over the sack of Constantinople and the subsequent conquests only embittered the Greeks against the "Latins" and perpetuated the schism.

8. **What the causes of the Schism of 1054 were and what precipitated it**

Though the Christians of the West and East held the same Faith, differences in language, culture, and the ways they expressed the mysteries of the Faith led to misunderstandings between them. The patriarch at Constantinople also began to claim greater authority in the Church while Rome insisted more and more on the authority of the popes as the successors of St. Peter. Controversy broke out between the pope and the patriarch of Constantinople, Michael Kerullarios. In 1053, Michael closed the Latin churches in Constantinople and condemned Latin customs. When Michael refused to recognize the pope's authority, the papal representative in Constantinople presented him with a document of excommunication from the pope. Michael, in turn, excommunicated the pope. The split between Rome and Constantinople gradually included the sees of Antioch, Jerusalem, and Alexandria, as well as churches in Russia and Eastern Europe, who all sided with Constantinople.

9. **What were the causes of the Iberian Crusade and how it ended**

A new Muslim power from North Africa, the Almohads, conquered Muslim Spain in the early 13th century and threatened the Christian Iberian states. Seeing the danger posed by the Almohads, Pope Innocent III called for a crusade against them. The crusader army gathered in 1212 and marched into Al Andalus from Toledo. At Las Navas de Tolosa on July 16, the Christians met the mighty Almohad host and utterly defeated it. This victory destroyed the Almohad power.

10. **What the Cathars or Albigenses were; in what part of France they flourished; what they believed and how they lived. How the Church first tried to deal with them**

The Cathars or Albigenses were a heretical group that flourished in the region of southern France called Languedoc. The Albigenses believed in two gods, one good and the other evil. The evil god created the physical world in which the human soul (created by the good god) is imprisoned. The soul is to be freed, they taught, only through denying all pleasures of the flesh. The Albigenses despised marriage, since it brought about new life. The Albigenses were popular since they lived lives of rigorous self-denial and asceticism; and their discipline made them appear as reformers of the Church.

Beginning in the mid-12th century, the Church tried peaceful means to deal with the Albigenses, sending preachers such as St. Bernard of Clairvaux to them. In 1198, Pope Innocent III called on the Cistercisans to re-evangelize Languedoc. Preaching, however, had little impact on the Albigenses.

11. **What caused the Albigensian Crusade and what were its results**

The Albigenses met Catholic preaching with violence. In 1207, Pope Innocent III's legate, Peter of Castelnau, excommunicated Count Raymond of Toulouse, who protected the Albigenses. When Raymond spoke out against "meddlesome priests," one of his knights killed Peter. The pope then called for a crusade against Raymond and the Albigenses.

Northern French lords joined the crusade under the leadership of Simon de Montfort. Raymond at first promised to punish the heretics; but after Simon's defeat of the count of Beziers, the southerners rallied to defend their lands. Raymond joined them. The northern lords again invaded the south. At the battle of Muret in 1213, Simon defeated the forces of Raymond of Toulouse and Peter II the Aragon. Simon became lord of Toulouse and of the southern lands, which he divided among the northern lords. The crusade ended, not as a religious war, but a war of conquest.

12. **What the medieval Inquisition was**

The medieval Inquisition was a tribunal established by Pope Gregory IX in 1231. Its purpose was to crush the Albigensian heresy and replace violence with the rule of law. It eventually spread from southern France to all of Europe.

The Inquisition was run by judges who generally were members of the Franciscan or Dominican orders. Those accused of heresy were tried before the court of the Inquisition, and if convicted of heresy, were given a chance to repent and a mild penance. Those whose repentance was insincere could be imprisoned. Relapsed heretics, if convicted, were turned over to the state for execution.

13. **What the last triumph of the crusades in Outremer was and how it was accomplished**

The last triumph of the crusades was the recovery of Jerusalem in 1229 after it had been under Muslim control for about 40 years. Emperor Frederick II had come to the Holy Land as the head of the Sixth Crusade; but, instead of fighting, he began negotiations with the Sultan of Egypt, who gave him control of Acre, Bethlehem, and Jerusalem. Jerusalem remained in Christian hands until 1244, when it was conquered by Muslim Turks.

14. **When the last Christian strongholds in the Holy Land fell**

    The last Christian strongholds in the Holy Land—Tripoli and Acre—fell, respectively, in 1289 and 1291. Henceforth, the "Kingdom of Jerusalem" was transferred to Cyprus.

15. **What the effects of the crusades to the Holy Land were**

    a) widening of the split between the Catholic Church and the Orthodox Churches

    b) reduction of feudal warfare in Europe by giving rival lords a common enemy

    c) growth of trade between Italian maritime cities (Venice and Genoa) and the East

    d) keeping the Mediterranean from being completely controlled by the Muslims

    e) Pushing back the Muslim advance against Eastern Europe

Questions for Review

1. **Why were the wars against the Turks in the Holy Land called "crusades"?**

   The wars against the Turks in the Holy Land were called "crusades," a word derived from the Latin word *crux* (meaning cross), because those engaged in the wars sewed a red cross to the front of their cloaks. The soldiers were also said to "take up the cross" when they went on crusade.

2. **Why did Pope Urban II call for a crusade in 1095?**

   Pope Urban II called for a crusade in 1095 because the Seljuk Turks had conquered Palestine and Jerusalem, had forbade Christians from entering the holy places in Jerusalem, and were threatening Constantinople and the Christian lands of the East.

3. **When did Jerusalem fall to the crusaders?**

   Jerusalem fell to the crusaders in July 1099.

Some Key Terms at a Glance

crusade: a war fought in defense of Christianity, named from the cross (Latin: *crux*) worn by the first crusaders

Holy Land: Palestine, called *Outremer* by the crusaders

Templars: the Knights of the Temple; crusader military order of knights, organized like a monastic order

Hospitallers: the Knights of St. John of the Hospital; crusader military order

sultan: the king or ruler of the Turks

Albigensian/Cathar: the name for someone who held to the heresy asserting that material existence is evil

The Inquisition: ecclesiastical court created after the Albigensian Crusade to deal with the threat of heresy

Who refused to take the title of king? Why?

Godfrey of Bouillon refused to take the title of king of Jerusalem because he refused to be "a king in Christ's kingdom."

4. **Describe what the Templars and Hospitallers were.**

The Templars and Hospitallers were soldiers who took monastic vows of poverty, chastity, and obedience. Living lives of austerity, they protected the Christian realms of Outremer as well as pilgrims who came to the holy places.

Why were they so called?

The Templars were so called because their house in Jerusalem was next to the ruined temple. The Hospitallers received their name from the fact that they originally operated a hospital in Jerusalem for poor pilgrims, dedicated to St. John the Baptist.

5. **Why did the crusaders not gain the help and affection of the Christians they had liberated in the Holy Land?**

The crusaders treated the Christians in the Holy Land like second-class citizens. They were excluded from government along with Muslims and paid high taxes to support the Christian feudal states. This treatment created hard feelings on the part of the native Christians towards the crusaders.

6. **When did crusader control of Jerusalem end?**

Jerusalem fell to the Muslims on October 2, 1187, thus ending crusader control of the city.

Who ended it?

Saladin, the sultan of Egypt, ended crusader control of Jerusalem.

7. **Why did the Fourth Crusade attack Christian Constantinople?**

Alexius, the son of the deposed Byzantine emperor, promised the crusaders that if they helped him regain the imperial throne, he would aid them in the crusade. So it was that the crusaders attacked Constantinople. Later, when Alexius delayed to fulfill his promises, and was then overthrown, the crusaders and the Venetian allies conquered and sacked Constantinople.

8. **Why did Pope Innocent III call for a crusade in Iberia?**

Pope Innocent called for a crusade in Iberia because the Muslim Almohads had crossed from North Africa, conquered Muslim Iberia (Al Andalus), and threatened the Christian realms in Iberia.

What were the results of this crusade?

The crusaders destroyed the Almohad power at the battle of Las Navas de Tolosa and pushed the Christian frontier further south.

9. **Why did the pope call for a crusade in the south of France?**

Count Raymond of Toulouse was protecting the heretics called Cathars or Albigenses. When the pope's legate excommunicated Raymond, one of the count's knights murdered the legate. The pope then called for a crusade against Raymond, whom he had deposed, and in order to stamp out the Albigensian heresy.

What were the results of this crusade?

The northern French lords defeated Raymond and Raymond Roger, viscount of Beziers. Simon de Montfort, the leader of the crusaders, divided the southern lands among the northern lords. Albigensianism, however, continued.

10. **What was the purpose of the medieval Inquisition?**

The Inquisition was called to crush heresy (originally Albigensianism) and to replace violence with the rule of law.

Ideas in Action

1. **Discuss: What is a crusade? For what other causes, besides military ones, do we now use this term? Why do we call these causes "crusades"?**

   Causes for which we use the term "crusade" include religious, political, and social endeavors. Because the medieval crusades were ostensibly undertaken not for personal or political gain but for the honor of Christ and the preservation of the Church, the word crusade has come to imply an altruistic struggle to promote a cause greater than oneself, whether it be an idea or a way of living and acting. So it is that evangelistic endeavors, struggles for justice, or causes such as temperance have been called *crusades*.

2. **Make a map of the Kingdom of Jerusalem and the other three crusader principalities of the Middle East. Make another map of the final coastal cities held by the crusader armies.**

   This can be a project divided among several groups of students or assigned to individual students.

3. **Find Languedoc on a map. Draw your own map showing the principal lands and cities of Languedoc: Toulouse, Carcassonne, Beziers, Marseilles, Avignon, and Albi.**

   This can be a project divided among several groups of students or assigned to individual students.

4. **Find a photo of the surviving walls of Carcassonne. Draw a picture of that fortress city and then write reports on its fortifications, its location in the countryside, and the great sieges it endured.**

   Photographs of Carcassonne can readily be found on the Internet.

5. **Find photos of the treasures of the Iberian Crusade: the tent of Miramamolin and the other relics and objects kept in Spain from that event. Find Las Navas de Tolosa on a map.**

6. **Report on the facts about Saladin. Was he the chivalrous gentleman that Western tradition has remembered?**

   This can be a project divided among several groups of students or assigned to individual students.

Sample Quiz for Pages 295–308

Please answer the following in complete sentences.

1. What was the name of the Muslim people whose conquests in Palestine caused Pope Urban II to call the First Crusade?

2. In what month and year did the forces of the First Crusade capture Jerusalem?

3. What made the Knights Templar and Knights Hospitaller differ from other knights?

4. Who was the sultan whose conquest of Jerusalem in 1187 led to the Third Crusade? What Christian king defeated him in battle?

5. What event in the Fourth Crusade widened the split between the Church of Constantinople and the Catholic Church?

6. In what year did the pope excommunicate Patriarch Michael Kerullarios of Constantinople and Michael excommunicate the pope?

Answer key to Sample Quiz I

Students' answers, of course, should only approximate the following.

1. *The Seljuk Turks* were the Muslim people whose conquests led to the calling of the First Crusade.
2. The crusaders captured Jerusalem in *July 1099*.
3. *Because they took monastic vows*, the Knights Templar and Knights Hospitaller differed from other knights.
4. *Sultan Saladin* took Jerusalem in 1187. The English *King Richard the Lion-Heart* defeated him in battle.
5. *The capture, pillage, and looting of Constantinople* during the Fourth Crusade widened the split between the Church of Constantinople and the Catholic Church.
6. The mutual excommunications between Rome and Constantinople occurred in *1054*.

Sample Quiz for Pages 309–322

Please answer the following in complete sentences.

1. **What was the name of the battle at which the Christian kings of the Iberian Peninsula defeated the Almohads? In what year was it fought?**
2. **Against what heretical group in Languedoc did Pope Innocent III call a crusade? Identify one of the teachings of this group.**
3. **Why did Pope Gregory IX establish the medieval inquisition?**
4. **Name two effects of the crusades.**

Answer key to Sample Quiz II

Students' answers, of course, should only approximate the following.

1. The battle at which the Christian Iberian kings defeated the Almohads is *the Battle of Las Navas de Tolosa*. It was fought in *1212*.
2. The group against which Pope Innocent III called a crusade were *the Albigenses or Cathars*. Possible answers for what this group believed are as follows:
   a) the existence of two gods: one good; the other, evil
   b) the evil god created the physical or material universe, and the good god the spiritual universe and the human soul
   c) marriage is evil because it brings new life
3. Pope Gregory IX established the inquisition *to crush the Albigensian heresy and replace violence with the rule of law.*
4. *Possible answers*:
   a) widening of the split between the Catholic Church and the Orthodox Churches
   b) reduction of feudal warfare in Europe by giving rival lords a common enemy
   c) growth of trade between Italian maritime cities (Venice and Genoa) and the East
   d) keeping the Mediterranean from being completely controlled by the Muslims
   e) pushing back the Muslim advance against eastern Europe

Sample Test

1. Why did Pope Urban II call the First Crusade?

2. What were the accomplishments of the First Crusade?

3. Why did native, Palestinian Christians resent the rule of the Western Christians in the Holy Land?

4. What event led to the calling of the Third Crusade? How did it end?

5. Identify the following:
   a) The wandering preacher who inspired the Peasants Crusade
   b) The year the crusaders captured Jerusalem
   c) The abbot and religious leader of Europe who preached the Second Crusade
   d) The English king who took the city of Acre in the Third Crusade
   e) The Muslim sultan who conquered Jerusalem in 1187
   f) The year the pope excommunicated the patriarch of Constantinople and the patriarch excommunicated the pope

6. Name two causes of the misunderstanding between the western and eastern Churches that ultimately led to the split between Rome and Constantinople in 1054.

7. Why did the crusaders of the Fourth Crusade go to Constantinople instead of Palestine? What did they do at Constantinople?

8. Were the Albigenses monotheists? Please explain.

9. How did the pope at first try to deal with the Albigenses? What did he finally resort to in order to free Languedoc from the heresy?

10. Give three effects of the crusades to the Holy Land.

Answer key to Sample Test

Students' answers, of course, should only approximate the following.

1. *Asked by the Byzantine emperor for aid*, Pope Urban II called the First Crusade *to deliver the Holy Land from the Seljuk Turks* who had conquered Jerusalem and were forbidding Christians to enter the holy places there.

2. The accomplishments of the First Crusade were *the capture of Jerusalem* by the crusaders and *the establishment of Christian crusader kingdoms in Palestine and Syria.*

3. Palestinians resented the rule of the western Christians because they treated natives of Palestine, Christians and Muslims alike, as second class citizens, excluded them from government, and made them pay high taxes.

4. *The capture of Jerusalem by Saladin* led to the calling of the Third Crusade. It ended *with a truce in which the Muslims remained in control of Jerusalem but Christians were allowed access to the holy places there.*

5. *Answers:*
    a) Peter the Hermit
    b) 1099
    c) St. Bernard of Clairvaux
    d) Richard the Lion-Heart
    e) Saladin
    f) 1054

6. *Possible answers:*
    a) differences in language
    b) differences in culture
    c) different ways of expressing the same mysteries of the Faith
    d) the patriarch of Constantinople's claims of greater authority in the Church
    e) Rome's increasing insistence on the authority of the popes as the successors of St. Peter

7. The crusaders of the Fourth Crusade went to Constantinople *because the son of the deposed emperor asked them to help him recover his throne. The crusaders captured Constantinople, sacked and pillaged it, and established a Latin empire there in place of the Greek, Byzantine empire.*

8. The Albigenses were *not monotheists. They believed in two gods: one good; the other, evil.*

9. The pope *at first tried peaceful means* to deal with the Albigenses—*sending preachers to Languedoc to convince the Albigenses and their followers to return to the Catholic Faith. When that failed, the pope called a crusade.*

10. *Possible answers:*
    a) widening of the split between the Catholic Church and the Orthodox Churches
    b) reduction of feudal warfare in Europe by giving rival lords a common enemy
    c) growth of trade between Italian maritime cities (Venice and Genoa) and the East
    d) keeping the Mediterranean from being completely controlled by the Muslims
    e) pushing back the Muslim advance against eastern Europe

CHAPTER 13: The Great Century

Chapter Overview

- Medieval architects raised cathedrals that were tributes to God. The cathedrals of the 11th and 12th centuries were built in two basic styles: Romanesque and Gothic.

- Veneration of the Blessed Virgin Mary affected all aspects of life in the Middle Ages, especially influencing attitudes toward women.

- During the late 12th century, cathedral schools replaced monastery schools as the most vibrant centers of study. Some cathedral schools began to associate with one another to form universities. The universities were divided into four faculties or colleges: arts, medicine, law, and theology. The predominant university centers at the beginning of the 13th century were at Bologna, Montpellier, Salerno, Oxford, and Paris.

- Pope Innocent III affected the life of Europe profoundly in the 13th century. His goal as pope was to reform society and the Church to make them truly Christian. He exercised great authority, even over kings.

- Pope Innocent's great triumph was the Fourth Lateran Council, which enacted many reform measures for the Church. However, the council is most significant for defining the doctrine of transubstantiation.

- Two new orders, the Franciscans and Dominicans, arose during the reign of Pope Innocent III. St. Francis of Assisi formed the Order of Friars Minor, men who were to be wandering preachers and evangelists living a life of strict poverty. St. Dominic de Guzmán formed the Order of Preachers, who would be learned enough to debate with learned Albigensians. These Dominicans, as they came to be called, began to teach in the schools and universities of Europe, as did the Franciscans.

- Fierce Mongol hordes invaded eastern Europe in the mid-13th century. Under their leader Ogodei Khan (son of Genghis Khan) and under the generalship of Batu, they swept into Hungary, defeating the Hungarian knights. But the death of Ogodei Khan turned back the invasion before it reached as far as Poland or Germany.

- King Fernando of Castile and León fought Islam for over a quarter of a century without losing a battle. In the territories he reconquered from the Moors, he restored Catholic dioceses and institutions.

- A method of study, called scholasticism, was developed in the medieval universities. The Dominicans and Franciscans, especially, contributed to the development of this method.

- Foremost among Franciscan scholars was St. Bonaventure, who saw the pursuit of truth as a road to God and used Aristotelian logic in his writings. From the Dominicans came St. Thomas Aquinas, who is famous for having constructed a vast synthesis of Aristotelian and Christian thought that he called the *Summa Theologica* (Theological Summary).

Chapter Goals

The 13th century is generally accepted as the high point of the Middle Ages. Called the "High Middle Ages," the 13th century revealed what medieval western Europe was capable of producing in the arts and what would have then been called the "sciences"—the mathematical disciplines, astronomy, philosophy and theology. The teacher should help students to understand how this century expressed, albeit imperfectly, the aspirations of the preceding centuries in the development of learning and art, guided by the principles of the Catholic Faith.

The development of the mendicant orders is also of great interest, for it shows the adaptability of Christian religious culture to changed circumstances and new needs. The development of monasticism showed how Christians found new ways of attaining holiness in an age where the society at large had become at least nominally Christian instead of being continually hostile to the Faith—a sort of "white martyrdom" to replace the "red martyrdom" Christians had faced in the pagan Roman Empire. Benedict's monasticism was, in turn, an adaptation of the monastic ideal to suit a new age—and it allowed monasticism to spread to more areas, giving pagans and lax Christians the experience of what a Christian life could be, as well as passing on the rudiments of civilization. The Dominicans and Franciscans arose at a time when charity had grown cold and Christians needed the example of lives lived in radical charity—casting all things away, even stability, for the sake of Christ.

Finally, Innocent III serves as an example of both the promise of the medieval reform movement and its contradictions. Under Innocent, the Church became the leader of the Christian world, at least in the West; but the confusion between spiritual and temporal power inherent in feudalism compromised the Church's reform by thrusting the pope too much into practical politics. Idealistic and with the best of intentions, Innocent III nevertheless made some grave mistakes. His attempt to reconcile the Eastern Church by permitting Greek clergy to be replaced by Latin clergy after the sack of Constantinople by the soldiers of the Fourth Crusade only deepened the rift between Rome and the Eastern patriarchates. The Albigensian Crusade quickly degenerated into a war of political ambition. The legacy of the confusion of papal political and spiritual power would bear bitter fruit in the coming centuries when men of a far less moral and intellectual stature than Innocent III ruled the Church—and when political leaders would use the confusion between temporal and spiritual authority as an excuse to rob the Church even of her spiritual powers. This is a theme we shall look at in the next chapter.

What Students Should Know

1. **What function public art played in the Middle Ages**

    Since many people in the Middle Ages could not read, they learned their philosophy, theology, and science through the public arts. Public arts were found in churches, both great cathedrals and humble village churches, which gathered under their roofs all the arts that adorned public worship—sculpture, painting, weaving (used in tapestries and vestments), and music (the chant and, later, sacred polyphony). Details in churches were meant to teach Gospel truth. Painting and sculpture told Bible stories or depicted holy saints and heroes of the Faith.

2. What the two major styles of medieval church architecture were and their characteristics

The two major styles of medieval architecture were the "Romanesque" and the "Gothic."

Romanesque churches are characterized by their use of the round Roman arch supporting a high, barrel-vaulted ceiling. Romanesque churches have heavy pillars and thick walls.

Gothic churches use pointed arches, which seem to draw the eye upward toward heaven. Gothic churches allow plenty of space for large windows of either stained or plain glass, which fill the church's interior with softly colored light. In the Middle Ages, church walls, vaults, pillars, and statues were painted in rich colors, including gold.

3. The effects of the veneration of the Blessed Virgin on medieval culture

Veneration of the Blessed Virgin gave women a new and unique status as equal companions to men on the journey to heaven. Motherhood came to be seen as a special gift to women. Veneration of Mary contributed to the code of chivalry: the chivalrous man was to be a man of his word, unfailingly courteous to ladies, and a protector of the weak and unfortunate.

4. How universities developed and what are the chief characteristics of universities

Before the 12th century, there were two kinds of schools—those attached to monasteries and those attached to cathedrals. During the 12th century, cathedral schools in such centers as Paris, Bec, London, Laon, Chartres, and Canterbury became the more vibrant centers of learning. Eventually, various cathedral schools began joining in associations among themselves to form larger institutions, called universities.

Medieval universities were divided into four faculties or colleges: liberal arts, medicine, law, and theology. (Not every university had all four.) Though individual schools in a university maintained their independence, they were joined in a larger organization that, among other things, conferred bachelor's, master's, and doctor's degrees.

Liberal arts, the basis of all learning in the Middle Ages, included the *trivium* (grammar, rhetoric, and logic) and the *quadrivium* (arithmetic, geometry, astronomy, and music).

5. Why the 13th century is called the "Great Century"

The 13th century is called the "Great Century" because it saw the full flowering of medieval art, architecture, and thought (especially in philosophy and theology).

6. How Pope Innocent III sought to reform Church and society and protect Christendom; and his significance

Innocent III (pope 1198–1216) sought to protect Christendom by calling two crusades to free Jerusalem (the Fourth and Fifth Crusades) as well as crusades against the Almohads and Albigenses.

Innocent worked to defend the rights of the Church and make sure Christian lords ruled justly. He sought to reform the Roman Empire of the Germans to make it what it was supposed to be—a defender of the Church and the secular leader of Christendom. He opposed kings who violated the sanctity of marriage and violated the independence of the Church.

The Fourth Lateran Council (1215) called by Innocent defined transubstantiation to describe how the bread and wine at Mass become the Body and Blood of Christ. It also enacted decrees to reform abuses in the Church.

Pope Innocent III approved the foundation of both the Franciscan and Dominican orders.

Pope Innocent III was perhaps the most powerful of all the medieval popes. For 20 years he shaped the history of all of Europe.

7. **Who St. Francis of Assisi was and his significance**

Francis was the son of a wealthy merchant of Assisi in Italy. As a young man, he pursued dreams of military glory; but after two illnesses, he resolved to turn from his former way of life and embrace a life of poverty for the love of God. He began giving alms to the poor, even giving away all his money and exchanging his clothes for a beggar's rags. Believing he received from God a command to rebuild a ruined church, Francis sold some of his father's cloth stocks to buy building materials. Accusing his son of theft, Francis's father brought him before the bishop, where Francis renounced his inheritance and took to living a life of prayer, poverty, and service to the poor.

Eventually, Francis gathered around him a number of followers, who became known as the Friars Minor or "Little Brothers." In 1209, Pope Innocent III approved the group as a new religious order. The order was the first of a new kind of religious (called mendicants) who do not live by the work of their hands but by alms of food and money given to them by the faithful. In return, they preach, teach, and minister to the spiritual needs of Christians. Eventually a group of women joined St. Clare to form a mendicant order of women.

Franciscans attended the new universities and began to provide them with professors.

8. **Who St. Dominic was and his significance**

Born in Castile, Dominic de Guzmán was dedicated by his family to the religious life of a canon. Ordained a priest, Dominic eventually decided that he was called to public teaching and preaching.

Pope Innocent III sent Dominic to preach to the Albigenses in Languedoc. Eventually, Dominic thought the time in which he lived required a new kind of preacher who would have the theological education and training in public speaking necessary to debate with the most learned Albigensian leaders. The preachers were to live lives of poverty and be subject to a centralized head, the master general, who would send them wherever he wished them to go. They would be mendicants, like the Franciscans.

Pope Innocent III approved this "Order of Preachers" or Dominicans in 1216. The Dominicans not only preached but began to supply teachers to the new universities. Both the Dominicans and the Franciscans helped renew and reform the Church of their time by inspiring Christians to love Christ and His Church. But their influence was not just spiritual, for they helped bring about a flowering of learning in western Europe.

9. **Who Genghis Khan and Ogodei Khan were**

Genghis Khan was the leader of the Mongols, leading them, in the early 13th century, in conquests of China, Samarkand, and the kingdom of Persia. After Genghis' death in 1227, his son, Ogodei sent the Mongols westward on a conquest of Novgorod and Kiev (in what is now Russia). Ogodei's general, Batu, led the Mongols into Poland and Hungary. When Batu was about to advance into Germany, Ogodei died (1241) and the Mongol horde returned to Mongolia. The Mongols were known for their great cruelty toward those they conquered.

10. **Who Fernando III was and what he accomplished**

Fernando was king of Castile and, later, of León. He was a just ruler, a great war leader, and a devout Catholic. (The Church remembers him as St. Fernando.) Throughout his 35-year reign, Fernando reconquered several cities of Al Andalus, bringing them under Christian rule. These cities were Córdoba (1246), Jaén, and Seville (1248—the largest city in Al Andalus). In the conquered lands, Fernando helped spread the Catholic Faith, building churches and monasteries.

11. How the philosophy of Aristotle came to Europe; what difficulties it posed

After conquering the ancient centers of the East (Antioch in Syria and Alexandria in Egypt), the Arabs came into contact with ancient Greek philosophy and science. In the 8th–10th centuries, the Arabs translated the works of the Greek philosopher Aristotle into Arabic. Through contact with Muslim scholars in Al Andalus, Christians in Western Europe rediscovered many of the works of the ancients, but especially those of Aristotle. The texts of Aristotle and other ancient thinkers were translated into Latin in the 12th–13th centuries. Aristotle's philosophy took Europe by storm in the 12th century. Many university scholars thought Aristotle offered a better explanation of the natural world than did the Platonic philosophy that had dominated schools in western Europe.

Many Christian scholars, however, adopted Aristotelian ideas that were contrary to the Catholic Faith—for instance, that the material universe was without beginning and will never end.

12. What scholasticism is

Scholasticism is the name for the method of philosophical inquiry and study developed in Europe in the 12th and 13th centuries. It is so called because it was the method of the *schola* or the school. It accompanied the discovery of Aristotle and developed a form of logical, rigorous argumentation.

13. Who St. Bonaventure was and what he accomplished

Born in Italy in 1221, Bonaventure entered the Franciscan order as a young man. As a Franciscan he studied at the University of Paris, where he received a master's degree. Bonaventure was a great scholar and became one of the greatest Franciscan scholastic philosophers and theologians of his day. He saw the pursuit of truth as a road to God and was a faithful student of the writings of St. Augustine of Hippo, though he drew as well on the writings of Aristotle. Elected minister general of the Franciscan order, Bonaventure made peace between two groups who had different ideas about how Franciscans should live their profession. In 1274, he took part in a Church council in Lyons, France, where he helped bring about a temporary reconciliation with the Eastern Orthodox churches. Bonaventure died during the council, in 1274.

14. Who St. Thomas Aquinas was and his importance

Born in Italy in 1225, Thomas Aquinas at an early age was sent to live with Benedictine monks at Monte Cassino. A brilliant student, Thomas was sent by the abbot to the University of Naples, where he studied the liberal arts and met members of the Dominican order. When Thomas became a Dominican in 1244, his parents had him kidnapped and tried to force him to abandon the Dominicans. Finally, they set him free.

Thomas studied under Albert the Great and at the University of Paris. After receiving his doctorate, he taught in the Dominican faculty at the University of Paris. Thomas achieved a complete mastery of Aristotle's philosophy and showed how it could be used to lead one to a deeper understanding of Divine Revelation. Thomas brought Aristotle's teaching together with Divine Revelation in a great work of theology, called the *Summa Theologica*. It was a textbook that sought to encompass all the questions asked by medieval theologians.

Thomas's theological writings have exerted a great influence on the teachings of the Catholic Church. In 1880, Pope Leo XIII declared Thomas's work the foundation of Catholic thought.

Questions for Review

1. **What were the two architectural styles that developed in the medieval centuries?**

   The two architectural styles that developed in the medieval centuries were the Gothic and Romanesque styles.

   What characterizes each style?

   The Romanesque churches are characterized by their use of the round Roman arches supporting a high, barrel-vaulted ceiling. They have heavy pillars and thick walls.

   Gothic churches use pointed arches, which seem to draw the eye upward toward heaven. Gothic churches allow plenty of space for large windows of either stained or plain glass.

2. **When did Pope Innocent III hold the papal office?**

   Pope Innocent held the papal office at the turn of the 13th century.

   Why was his reign as pope so important?

   Innocent III was probably the most powerful pope of the Middle Ages. For 20 years he shaped the history of Europe.

3. **How does the Fourth Lateran Council still influence the Church today?**

   The Fourth Lateran Council defined the term *transubstantiation*, describing how the bread and the wine in the Eucharist become the Body and Blood of Christ. This teaching still forms the substance of the Catholic Church's teaching about the Eucharist today.

4. **What did St. Francis want his order to be and do?**

   St. Francis wanted his order to live a common life in poverty. His brothers were to go out in

Some Key Terms at a Glance

Romanesque: architectural style characterized by its use of the Roman arch

Gothic: architectural style characterized by its pointed arches

cathedral schools: schools that followed the monastic schools of the earliest Middle Ages and from which universities were formed

universities: larger unions of small colleges and schools

Seven Liberal Arts: grammar, logic, rhetoric, arithmetic, geometry, astronomy, and music

friar: "brother," the name given to members of the Franciscan and Dominican orders and eventually to members of other orders

Franciscans: the Order of Little Brothers, founded by St. Francis of Assisi

Dominicans: the Order of Preachers, founded by St. Dominic de Guzmán

Aristotelianism: the philosophy derived from the works of the Greek philosopher Aristotle

transubstantiation: the doctrine of the change in substance (essence) of the elements of the Mass, the bread and wine, into the body and blood of Christ

twos to preach to the people about the Kingdom of God and the call to repentance. His brothers were to live by manual labor or by alms given them by the people. The Franciscans were the first of the mendicant orders.

What did he call it? Why?

St. Francis called his order the *Fratres Minores* or "Little Brothers," because they were to live humbly and in poverty.

5. **What sort of order did St. Dominic want to form?**

St. Dominic wanted to form an order to preach the Gospel to the Muslims in the East.

What kind of work did they end up doing?

By request of Pope Innocent III, the Dominicans went to preach against the Albigenses in Languedoc. The Dominicans ended up being an order of preachers and teachers.

6. **What is the *Summa Theologica*?**

The *Summa Theologica* is a textbook written to encompass all the questions asked by medieval theologians.

What did St. Thomas want it to be used for?

He intended it to be used as a textbook in theology for his fellow Dominicans.

Ideas in Action

1. **Photocopy from books, or cut from magazines, pictures of Gothic and Romanesque cathedrals. Mount them on separate boards, one for Gothic and the other for Romanesque. Indicate when the churches were built and where. Discuss how the Gothic and Romanesque churches differ and how particular Gothic churches differ from other Gothic churches and Romanesque churches from other Romanesque churches. Are there any examples of Gothic or Romanesque architecture near where you live?**

2. **Pope Innocent III believed it was his duty to influence the social and political life of the world. The popes of our day continue in this tradition. Collect news stories that describe various things the pope, the Holy See, and the bishops do and say to influence the social and political life of our time. How do the Church's actions today in this regard differ from those of Pope Innocent III? Why do they differ in these ways?**

One reason the Church's actions today differ from what they were in the days of Innocent III is that the Church holds a different place in the modern than in the medieval world. The medieval world was Catholic and looked to the Church as the teacher of the truths that nearly everyone accepted. The Church today faces a world that is not uniform in its acceptance of the Catholic Faith but views it as one religion among many. Even formerly Catholic countries no longer see the Catholic Church as the source of the truth about God and man.

3. **Discuss how a modern St. Francis might live. How would he dress? Where would he live? What might you think of him if you saw him? Do you think he would attract many followers in our day? Why or why not? Discuss where a modern St. Thomas might live and where he would work.**

Students should give reasons for their responses to these questions. The class can discuss whether the reasons given make sense, and why.

4. **Learn one of St. Thomas's hymns and prepare to sing it with your class. Consult a hymnal.**

Sample Quiz for Pages 327–342

Please answer the following in complete sentences.

1. What are the names for the two major architectural styles in medieval Europe?

2. Name two of the four faculties or colleges into which medieval universities were divided.

3. Name one of the arts in the *trivium*. Name one of the arts in the *quadrivium*.

4. What was the term the Fourth Lateran Council used to describe how the bread and wine in the Eucharist becomes the Body and Blood of Christ?

5. What is the name for members of religious orders who do not live by the work of their hands but by gifts of food and money from the faithful? What does this name mean?

6. What is the name St. Francis of Assisi gave his order? What is another name, besides the "Dominicans," for St. Dominic's order?

Answer key to Sample Quiz I

Students' answers, of course, should only approximate the following.

1. The names for the two major medieval architectural styles are *Gothic and Romanesque*.

2. Possible answers:
   a) liberal arts
   b) medicine
   c) law
   d) theology

3. Possible answers:

   For the trivium:
   a) grammar
   b) rhetoric
   c) logic

   For the quadrivium:
   a) arithmetic
   b) geometry
   c) astronomy
   d) music

4. The Fourth Lateran Council called the bread and wine becoming the Body and Blood of Christ *transubstantiation*.

5. Members of religious orders who live by gifts of food and money from the faithful are called *mendicants*. The word means *"beggars."*

6. St. Francis of Assisi called his order the *Order of Friars Minor* or *"Little Brothers."* St. Dominic's order is called *the Order of Preachers*.

Sample Quiz for Pages 342–354

Please answer the following in complete sentences.

1. Who was the founder of the Mongol Empire?
2. What is the name of the king of Castile and León who conquered Córdoba, Jaén, and Seville?
3. What is the name for the method of philosophical inquiry and study that developed in Europe in the 12th and 13th centuries? It used a form of logical, rigorous argumentation and followed the discovery of Aristotle by western Europeans.
4. What great work of theology did Thomas Aquinas write?

Answer key to Sample Quiz II

Students' answers, of course, should only approximate the following.

1. *Genghis Khan* was the founder of the Mongol Empire.
2. The conqueror of Córdoba, Jaén, and Seville was *Fernando III*.
3. The method of philosophical inquiry developed in the 12th and 13th centuries is *scholasticism*.
4. St. Thomas Aquinas wrote the *Summa Theologica*.

Sample Test

1. What were the two major architectural styles of the Middle Ages? Give a characteristic of each.
2. In the Middle Ages, the liberal arts were divided into the *trivium* and *quadrivium*. What arts were in the *trivium*? What arts were in the *quadrivium*?
3. What were the two kinds of schools found in the Middle Ages? Which developed into universities? How?
4. What were the four faculties or colleges in medieval universities?
5. What is a mendicant? Who formed the first mendicant order? What was it named?
6. Which of the new mendicant orders did the pope send to convert the Albigenses in Languedoc? Who founded this order? What was its chief work?
7. Identify the following:
   a) The pope who called the Fourth Lateran Council
   b) The term, defined by the Fourth Lateran Council, that indicates that the bread and the wine in the Eucharist become the Body and Blood of Christ
   c) The people whom Ogodei Khan and his general, Batu, led into Russia, Poland, and Hungary

d) The king of Castile and León who reconquered Cordoba from the Muslims in 1246

e) The ancient Greek philosopher whose works, rediscovered in the 12th century, led to the development of scholasticism

f) The Italian scholastic scholar who took part in a Church council in Lyons, France and helped bring about a reconciliation between the Catholic Church and the Orthodox churches

8. What is the *Summa Theologica*? Who wrote it? Why are the works of this author so important?

Answer key to Sample Test

Students' answers, of course, should only approximate the following.

1. The two major architectural styles of the Middle Ages were the *Romanesque* and the *Gothic*.

   Possible answer for the second part of the question:

   For Romanesque:

   a) round Roman arches
   b) high, barrel-vaulted ceiling
   c) heavy pillars
   d) thick walls

   For Gothic:

   a) pointed arches
   b) space for large windows, either of stained or clear glass

2. The *trivium* consisted of:

   a) grammar
   b) rhetoric
   c) logic

   The *quadrivium* consisted of:

   a) arithmetic
   b) geometry
   c) astronomy
   d) music

3. The two types of schools found in the Middle Ages were *cathedral* and *monastic* schools.

   Cathedral schools developed into universities.
   Cathedral schools in particular *areas joined together in associations and thus became universities.*

4. The four faculties or colleges in medieval universities were *liberal arts, medicine, law,* and *theology.*

5. A mendicant is *a kind of religious brother or sister who does not live by the work of his or her hands but relies on alms of food and money given by the faithful* in return for preaching, teaching, and ministering to the spiritual or material needs of the people.

   The first mendicant order was founded by *St. Francis of Assisi.*

   It was called the *Order of Friars Minor* (or Little Brothers, or Franciscans.)

6. The pope sent *the Dominicans (or Order of Preachers)* to convert the Albigenses.

   St. Dominic founded the Dominicans.

   The Dominicans chief work was *preaching and teaching.*

7. Answers:

   a) Innocent III

   b) transubstantiation

   c) Mongols

   d) Fernando III

   e) Aristotle

   f) St. Bonaventure

8. The *Summa Theologica* is *a textbook that sought to cover all the questions asked by medieval theologians*

    It was written by *St. Thomas Aquinas.*

    Thomas's writings *have exerted a great influence on the teachings of the Catholic Church. A pope has declared Thomas's work the foundation of Catholic thought.*

CHAPTER 14: Decline and Decay of the Middle Ages

Chapter Overview

- When King Philip the Fair of France decided to tax the clergy of his realm, Pope Boniface VIII protested. Boniface issued the famous bull, *Unam Sanctam*, in which he reasserted his moral authority over church and state. King Philip's response was to send henchmen to mistreat and insult the pope at Anagni.

- Pope Clement V, made pope in France, was a weak man who did what King Philip the Fair wanted him to do. Clement established an elaborate papal court at Avignon, from where Clement and several of his successors ruled the Church. This period has been called the "Babylonian Captivity" of the papacy.

- The Avignon papacy resorted to many new and ingenious devices to raise the money to support the growing papal government. This, along with the fact that the Avignon popes were seen as servants of the French king, led to much resentment in the rest of Europe toward the papacy.

- Under King Edward III, England proposed withholding tithes from the Avignon popes. This policy of the king and his son, John of Gaunt, was supported by a preacher at Oxford, John Wycliffe, who promoted heretical teachings on the Eucharist and the authority of priests and bishops.

- In 1377, Pope Gregory XI returned the papal court to Rome. The French cardinals, however, were dissatisfied with Urban VI, his successor. They elected an antipope, Clement VII, who established himself at Avignon. For 40 years, there were two lines of claimants to the papacy, one at Rome and the other at Avignon. In 1409, a council at Pisa voted to depose both popes and elected another, Alexander V. But when the two other popes refused to abdicate, the Church was further split between three rival claimants to the papal throne. This "Great Schism" was ended by the Council of Constance, which elected Martin V as pope.

- Beginning in 1347, the bubonic plague—called the Black Death—swept across Europe and killed vast numbers of people. The plague had devastating effects on both Church and state in Europe.

- With the end of the Hohenstaufen line in the Western Roman Empire, Germany went from a united state to a collection of small, rival states. The empire remained, but the influence of the emperor was diminished. France, on the other hand, under Philip the Fair, became more united. Under the reigns of Philip's two sons, however, the great lords of France forced the monarchy to recognize their traditional rights. After the death of Philip's sons, the crown passed to their cousin, Philip of Valois—thus ending the Capetian line of kings and establishing the house of Valois.

Chapter Goals

The 14th century was a turning point in the history of Europe. Students should understand how Europe was becoming more secularized—with secular rulers insisting not only on their independence from the Church but on their dominance of the Church. The eclipse of the authority of the papacy during the "Babylonian Captivity" and the Great Schism and the corruption in Church government that arose during these periods also helped to weaken the sense of papal authority in Europe. The role of the Black Death in weakening the great moral and religious sense of unity under the Church must also be emphasized.

What Students Should Know

1. **What caused the quarrel between Pope Boniface VIII and King Philip the Fair of France and how it progressed**

   The quarrel between Boniface and Philip arose over the question whether kings have the authority to tax the clergy in their realms. Philip had begun to tax the clergy to finance a war with the English. Boniface declared in a papal bull that no king or prince had the right to tax the clergy without the pope's permission.

   The arrest of a French bishop, against which Boniface protested, and the king's forging of a papal bull, which turned the French people against Boniface, only increased tensions between the king and pope. The final straw for Philip was the pope's issuing in 1302 of the bull *Unam Sanctam*, in which the pope reasserted his authority as the spiritual leader of Christendom to correct what was morally wrong, even in the conduct of kings. The bull ends with the words: "We declare, say, define, and pronounce that it is necessary for salvation for every human creature to be subject to the Roman Pontiff."

   In 1303, Philip called a council of French bishops, which condemned Boniface on a number of trumped-up crimes.

2. **What happened at Anagni and what it signified**

   After the council of French bishops had condemned Boniface VIII, King Philip sent a force of cavalry and infantry to kidnap the pope. They found Boniface at the Italian city of Anagni. They treated him roughly but were stopped by the citizens from abducting him to France. Boniface returned to Rome but died three weeks later.

   What happened to Boniface at Anagni symbolized the downfall of the medieval reform movement and of the pope's influence in Europe. What happened at Anagni and the reaction to it indicated that a new attitude was arising in Europe. Kings, not churchmen, were becoming the leaders of Christendom and the things of the world were growing more important than the things of the Faith.

3. **What the "Babylonian Captivity" of the popes was, how it came about, and how it ended**

   The "Babylonian Captivity" refers to the roughly 70-year period during which the popes reigned from Avignon in France instead of Rome. During this period, the popes were all French.

   After the death of Boniface VIII and the short reign of Benedict XI, the cardinals (in order to please Philip the Fair, it seems) elected a Frenchman as pope. This pope, Clement V, was crowned in France and remained there, appointing mostly French cardinals. Clement finally settled on Avignon as his place of residence.

   The popes reigned from France and Avignon from 1305–1377. One reason they did not return to Rome was that Italy and, in particular, the Papal States, were torn by struggles between rival lords. Moved by the entreaties of St. Catherine of Siena, Pope Gregory XI returned to Rome on

January 17, 1377, thus ending the "Babylonian Captivity."

4. **What evils in the Church arose during the "Babylonian Captivity"**

Seemingly more concerned about the worldly aspects of the Church than its spiritual welfare, the Avignon popes lived a luxurious life and set up a large bureaucracy to rule the Church. To pay for this extravagance, the Avignon popes levied new taxes that became burdensome to dioceses and common priests, who sometimes charged fees for offering the sacraments. Among the other abuses that the Avignon papal court instituted were:

a) the granting of more than one benefice to a cardinal or member of the papal court, so that one man would be the bishop of more than one diocese

b) granting episcopal sees to men foreign to the regions in which the sees were located because these men could pay the high costs of the office

Such abuses led many Europeans to believe that the papacy was no longer an authority for all Christians but had become a servant of the French king.

5. **What the Great Schism was, how it developed, and how it ended**

The Great Schism refers to the nearly 40-year period when the Church was split between at first two and then three claimants to the papal throne. It began in 1378 when the French cardinals left Rome, saying that they had been forced to elect Urban VI pope and that, thus, the election was invalid. They went to Avignon, where they elected Clement VII pope. Urban and Clement excommunicated each other. Thus were established two lines of claimants to the papal throne, one at Avignon and the other at Rome. The schism between Avignon and Rome spread to the rest of Europe, with some individuals, churches, and even nations siding with Rome and others with Avignon.

To end the schism, a Church council met in Pisa and in 1409 voted to depose both popes and elect another to replace them. The council elected Alexander V and, after he died, John XXIII. But when the Rome and Avignon popes refused to step down, a new schism between three claimants to the papacy developed.

Finally, another council met at Constance in 1414. It deposed the antipope John XXIII (who had earlier agreed to resign, but then had fled). When the pope at Rome, Gregory XII, agreed to step down, the council had only to deal with the Avignon pope, Benedict XIII. When Benedict refused to resign, the council deposed him. Finally, on November 11, 1417, the council elected Martin V, and the Great Schism came to an end.

6. **What the conciliar theory was**

The conciliar theory, which arose during the time of the Great Schism, was the idea that Church councils have the highest authority in the Church, superior even to that of the pope.

7. **What the effects of the Great Schism were**

The Great Schism, following as it did the "Babylonian Captivity," seriously damaged the unity of the Church.

a) During the schism, kings and other temporal lords had cut away at the power of the Church courts in their dominions, had seized the wealth of the clergy, and taxed the Church.

b) Temporal rulers had become effectively the rulers of the Church in their lands, forming national churches that tore at the unity of the Catholic Church.

c) The papacy lost much of the respect formerly accorded it. It thus could not as effectively reform the Church.

8. **Who John Wycliffe and John Hus were and what they taught**

John Wycliffe was an English preacher and Oxford scholar who, in the late 14th century, began teaching doctrines that contradicted Catholic teaching.

Wycliffe taught:

a) Only righteous clergy had any authority from God—implying that unrighteous clergy had no authority to administer the sacraments or even own property. Kings and lords thus could refuse to pay taxes to popes whom they deemed unrighteous and could seize the property of clergy judged unfit for their office.

b) The bread and wine in the Eucharist do not become the Body and Blood of Christ, but Christ is only present in the bread and the wine.

c) The pope and bishops are not the real Church, which is invisible and made up only of true believers.

d) The Bible—not tradition or the Church—is the sole source of doctrine.

John Hus was a Bohemian priest, preacher, and professor at the University of Prague. He became an enthusiastic promoter of the teachings of Wycliffe, though, unlike Wycliffe, he did not deny transubstantiation. Hus attended the Council of Constance in 1415, where he had been summoned under a safe conduct. The council condemned Hus as a heretic and, despite the promise of safe conduct he had received, ordered him to be executed. Hus was burnt at the stake in July 1415.

9. **What the Black Death was and its effects on Europe**

The Black Death was a plague that began to spread across Europe in 1347. It killed about half the population in northern Europe and vast numbers in other parts of Europe. Outbreaks of the disease continued between 1350 and 1400.

The plague helped change the economic and social life of Europe. Because so many laborers had died, workers could demand higher wages and serfs could buy their freedom. A new class of freedmen arose in Europe, and many moved to the towns and cities, swelling their population.

Because many good clergy had died during the plague (catching the disease from tending the sick), the Church accepted less worthy men to fill their ranks. This is one explanation for the sad state of the Church in the late 14th century.

10. **What happened to the Roman Empire of the Germans after the death of Emperor Frederick Barbarossa**

After Barbarossa's death, his grandson, Frederick II, became emperor. But Frederick II, concerned more for his domains of Sicily and southern Italy, was not the strong German king and emperor his grandfather had been. When the Hohenstaufen line died out in 1254, Germany was left basically without an emperor, since the men elected emperor were foreigners and did not even visit Germany. During this period, the German princes became more and more independent so that, by the end of the 13th century, Germany was divided into many duchies and little principalities that were powerful enough to resist the emperor if they wanted to. The emperors that were elected no longer tried to control Italy, and the empire became merely a German thing. It was no longer regarded as an authority for all Europe.

11. **The development of the kingdom of France**

    Under Louis IX, from a loose collection of nearly independent feudal principalities, France had become a powerful state. Philip IV "the Fair," Louis IX's grandson, became king in 1285 and reigned for nearly 30 years. Philip increased the power of the king, even bringing the papacy under his control (the papal court at Avignon). But after Philip's death, the French lords forced King Louis X to issue a series of charters confirming their traditional rights.

Questions for Review

1. **Why did King Philip the Fair of France and Pope Boniface VIII quarrel?**

    The king and the pope quarreled at first because Philip wanted to tax the clergy of France and Boniface insisted that the clergy might not be taxed without the consent of the pope. Basically, the king insisted that he had authority over the Church in his realm, and Boniface countered that the Church must not be subject to the king

    What resulted from their quarrel?

    As a result of the quarrel between Boniface and Philip, the king sent a force of 600 cavalry and 1,500 infantry to the town of Anagni, where Boniface was, to kidnap him. The king's troops mistreated the pope but were unable to kidnap him because the citizens of Anagni rose in defense of the pope. The insult to Boniface, however, symbolized the end of the medieval reform of the Church and of the pope's influence in Europe.

2. **Why is Dante's great poem about a journey through hell and purgatory and into paradise called a "comedy"?**

    It is called a comedy because it begins badly for the chief character but ends happily.

3. **Who was John Wycliffe?**

    John Wycliffe was an English preacher and Oxford scholar who, in the late 14th century, began teaching doctrines that contradicted Catholic teaching.

    What were his teachings?

    Wycliffe taught:

    a) Only righteous clergy had any authority from God—implying that unrighteous clergy had no authority to administer the sacraments or even own property. Kings and lords thus could refuse to pay taxes to popes whom they deemed unrighteous and could seize the property of clergy judged unfit for their office.

Some Key Terms at a Glance

bull: (from Latin *bulla*, "seal") a decree or law sealed with a heavy official seal and its ribbon

Lollards: the followers of John Wycliffe's ideas

conciliar theory: the idea that Church councils have the highest authority in the Church, superior even to that of the pope

Black Death: the bubonic plague, a terrible disease that ravaged Europe for some 60 years and killed half the population

b) The bread and wine in the Eucharist do not become the Body and Blood of Christ, but Christ is only present in the bread and the wine.

c) The pope and bishops are not the real Church, which is invisible and made up only of true believers.

d) The Bible—not tradition or the Church—is the sole source of doctrine.

4. **How many men claimed to be pope during the Great Schism?**

During the Great Schism, at first two and then three men at one time claimed to be pope.

How did having more than one man claiming to be pope divide and weaken the Church?

The Great Schism divided the Church because, since no one could be certain who the real pope was, different individuals and the various nations sided with one pope or the other. The schism weakened the Church because:

a) During the schism, kings and other temporal lords had cut away at the power of the Church courts in their dominions, seized the wealth of the clergy, and taxed the Church.

b) Temporal rulers had become effectively the rulers of the Church in their lands, forming national churches, which tore at the unity of the Catholic Church.

c) The papacy lost much of the respect formerly accorded it. It thus could not as effectively reform the Church.

5. **What was the conciliar theory?**

The conciliar theory was the idea that Church councils have the highest authority in the Church, superior even to that of the pope.

How does it differ from Church teaching about the authority of the pope?

The Church teaches that the pope exercises the highest authority in the Church and that an ecumenical council or any other authority may not stand in judgment over him.

6. **What was the Black Death, and what were its consequences?**

The Black Death was a plague that began to spread across Europe in 1347. It killed about half the population in northern Europe and vast numbers in other parts of Europe. Outbreaks of the disease continued between 1350 and 1400.

The plague helped change the economic and social life of Europe. Because so many laborers had died, workers could demand higher wages and serfs could buy their freedom. A new class of freedmen arose in Europe, and many moved to the towns and cities, swelling their population.

Because many good clergy had died during the plague (catching the disease from tending the sick), the Church accepted less worthy men to fill their ranks. This is one explanation for the sad state of the Church in the late 14th century.

Ideas in Action

1. **Report on Dante's *Divine Comedy*.** Take a small passage or section from the poem, read it, and discuss its imagery and what it represents. How, for instance, do the punishments described in the *Inferno* and the *Purgatorio* fit the sins of those who are punished?

2. **Read in class "The Nun's Priest's Tale" from *The Canterbury Tales*,** and discuss the characters (Chanticleer and his wife) and the human situation the tale describes.

Sample Quiz for Pages 359–368

Please answer the following in complete sentences.

1. At what French city did the popes reside during what is called the "Babylonian Captivity" of the papacy?

2. Please identify:

    a) The pope who quarreled with the king of France and was assaulted in Anagni by the king's soldiers

    b) The king of France who ordered his soldiers to assault and kidnap the pope at Anagni

    c) The name of the papal bull that ended with the words, "We declare, say, define, and pronounce that it is necessary for salvation for every human creature to be subject to the Roman Pontiff."

3. Why did popes raise new taxes during the "Babylonian Captivity"?

4. What saint urged the popes to return to Rome during the Babylonian Captivity? In what year did the pope finally return permanently to Rome?

5. Who was John Wycliffe?

Answer key to Sample Quiz I

Students' answers, of course, should only approximate the following.

1. The popes resided at *Avignon* during the "Babylonian Captivity" of the papacy.

2. Answers:

    a) Boniface VIII

    b) King Philip the Fair

    c) *Unam Sanctam*

3. During their "Babylonian Captivity," the popes raised new taxes *to pay for the luxurious or rich lifestyle they lived and to pay for the huge bureaucracy they established.*

4. *St. Catherine of Siena* urged the pope to return to Rome. The pope returned to Rome in *1377.*

5. John Wycliffe was *an English preacher and Oxford scholar who in the late 14th century began teaching doctrines that contradicted Catholic teaching.*

Sample Quiz for Pages 369–376

Please answer the following in complete sentences.

1. Describe one effect of the Great Schism on the Church.

2. What do we call the theory that Church councils have more authority than the pope?

3. What was the name of the Bohemian priest, preacher, and professor at the University of Prague who followed the teachings of John Wycliffe? What finally happened to him?

4. What is the name given to the plague that swept across Europe in the late 14th century, killing up to half the population in some European countries?

Answer key to Sample Quiz II

Students' answers, of course, should only approximate the following.

1. *Possible answers:*

    a) Kings and other temporal lords during the schism cut away at the power of the Church courts in their dominions, seized the wealth of the clergy, and taxed the Church.

    b) Temporal rulers became effectively the rulers of the Church in their lands, forming national churches, which tore at the unity of the Catholic Church.

    c) The papacy lost much of the respect formerly accorded it. It thus could not as effectively reform the Church.

2. The theory that Church councils have more authority than the pope is called *the conciliar theory.*

3. The Bohemian priest, preacher and professor was *John Hus. He was burnt at the stake* by order of the Council of Constance.

4. The plague that swept across Europe in the late 14th century was *the Black Death.*

Sample Test

1. What was the cause of the quarrel between Pope Boniface VIII and King Philip the Fair of France? Describe what the king finally did to Boniface.

2. What was the "Babylonian Captivity" of the papacy? What events brought it about?

3. Why did respect for the papacy decline in Europe during the "Babylonian Captivity" of the pope?

4. How many men claimed to be pope during the Great Schism? Describe one evil that came about because of the Great Schism.

5. Identify the following:

    a) The English preacher and scholar who taught that the Bible was the sole source of doctrine

    b) The Bohemian priest and university professor who was burnt at the stake for heresy

    c) The council that ended the Great Schism

    d) The name of the papal bull that ended with the words, "We declare, say, define, and pronounce that it is necessary for salvation for every human creature to be subject to the Roman Pontiff."

    e) The saint who urged the pope to return to Rome from Avignon

6. What happened to the power of the German Roman emperor after the death of Frederick Barbarossa? Compare and contrast the change in the emperor's power in Germany with the power of the French king during the reign of Philip the Fair.

7. What happened to the power of the French king after King Philip the Fair's death?

Answer key to Sample Test

Students' answers, of course, should only approximate the following.

1. The cause of the quarrel between Boniface and Philip was *the king's insistence on taxing the clergy of France.* The quarrel ended *with Philip sending troops to Anagni to kidnap the pope* and bring him to France. *Philip's troops insulted the pope but were unable to kidnap him because the people of Anagni rose up to defend him.*

2. The Babylonian Captivity of the papacy was *the roughly 70-year period the popes spent in Avignon.* After the death of Boniface VIII and the short reign of Benedict XI, *the cardinals elected an Italian pope, Urban VI. When this pope angered the French cardinals, they withdrew from Rome and went to France where they elected a Frenchman as pope.* This pope, Clement V, was crowned in France and remained there, appointing mostly French cardinals. *Clement finally decided Avignon would be his place of settlement.*

3. Respect for the papacy declined in Europe during the "Babylonian Captivity" *because many in Europe began to think that the papacy was no longer an authority for all Christians but had become a servant of the French king.*

4. In the Great Schism, *at first two and then three men* claimed to be pope

   Possible answers:

   a) During the schism, kings and other temporal lords had cut away at the power of the Church courts in their dominions, seized the wealth of the clergy, and taxed the Church.

   b) Temporal rulers had become effectively the rulers of the Church in their lands, forming national churches, which tore at the unity of the Catholic Church.

   c) The papacy lost much of the respect formerly accorded it. It thus could not as effectively reform the Church.

5. *Answers:*

   a) John Wycliffe

   b) John Hus

   c) Council of Constance

   d) *Unam Sanctam*

   e) St. Catherine of Siena

6. After the death of Frederick Barbarossa, *the power of the emperor decreased and the power of the dukes increased.* Philip the Fair, by contrast, *was able to increase royal power over the French lords.*

7. After Philip's death, the power of the French king was weakened *because the French lords forced the king to issue a series of charters confirming their traditional rights.*

CHAPTER 15: Two Centuries of Conflict

Chapter Overview

- The Rus, under their chief, Rurik, founded Novgorod in what is now northern Russia. One of Rurik's companions, Oleg, founded Kiev on the Dnieper River.

- Two brothers, Cyril and Methodius, preached the Gospel to the Slavs in Moravia, translating the liturgy into Slavonic. They translated the Scriptures into Slavonic, developing an alphabet based on Greek and called Cyrillic script.

- Vladimir, who became Grand Prince of Kiev in 980, accepted the Christian Faith from Constantinople. Vladimir was baptized in 988 and immediately set about converting the people of Russia to the Christian religion.

- During the reign of Grand Prince Yaroslav, Kiev became famous as a center of culture. So beautiful was the city that it became known as "Kiev the Golden."

- Kievan Russia had to face many invaders from across the steppe. In the early 13th century the Mongols, under Batu Khan, conquered all of Kievan Russia. The khan, from his encampment called the Golden Horde, forced the Russian princes to pay tribute.

- The city and realm of Novgorod had to contend not only with the Mongols, but with Christian powers to the west. For his victory over the Swedes at the Neva River, Prince Alexander of Novgorod received the name "Nevski." Alexander Nevski was able to defeat the invading Teutonic Knights. However, because of these Christian enemies, Alexander was forced to make peace with the Mongols. In return, the Mongols named him Grand Prince of all Russia.

- Under Ivan I ("Money Bag"), the formerly insignificant city of Moscow began to become an important power in Russia, and the ruler of Russia began to be called "Grand Prince." In 1328, the city became the seat of the metropolitan archbishop of all Russia. In 1380, Moscow's Grand Prince Dmitri Donskoi defeated the Mongols at Kulikovo Pole. This victory showed Russians that the Mongols were not invincible.

- A dynastic struggle called the Hundred Years' War began when England's King Edward III claimed the throne of France. English troops landed in France in 1339. Using the longbow and a new invention, the cannon, the English won great victories over the French at Crécy (1346) and at Poitiers (1356).

- Joan of Arc, the daughter of peasants, heard heavenly voices calling on her to rise in defense of the French kingdom against the invading English. Winning the confidence of Charles VII, the uncrowned king of France, Joan led troops to the besieged city of Orléans, capturing the English forts around the city and lifting the siege. After a stunning success in a short campaign along the Loire River, Joan accompanied Charles VII to Reims, where he was crowned king on July 17, 1429. Almost a year later, Joan was captured by the Burgundians, who turned her over to the English. After being tried by English judges as a sorceress and a heretic, Joan was burned at the stake on May 30, 1431.

- The Hundred Years' War ended with England losing all its French possessions except for the channel port of Calais. Under King Louis XI, the French state became as strong as it was under Philip the Fair 100 years earlier.

- King Richard II succeeded his grandfather, Edward III, as king of England. He was overthrown by his cousin, who became king as Henry IV, establishing the House of Lancaster on the English throne. Henry IV's son, Henry V, reasserted his claims to the French throne, winning an important victory against the French at Agincourt in 1415.

- During the 14th and 15th centuries, the English Parliament gained more and more power and authority over the English kings. Parliament's approval became essential for every important change in law or policy.

- After the death of King Henry V, England was torn by a series of civil wars. Called the "Wars of the Roses," they pitted the House of York against the House of Lancaster for control of the English crown. In 1485 Henry Tudor, a Welsh prince and last surviving member of the House of Lancaster, defeated King Richard III and the Yorkists at the Battle of Bosworth Field. Henry Tudor became king as King Henry VII.

- The Muslim Ottoman Turks threatened Christian civilization in the 15th century. In 1337, the Ottoman sultan Orkhan conquered Nicomedia, the last Byzantine stronghold in Asia. Osman's successor, Orkhan, invaded Europe. Orkhan's son, Murad, took the old city of Adrianople—which he made the chief Ottoman base in Europe—thus opening up the Balkans for Muslim conquest.

- To supply his armies, Murad demanded that Christian villagers give up their young boys to him. These boys were indoctrinated in Islamic beliefs and as young men were organized in an infantry corps that became known as the "New Force," or Janissaries.

- Seeing the Balkans fall to Murad's armies, Prince Lazar of Serbia brought together Christian Serbian princes to drive the Turks out. At Kosovo in 1389, however, the Ottomans destroyed the Serbian army, and Prince Lazar was killed.

Chapter Goals

This chapter deals with a very important topic—the growth of a nationalist sense among Europeans. Though influenced by very different factors than western Europe, Russia's development, with the growing hegemony of Moscow, could be seen as harboring the germ of nationalism. Students need to grasp what nationalism is and how it developed and spread because of the events outlined in this chapter.

What Students Should Know

1. **How Kievan Russia was founded**

   In the ninth century, a Viking named Rurik led his people, the Rus, into what is today northern Russia and settled there. One of Rurik's companions, Oleg, moved southward to the Dnieper River, which flows into the Black Sea, and on the banks of the Dnieper founded the settlement of Kiev. Though the Rus were Scandinavian, the people among whom they settled were Slavs.

2. How Russia became Christian and what was the character of its Christianity

Though, in the late ninth century, the Slavs of Moravia had been converted to the Christian Faith through the missionary work of Sts. Cyril and Methodius, in the late tenth century the people of Novgorod and Kiev were still pagan. Then in 980, Vladimir became Grand Prince of all the Rus (including Novgorod and Kiev) and established his capital at Kiev. Vladimir, like his predecessors, was a pagan; however, in 987, he sent out emissaries to the Jews, Muslims, Latin Catholics, and the Christian Greeks to find out about each religion in order that he might decide which one he wanted to follow. Moved by a report of the splendor of the liturgy in Constantinople, Vladimir decided to adopt the Byzantine form of the Christian Faith. Accordingly, Vladimir was baptized in 988. As a Christian prince, Vladimir ordered the destruction of idols in his realms. Many of his subjects accepted baptism.

Vladimir received missionaries from Constantinople; thus, Kievan Russia accepted the Byzantine rite of the liturgy and the structure of the Byzantine Church. Russian artists imitated Byzantine icon painting, liturgical music, church mosaics, and church architecture.

3. What the cultural and political life of Kievan Russia was like

Byzantine culture influenced Russia's cultural and political life as well as its religious culture. Yet, unlike the absolutist government of the Byzantine emperors, the grand prince of Kiev shared power with a council of advisors, called the *duma*, made up of wealthy landowners, called *boyars*. Towns had had an assembly, called the *veche*, in which all freemen could participate. In the countryside, the common farmer was not a serf but a free property holder.

Growing wealthy through trade, Kiev became a center of culture. It became known as "Kiev the Golden." During the reign of Yaroslav the Wise, the glory of Kiev was famous from Constantinople to France.

4. How the Mongols conquered Kievan Russia and the effects of that conquest

Kievan Russia continually faced invasions from the east, across the Steppe. Though the Russians had been able to stave off many invasions, they could not stop the Mongols. At a battle on the Kalka River in 1223, the Mongols overwhelmed and destroyed the Russian forces. The Mongols then went on a spree of destruction, laying waste to lands all the way to the Dnieper River. After sacking Kiev, they left Russia. But in 1237, the Mongols under Batu Khan returned to Russia. Within three years, Batu conquered all of Kievan Russia, except for Novgorod. Thenceforth, the Mongols, reigning from the encampment called the "Golden Horde," kept Russia in subjection. Though the Mongols allowed Russian principalities and cities to keep their governments and permitted the Church to exist, they demanded a heavy tribute that reduced the Russians to poverty.

The Mongol conquest of Russia cut that land off from Constantinople and western Europe for two centuries. Over time, free peasants, seeking protection, traded their freedom to the boyars for security. Some peasants fled into the forested lands in the cold north or into the broad valleys of the Dnieper and Volga Rivers. These peasant frontiersmen were called *Cossacks,* meaning "adventurers" or "pioneers." Rulers in Russia began to adopt the harsh ways of their Mongol masters.

5. Who Alexander Nevski was and what he accomplished

Novgorod, the center of a large and rich territory, faced not only the Mongols in the east but Christian enemies to the west. In 1240, the Swedes tried to cut off Novgorod's access to the sea by blockading the mouth of the Neva River. The same year, Alexander, the prince of Novogorod, defeated the Swedes in a battle on the Neva—for which he was called *Nevski*. In 1242, Alexander Nevski, leading an army from Novgorod, defeated the Teutonic Knights in a battle on Lake Peipus, not far from Novgorod.

In order to protect himself from his western enemies, Alexander Nevski was forced to make peace with the Mongols. In return for tribute payments, Batu Khan gave Alexander the title, "Grand Prince of All Russia."

6. **How Moscow rose to become one of the most important cities in Russia**

When Alexander Nevski gave Moscow to his youngest son, Daniel, to rule, it was a minor, unimportant city. Daniel, however, expanded Moscow's holdings by conquest and inheritance. His descendant, Ivan I "Money Bag," by taking more in taxes than what was owed to the Mongols, bought more and more land until Moscow was five times larger than what it had been under Daniel. Then, in 1328, the metropolitan archbishop of Russia moved his seat from Vladimir to Moscow, making the latter city the head of all the churches in Russia. In 1378, Moscow's Prince Dmitri gathered a large force of Russians and met the Mongols in battle at Kulikovo Pole, where the Don and Nepryavda Rivers meet. Though suffering serious losses, the Russians routed the Mongols—for which Dmitri received the title *Donskoi* ("of the Don.") The victory at Kulikovo Pole made Dmitri Donskoi a hero to all Russians and increased Moscow's prestige.

7. **What were the causes of the Hundred Years' War**

In 1328, when the last Capetian king died, the French chose Philip of Valois to succeed him as king. Philip was not the closest male relative to the late king—Edward III of England was. But Edward was related to the Capetians only through his mother; and, according to French law, the royal succession could not pass through a woman. Nevertheless, Edward claimed to be the rightful king of France. In addition to claims to the French throne, the English kings held territories in southern France as vassals of the French king.

In 1337, Edward claimed his supposed right to the French crown. This began a series of wars, called collectively the Hundred Years' War.

8. **What happened during the first phase of the Hundred Years' War, 1340–1360**

Several years passed after the first battle of the war, a sea fight at Sluys, which the French lost. Then in 1345, Edward III invaded France. On August 26, 1346, the English and French forces met at Crécy, near the Flemish border. Though outnumbered, the English use of the longbow and the cannon gave them the victory. For another ten years, the English and French fought no great battles. Then, in 1356, Edward the "Black Prince" led the English to victory over the French at Poitiers in southern France, where the French king John II was captured. Again, it was the longbow that gave the English the victory.

With King John a prisoner in England, his son, Charles the Dauphin, successfully resisted the English. Finally, in 1360, Charles and Edward III signed the Treaty of Calais, in which Edward III received three French territories and, in return, gave up his claim to the French crown.

9. **What happened during the second phase of the war, 1369–1389**

The dauphin, when he became king (Charles V), proved an able ruler. He was able to take back many of the lands given to England in the

Treaty of Calais. By the time Charles V died in 1380, England held only three coastal towns in France.

10. What happened during the third phase of the war, 1415–1453; the role of St. Joan of Arc

The new French king, Charles VI, however, was weak, and France was torn by civil war. Taking advantage of this, King Henry V of England landed in France in 1415, and his troops, using the longbow, defeated the French at the Battle of Agincourt. When the Burgundians, one of the warring French factions, made an alliance with Henry, Charles VI made peace with the English. In the Treaty of Troyes in 1420, Charles agreed to give his daughter in marriage to Henry and named Henry the next king of France.

When both Henry V and Charles VI died in 1422, Charles's son, ignoring the Treaty of Troyes, proclaimed himself king of France as Charles VII. In carrying on his war against the English and the Burgundians, however, Charles was not successful. It was about this time that Joan of Arc began hearing voices telling her to help Charles VII in his struggle against the English. In 1429, she was brought before Charles, who, after she had recognized him and told him a secret only he would know, had her examined by theologians. When the theologians gave their approval to Joan, the king accepted her services.

After Joan led the French to two victories over the English, she accompanied Charles to Reims, where he was crowned king. Joan was eventually taken prisoner by the Burgundians. Tried by the English, Joan was declared a heretic and was burned at the stake on May 30, 1431.

Despite her early death, Joan inspired new spirit in the hearts of the French. Even King Charles VII threw off his lethargy and convinced the Burgundians to break their alliance with the English. Charles led the French to victories over the English. By 1453, the end of the Hundred Years' War, the English had abandoned all of France except the northern port city of Calais.

11. What the results of the Hundred Years' War were

The Hundred Years' War ended England's dominion in France. Henceforth, England and France were clearly and definitely two separate kingdoms. The Hundred Years' War also helped to develop among the French and English the spirit of nationalism—the devotion to a people or nation based on a shared language, history, and customs. The spirit of nationalism, however, indicated that the people of Europe were thinking of themselves less and less as belonging to one Christian society—Christendom.

The power of the French king increased after the Hundred Years' War, especially under Louis XI, who was called the "Spider King" because of his craftiness. Under Louis XI, the French state attained the strength it had possessed under King Philip the Fair.

12. How the Hundred Years' War contributed to the growth of Parliament's power in England

In order to get the funds to fight the war in France, England's King Edward III and his successors had to turn to Parliament, on which, since the days of King Edward Longshanks, the kings had been relying for funds to fight their foreign wars. This gave Parliament leverage over the king. In return for money, Parliament asked favors that increased its power; for instance, the right to petition the king to make laws and the power to impeach royal officials.

Parliament was made up of an upper house, the House of Lords, comprised of the feudal aristocracy, and a lower house, the House of Commons, comprised of the knights, burgesses, and lesser nobility.

Parliament became a king maker when Henry Hereford revolted against the Plantagenet king,

Richard II. Barons in Parliament helped topple the king and chose Henry IV as his successor.

13. What the Wars of the Roses were, how they proceeded, and what was their result

The Wars of the Roses were struggles between two houses—the House of Lancaster and the House of York—each of which claimed the kingship of England. The House of Lancaster had been established by Henry IV, whose son was the great conqueror of France, Henry V. Henry V's son, Henry VI, however, was a weak ruler, who ended up losing most of the lands his father had won in France.

In 1455, Richard, Duke of York, rose in rebellion against Henry VI in a struggle that became known as the Wars of the Roses on account of the rose each side took as its symbol. The party of Henry VI, the Lancastrians, took the red rose as their symbol, while the Yorkists took the white rose.

During the Wars of the Roses, each side fought for the extermination of the other, and a significant portion of England's feudal nobility was destroyed. Richard of York's son, Edward, drove Henry VI out of England and became king in 1461. After Edward IV's death in 1483, his brother, Richard of York, was named the protector of the new king, Edward V, and Edward's brother. When Parliament declared that Edward V was not the legitimate son of Edward IV, it offered the crown to Richard, who became England's king as Richard III.

Accused of killing Edward V and his brother, Richard III faced a revolt. Henry Tudor, descended from the House of Lancaster, received Parliament's support, and on August 22, 1485, defeated Richard in battle. The same year, Henry Tudor was crowned King Henry VII. Marrying the daughter of Edward IV, Henry VII united in himself the warring houses of Lancaster and of York.

13. What the new Muslim threat in the 14th century was and what progress it made

Though Greek emperors had regained Constantinople from the Latin-French emperors established there after the Fourth Crusade, the restored Byzantine Empire was extremely weak. In the 14th century, it met a new Muslim threat, the Ottoman Turks. By the mid-14th century, the Ottomans had conquered all of Asia Minor and stood poised to invade Europe itself.

Some Key Terms at a Glance

Ottomans: Turkish Muslim people organized by Sultan Osman

Hundred Years' War: war between England and France over the right to the crown of France

nationalism: devotion to a group, sharing a common language, history, and customs. At times, nationalism includes a sense that one's nation is superior to or more important than all other nations.

Parliament: the representative assembly of England

House of Lords: the upper house of Parliament, comprised of the feudal aristocracy

House of Commons: the lower house of Parliament, comprised of the knights, burgesses, and lesser nobility

Wars of the Roses: civil war between the Houses of Lancaster and of York for possession of the English crown

In 1356, the Ottoman sultan, Orkhan, crossed the Dardanelles and established a foothold in Europe and his forces poured into Greece. Under Orkhan's son, Murad, the Ottomans conquered Adrianople, which became the Ottoman capital. From Adrianople, Murad conquered Bulgaria, and his forces defeated the army of King Lazar of Serbia at the Battle of Kosovo on June 15, 1389.

Questions for Review

1. **Why did Vladimir decide to receive the Christian Faith from the Church in Constantinople?**

Vladimir was drawn to Constantinople because of reports of the splendors of its liturgy, its art, and its great churches.

2. **What effects did the Mongol conquest have on Russia?**

The Mongol conquest cut Russia off from Byzantium and the West for two centuries. Over time, Russian free peasants, seeking protection, traded their freedom to the boyars for security. Some peasants fled into the forested lands in the cold north or into the broad valleys of the Dnieper and Volga Rivers. These peasant frontiersmen were called *Cossacks,* meaning "adventurers" or "pioneers."

3. **Why was the Hundred Years' War fought?**

The king of England, Edward II, claimed the throne of France and invaded France to assert his claims. The French king resisted these claims, and this led to warfare.

4. **When did the Battle of Crécy occur?**

The Battle of Crécy occurred on August 26, 1346.

What new weapons, used in this battle, changed the nature of warfare in Europe?

The new weapons used in the battle were the longbow and cannon.

5. **How did the Hundred Years' War change France?**

France came out of the Hundred Years' War with its government more firmly centralized under the French king.

How did it change England?

The Hundred Years' War ended forever English control of any significant part of France.

For both France and England, the Hundred Years' War gave rise to a new spirit of nationalism.

6. **What changes in English government came about because of the Hundred Years' War?**

In part, because of the Hundred Years' War, England plunged into the Wars of the Roses, which resulted in the House of Lancaster being overthrown by the House of York, which, in turn was overthrown by Henry VII, who founded the Tudor dynasty. Parliament gained more power in the English government.

Why did Edward III have to give Parliament more power?

The need for money to carry on the Hundred Years' War forced the English kings to request money from Parliament, which increased the power of that body, weakening the king's power.

7. **What did St. Joan of Arc see as the purpose of her mission?**

Joan saw helping King Charles VII drive the English from France and his coronation in Reims as king of France as the purpose of her mission.

Was she successful? Please explain.

Joan led the French to some victories and she was present when Charles was crowned king in Reims. But she was executed before the final victory over the English. Her chief contribution was to inspire the French with the will to resist the English and, ultimately, drive them from France.

8. **Who were the combatants in the Wars of the Roses?**

The combatants in the Wars of the Roses were the House of York and the House of Lancaster.

Why are they called the Wars of the Roses?

The wars were called "of the Roses" because each faction took a rose (one white, one red) as its symbol.

What were results of these wars?

The Wars of the Roses resulted, first, in the defeat of the House of Lancaster and the loss of the throne to its rival, the House of York. The House of York, however, was ultimately overthrown by the Henry Tudor, who became king as Henry VII and established the House of Tudor. The wars helped increase the power of Parliament yet further.

9. **What is nationalism?**

Nationalism is the devotion to a people or nation based on a shared language, history, and customs.

What effect did the spirit of nationalism have on Christendom?

The spirit of nationalism made the people of Europe think of themselves less and less as belonging to one Christian society—Christendom—and more as belonging to particular nations.

10. **What new threat to Europe arose in the East during the 14th century?**

The new threat to Europe in the East was the Ottoman Turks.

What parts of Europe were threatened?

The Ottoman Turks threatened primarily Greece and the countries of the Balkan Peninsula.

Ideas in Action

1. **Learn as a class the English medieval song, "Our King Went Forth to Normandy."**

The words for the song are as follows:

Our king went forth to Normandy
With grace and might of chivalry.
There God for him wrought marvellously,
Wherefore England may call and cry
   Deo Gratias Anglia
   *Redde pro victoria.**

He set a siege, for sooth to say,
To Harfleur town with royal array,
That town he won and made a fray
That France shall rue till doomesday.
   Deo Gratias etc.

Then went him forth our king comely,
In Agincourt field he fought manly,
Through grace of God most marvellously
He had the field and victory.
   Deo Gratias etc.

There many a Lord, Earl, and Baron
Were slain and taken and that full soon
And some were brought into London
With joy and bliss and great renown.
   Deo Gratias etc.

Almighty God, O keep our king,
His people and all those well willing,
And give them grace without ending;
Then may we call and safely sing
   Deo Gratias etc.

*Give thanks O England for the victory. (Latin pronunciation: *DAY-oh GRAH-tsi-ahs AHNG-lee-ah RAY-day proh vik-TOR-ee-ah*)

2. Study the battles of Crécy and Poitiers. What happened? What were their results? Who led the English? Who led the French?

3. Read the young people's novel, *The Black Arrow* (by Robert Louis Stevenson), set during the Wars of the Roses. What does such a novel teach about history?

4. Watch a dramatization of Shakespeare's play, *Richard III*. A good version is one by Sir Laurence Olivier. Discuss what Shakespeare's drama depicts about history.

5. As a class, study the life of St. Joan of Arc. Why would God choose a young girl like Joan to save France?

Sample Quiz for Pages 381–395

Please answer the following in complete sentences.

1. What was the name of the Scandinavian people who settled in what is now Russia? Who led them there?

2. Who was the grand prince of Kiev who became Christian in 988? From what city did he receive missionaries?

3. What Asiatic people from over the steppes overwhelmed and destroyed the Russians at the Kalka River in 1223? What was the name of the encampment from which they ruled Russia?

4. Please identify:

   a) The prince of Moscow who won a great victory at Kalikovo Pole

   b) The prince of Novgorod who defeated the Swedes in a battle on the Neva River and the Teutonic Knights in a battle on Lake Peipus

5. What new weapon used by the English was chiefly responsible for their victory over the French at Crécy and Poitiers?

6. What was the name of the war fought because King Edward III of England claimed the throne of France?

Answer key to Sample Quiz I

Students' answers, of course, should only approximate the following.

1. The Scandinavian people who settled Russia was the *Rus*. *Rurik* led them there

2. The grand prince of Kiev who became Christian in 988 was *Vladimir*. He received missionaries from *Constantinople*.

3. The Asiatic people who were victorious over the Russians at the Kalka River was *the Mongols*. They ruled Russia from an encampment called *the Golden Horde*.

4. Answers:

   a) Dmitri Donskoi   b) Alexander Nevski

5. The *longbow* was chiefly responsible for the English victories at Crécy and Poitiers.

6. The name of the war fought by Edward III to gain the French throne was *the Hundred Years' War*.

Sample Quiz for Pages 395–407

Please answer the following in complete sentences.

1. At what battle did the army of Henry V of England, using the longbow, defeat the French? When was it fought?

2. What did King Charles VI of France promise King Henry V in the Treaty of Troyes in 1422? Why was this promise never fulfilled?

3. Why did St. Joan of Arc think she was sent to help King Charles VII against the English?

4. Between which two English noble houses was the War of the Roses fought? What ruling house held the throne at the end of the war?

5. What Muslim people had conquered all of Asia Minor by the mid-14th century.

Answer key to Sample Quiz II

Students' answers, of course, should only approximate the following.

1. The battle at which the army of Henry V defeated the French was *the Battle of Agincourt*, fought in *1415*.

2. In the Treaty of Troyes, Charles VI promised Henry V *that he would succeed to the French throne after Charles's death*. This promise was never fulfilled, *for Charles and Henry died the same year and Charles VI's son, Charles VII, claimed the French throne.*

3. *Voices of saints and angels* told Joan that she had been chosen to aid Charles VII against the English.

4. The War of the Roses was fought between *the Houses of York and Lancaster*. At the end of the war, the *House of Tudor* held the English throne.

5. The Muslim people who had conquered all of Asia Minor by the end of the 14th century were the *Ottoman Turks*.

Sample Test

1. List two ways the Mongol conquest changed the cultural and political life of Russia?

2. Why did England and France fight the Hundred Years' War? Who was most successful in the war—the king of France or the king of England?

3. What was St. Joan of Arc's chief contribution to the French cause during the Hundred Years' War?

4. What is nationalism? Why did nationalism harm the unity of Christendom?

5. Why did the power of England's Parliament grow during the Hundred Years' War? What effect did the Hundred Years' War have on the power of the French king?

6. Who became king of England at the end of the Wars of the Roses? What ruling house did he establish? What effect did the Wars of the Roses have on the English nobility?

7. Identify the following:

   a) The city on the Dnieper River in Russia, called "the Golden"

   b) The brother missionaries who preached the gospel among the Slavs of Moravia and translated the Divine Liturgy and the Scriptures into Slavonic

   c) The first Russian grand prince to become Christian

   d) The first battle in which the English used the longbow against the French and defeated them

   e) The Muslim people who became a great threat to the Byzantine Empire in the 14th century and who conquered large parts of Greece and the Balkan Peninsula

   f) The English king who claimed the throne of France when Philip of Valois became the French king

   g) What Louis XI was called for his craftiness

Answer key to Sample Test

Students' answers, of course, should only approximate the following.

1. *Possible answers:*

   a) Before the Mongol conquest, Kievan Russia had a mild government, with town assemblies alongside the grand prince and noblemen (boyars). After the conquest, rulers in Russia began to adopt the harsh ways of their Mongol masters.

   b) Before the conquest, the Russian farmer was not a serf but a freeman. After the conquest, free peasants, seeking protection, traded their freedom to the boyars for security.

   c) Before the conquest, the land enjoyed prosperity. After the conquest, the Russians became poor because of the tribute they had to pay to the Mongols.

   d) The conquest cut Russia off from Constantinople and western Europe for two centuries.

2. England and France fought the Hundred Years' War *because the king of England claimed the French throne for himself. The French king was most successful in the war* because, by the time it ended, he had driven the English almost entirely out of France, ending English rule in France forever.

3. Joan of Arc's chief contribution to the French cause during the Hundred Years' War was that *she inspired new spirit in the hearts of the French.* Even King Charles VII threw off his lethargy and led the French to new victories, ultimately driving the English almost entirely from France.

4. Nationalism is *the devotion to a people or nation based on a shared language, history, and customs.* The spirit of nationalism harmed the unity of *Christendom because the people of Europe began thinking of themselves less and less as belonging to one Christian society*—Christendom.

5. In order to fight the war in France, the king of England needed money. To obtain it, he had to ask Parliament for funds. *In return for*

money, Parliament asked favors from the king that increased its power.

The power of the French *king increased because of the Hundred Years' War.*

6. *Henry Tudor (Henry VII)* became king at the end of the Wars of the Roses. He established *the House of Tudor.* During the Wars of the Roses, each side fought for the extermination of the other, and *a significant portion of England's feudal nobility was destroyed.*

7. *Answers:*

   a) Kiev

   b) Sts. Cyril and Methodius

   c) Vladimir

   d) Battle of Crécy

   e) Ottoman Turks

   f) Edward III

   g) Spider King

CHAPTER 16: The Birth of a New World

Chapter Overview

- "Renaissance" is the name that later generations gave to the period of history when Europeans developed a renewed respect for the literature, architecture, and art of ancient Rome and Greece. The Renaissance began in Italy and then spread to the rest of Europe.

- Humanism, the philosophy of the Renaissance, tended to see man, not God, as the center of the world. Human ideas and ideals, it was thought, should be the guides of human society.

- Francesco Petrarca (Petrarch), called the "father of Humanism," collected and published classical works and began modeling his Latin prose after the style of Cicero and other ancient Roman authors. Others soon followed his example.

- The Humanists at first thought Humanism and the Christian Faith complemented each other. Soon, however, a pagan spirit began to characterize Humanism.

- The first center of the Renaissance was Florence. In the 16th century, Rome became the center of the Renaissance.

- The first pope to patronize Renaissance artists and Humanist thinkers was Nicholas V. He planned the demolition and rebuilding of St. Peter's Basilica in Rome and founded the Vatican Library.

- At the Council of Florence in 1439, representatives of the Orthodox Church of Constantinople and the pope signed a declaration of union, ending the schism that had begun in 1054. The union between the churches, however, did not last.

- The Ottoman sultan, Mahomet II, laid siege to Constantinople in April 1453. On May 29, 1453, the Turks broke through the walls and took the city. Thenceforth, Constantinople was a Muslim city and the capital of the Ottoman Empire.

- John Hunyadi, with the help of the Franciscan priest, St. John Capistrano, broke the Turkish siege of Belgrade, Hungary, in 1456.

- Ivan the Great, the grand prince of Moscow, expanded his power over neighboring principalities, such as Novgorod, Tver, and lands once belonging to Kiev. Ivan ended all tribute payments to the Mongol khan.

- In 1472, Ivan the Great married the niece of the last Byzantine emperor. On account of this marriage, Ivan proclaimed himself tsar and autocrat of the East—the successor to the Byzantine emperors. The Russian Orthodox leaders followed along with Ivan's plan and proclaimed Moscow the Third Rome.

- Johannes Gutenberg invented the printing press in 1453. His first full book using the invention was a Latin Bible.

- The "Catholic Monarchs" of Spain, Fernando and Isabel, began a war against Granada, the last Muslim kingdom in Iberia, in 1481. The war ended when the Spanish rulers took the city of Granada on January 2, 1492, thus ending the 800-year Reconquest of the Iberian Peninsula.

- Portugal began to search for a sea route to the Indies. On May 28, 1498, the Portuguese captain, Vasco da Gama, reached Calicut, India, after a voyage around the southern tip of Africa.

- Following the conquest of Granada, the mariner Christopher Columbus received Queen Isabel's backing for a sea voyage to discover the Indies by sailing westward across the ocean. On October 12, 1492, Columbus and his crew landed on an island lying off the coast of a continent they had not known existed. They had discovered North America.

Chapter Goals

History has many watershed periods, turning-point times where the character of a society begins to change and to depart from older, more tried ways. Sometimes such times appear as decay to the people living through them; and often they truly are periods of decay. Other periods appear to those living through them to be openings to a new and better existence. Sometimes they are; other times, they are not.

To the people living through the "Babylonian Captivity" of the Church and the Great Schism, times seemed quite dark. The Black Death contributed to the sense that all was in decay and that, even, the end of the world was approaching.

The Renaissance, however, was a time of great optimism. It seemed to Europeans that they were coming of age. Developments in art and architecture, the perception that Europeans had rediscovered the classical ages and that mankind could hope to be free from what was perceived as superstition, filled many with feelings of exhilaration. A new world—America—had been discovered and a new and more humane world seemed to be dawning.

The teacher should help students to understand what the Renaissance meant to those living through it, to imagine the dismay Europe felt at the fall of Constantinople and the sense of wonder and adventure Europeans had hearing of the discovery of lands they had never known existed. At the same time, the teacher needs to help students see what the people of the Renaissance were losing in terms of their perception of higher, religious truth and the dangers they faced in embracing ideas about men and women—ideas that departed more and more from a notion of their high calling in Christ.

As far as Russia and Spain are concerned, students should see how these nations—which, before, had not had much effect on Europe outside their own borders—were now taking on important roles in Europe as a whole. Spain would become quite important as the nation that first controlled the lion's share of the New World; indeed, Spain was to become the most powerful nation in Europe.

Though Russia did not at this time play a key role in European affairs, it nevertheless is important as the successor in the East to Constantinople. The rise of Moscow, its role as the "Third Rome," its centralization under the tsar, were all developments that would make Russia the most important eastern European nation and, later, an important player in European politics.

What Students Should Know

1. **What the Renaissance was**

    "Renaissance" means "rebirth" and is the name given to the time when Europeans developed a renewed respect for the literature, art, and architecture of ancient Rome and Greece. To later generations, the Renaissance was the time when the creativity and spirit of the classical ages were reborn in the arts and philosophy.

2. How medieval and Renaissance ideals differed

During the Middle Ages, everything in art, politics, poetry, religion, and everyday life reflected the belief that God exists and man has a unique dignity among all the creatures of the world. Life and nature were not thought about apart from God. Belief in the Incarnation caused medieval people to think of all life as reflecting God and his will, as we learn of it through the Church. Everything was to be done for God's glory and to fulfill man's purpose, which is union with God. The Church was seen as the center of life and the worship of God as the very thing for which everything else in life was done.

The philosophy of the Renaissance—Humanism—tended to see man, not God, as the center of the world. It was thought that human ideas and ideals, not the ideals of divine revelation or the Church, were to guide the life of people and of human society. Humanism emphasized human virtue and human perfection in the arts and sciences, but looked to the perfection of these, not in Christian, but in ancient, pagan civilization.

3. How Renaissance Humanism related to the Christian Faith

Many of the ideals of Renaissance Humanism were compatible and complementary to medieval Christian notions. The emphasis on human perfection—not only moral but intellectual and artistic perfection—was quite consonant with the Christian Faith. And many early Humanists were serious and devout Catholics.

Other Humanists, however, became so fond of the pagan spirit of the classical world that they began to ignore the Christian religion. Their love of beauty became mere sensualism. Separated from the idea that man is created for God, the Renaissance emphasis on man's dignity led to conclusions contrary to the Christian Faith. Many Humanists wanted to ignore God when they thought about how man should live. An example of such a Humanist is Niccolò Machiavelli of Florence who, in his famous work, *The Prince*, claimed that the best ruler is one who makes his decisions based only on what benefits himself and his realm. He does not consider moral principles but uses fear, bullying, and even terror to subject others to his will.

Because of Humanism, the Renaissance had a corrosive effect on political and social life, leading, for instance, to a lack of consideration of justice in economic life and to autocracy in political life.

4. Why the Renaissance first occurred in Italy. What Italian cities were the centers of the Renaissance and why

As the center of the ancient Roman Empire, Italy had more visible reminders of classical civilization than did any other European land. Italy, thus, became the first center of Europe's revival of classical culture.

An important trade center, Florence became the first major center of the Renaissance. Beginning in the 15th century, the wealthy Medici family (who were merchants) collected beautiful works of art, commissioned paintings and sculptures, and patronized writers, philosophers, artists, architects. The Medici founded schools, built magnificent public buildings, and sponsored architectural digs to recover classical statues and ancient architectural forms. Under Lorenzo de Medici (the "Magnificent"), Florence became the richest cultural and artistic center in Europe.

When Nicholas V, a Humanist scholar, became pope in 1447, he worked to make Rome the center of art and literature. Nicholas began the process that ended in the rebuilding of St. Peter's Basilica many years later; but, perhaps, his greatest cultural achievement was the founding of the Vatican Library, which has preserved ancient works that might otherwise have been lost. After Nicholas's death in 1455, Renaissance artists and thinkers continued flocking to Rome. By the early 16th century, the city had become the center of the Italian art world.

5. **The characteristics of Renaissance painting**

    Whereas medieval visual arts had tried to represent the spiritual world that lies behind and gives meaning to the physical world, Renaissance art, in imitation of classical Greek and Roman art, sought to portray the world realistically as it is perceived through the senses. But Renaissance artists did not simply wish to imitate what they saw, but to bring out the beauty of what they saw. They wanted to portray the created world as God had meant it to be.

    An important device of Renaissance art was the use of perspective. In perspective, figures in a painting are made to appear farther away than other figures, just as in real life, things farther away from us appear smaller than things closer by. Medieval art did not use perspective.

6. **What unions occurred between the Catholic and Orthodox Churches and why they failed**

    The need to defend Constantinople against the Turks convinced the Byzantine emperor that he needed to seek a union between the Church of Constantinople and Rome. In 1439, representatives of the Church of Constantinople met with representatives of the Catholic Church at the Council of Florence, where they signed a declaration of union that, among other things, acknowledged the pope as head of the Church. After a failed crusade by western powers against the Turks, however, under pressure by their people, the priests, and the monks, the Greek bishops who had signed the union of Florence rejected the union.

    Representatives of the pope and of the Church of Constantinople and the emperor proclaimed a union of the Churches at Hagia Sophia in 1452. But, again, the monks, the Greek priests, and the people rejected the union.

7. **When Constantinople fell and to whom**

    Under their new sultan, Mahomet II, the Ottoman Turks laid siege to Constantinople in early April 1453. Though the city was strongly fortified, Mahomet had a new weapon—enormous bronze cannons against which the city's walls could not stand. Under their emperor, Constantine XI, the people of Constantinople bravely resisted the enemy. But on May 29, 1453, Mahomet directed an assault on the city, overwhelming its defenses. Constantine died in battle and the Turks took the city. Mahomet made Constantinople (now Istanbul) his capital and turned Hagia Sophia into a mosque.

8. **Who Ivan the Great was and what he accomplished**

    Ivan was an able but ruthless ruler who established himself as an autocrat by breaking the power of the boyars. Ivan greatly extended the territory of his principality, Muscovy. In 1478 he conquered Novgorod, abolishing its *veche* and elected mayor. He added other lands to Muscovy as well and, after refusing to pay tribute to the Mongols, he forced the khanate of Kazan to become his vassal.

    After his marriage to the niece of the last Byzantine emperor, Ivan proclaimed himself the rightful heir to the Byzantine Empire. He thus added the double-headed eagle to his family crest and called himself autocrat and tsar (Caesar). The Russian Orthodox clergy and theologians helped Ivan realize his claims. They proclaimed Moscow the "Third Rome."

9. **The importance of the invention of the printing press**

    In 1454, Johannes Gutenberg began printing works on his new invention, the printing press. Gutenberg's press printed the Bible, as well as other books and pamphlets. The printing press allowed printed material to be available to ordinary people. Unlike hand-copied works, printed works could be printed and reprinted in large numbers.

10. **Who Isabel and Fernando were and what they accomplished**

Isabel was the sister of the king of Castile and León and became queen of these lands in 1474. In 1469 Isabel married Fernando, who became king of Aragon in 1479. Though their two kingdoms remained formally separate, the monarchs ruled them as if they were one kingdom. Thus, nearly all of the Iberian Peninsula came under Isabel and Fernando's control.

In 1482, Isabel and Fernando began the reconquest of Granada. Through many difficulties and for over a decade, the "Catholic Monarchs" conquered Granada city by city. Finally, on November 25, 1491, the last Muslim ruler in Spain surrendered the city of Granada. This conquest marked the end of the centuries-long reconquest of Spain from the Muslims.

11. **Why Europeans were interested in finding a new trade route to the Indies. Who was the first to discover a new trade route, and when?**

European merchants for centuries had traded with the lands of the Far East to obtain luxury products—silks and spices. With the conquest of Constantinople, Europeans were forced to trade with the Muslims to obtain these goods. To bypass these middlemen, Europeans wanted to find a trade route to the Indies by sea.

Portugal began the search for new trade routes. In 1497, the Portuguese captain Vasco da Gama led an expedition down the west coast of Africa, rounding the southern tip of Africa, and then sailing up the east coast of the continent. Crossing the Indian Ocean, da Gama's fleet sailed into Calicut port in India on May 20, 1498, thus opening up a rich trade route between Portugal and the Far East.

12. **What the Enterprise of the Indies was and what it resulted in**

The Genoese mariner, Christopher Columbus, came up with a plan to reach the Far East, or the Indies, by another route than that followed by da Gama. He presented this "Enterprise of the Indies," as he called it, to Queen Isabel and King Fernando. Following the conquest of Granada, Columbus received Queen Isabel's backing for a sea voyage to discover the Indies by sailing

Some Key Terms at a Glance

Renaissance: a word meaning "rebirth" and the name later generations gave to the period of history when Europeans developed a renewed respect for the literature, architecture, and art of ancient Rome and Greece

Humanism: the philosophy of the Renaissance, which tended to see man, not God, as the center of the world and held that human ideas and ideals, not the Church, should guide the life of people and human society

autocracy: rule by one having absolute or unrestricted power; a ruler in an autocracy is called an *autocrat*

Third Rome: Russian Orthodox theological claim that Moscow had succeeded Rome and Constantinople as the chief center of Christendom

westward across the ocean. On October 12, 1492, Columbus and his crew landed on an island lying off the coast of a continent they had not known existed. They had discovered North America.

Questions for Review

1. **What was thought to be "reborn" in the Renaissance?**

   The creativity and spirit of the classical ages were thought to have been reborn during the Renaissance.

2. **How did Renaissance Humanism's way of looking at God, man, and the world differ from the way medieval people looked at these things?**

   For medieval Europeans, the Church was seen as the center of life and the worship of God in the Church was the purpose for which everything in life was done. Renaissance Humanism, in contrast, saw man as the center of the world and thought human ideas and ideals were what should guide the life of people and human society.

3. **What role did the Medici family play in the development of the Florentine Renaissance?**

   The Medicis of Florence were the patrons of writers, philosophers, artists, and architects. They commissioned paintings and sculptures, founded schools, built magnificent public buildings, and added to the cathedral in Florence.

4. **What sort of man made a good ruler, according to Machiavelli's *The Prince*?**

   Machiavelli claimed that the best ruler makes decisions based only on what benefits himself and his realm. Machiavelli said the successful ruler is one who does not pay attention to moral principles but uses immoral means to subject others to his will.

   What did this work reveal about the character of the Renaissance?

   This work revealed that many in the Renaissance wanted a world in which they did not have to pay heed to God or what he commands.

5. **When did Constantinople fall to the Turks?**

   Constantinople fell on May 29, 1453.

   Why did the attempt to reunite the Churches of Rome and Constantinople fail?

   The attempt at reunion failed because the eastern clergy and monks, along with the people of Constantinople, opposed union with those they thought of as heretics and schismatics.

6. **Why did Ivan III think he was the successor of the Byzantine emperors?**

   Ivan II thought he was the successor of the Byzantine emperors because he had married Sophia, the niece of the last Byzantine emperor. This union, he claimed, made him the heir of the Byzantine emperors.

7. **What was the idea of the "Third Rome"?**

   The idea of the "Third Rome" was that Moscow had succeeded Rome itself and then Constantinople as the center of the Christian Faith.

   Who developed the idea, and why?

   The Russian Orthodox clergy and theologians developed the idea to further the glory of Moscow. The first Rome had fallen because of heresy, they said; the second Rome (Constantinople) had fallen because of immorality. The Third Rome will stand, said the theologians. "And a fourth there will not be."

8. **Who invented the printing press?**

   Johannes Gutenberg invented the printing press.

   What have been its effects on civilization?

   The printing press made books affordable to common people rather than just to the wealthiest and greatest churches and helped spread new ideas more widely in society.

9. **Who were Fernando and Isabel?**

   Fernando was the king of Aragon who married Isabel, the queen of Castile and León.

   When did the last Moorish city fall to Fernando and Isabel?

   The last Moorish city in Spain, Granada, fell to the monarchs on November 25, 1491.

10. **What did Columbus seek to do in sailing west across the ocean?**

    By sailing west across the ocean, Columbus hoped to find a direct trading route with India and China.

    What did Columbus really find or sail to in his first voyage? What lands did he think he had found?

    What he really found was a new continent—the Americas—though he thought he had reached the Indies.

Ideas in Action

1. **Discuss in class what the highest ideals of human behavior and creativity might be. Do we, in our time, achieve these ideals? Why or why not?**

   If one considers that human beings are created with a purpose in life, and that purpose is common to all human beings, then he might understand that the highest ideals of human behavior have to do with that purpose. If, as people in the Middle Ages thought, the purpose of human beings is to glorify God and to achieve eternal union with him, then the highest ideals of human behavior are those which direct us to achieving our purpose. Under such an understanding, the highest ideals of human behavior would have to do with virtue—but not just natural virtue, but finally the supernatural virtues: faith, hope, and charity. The highest ideals of creativity would be those works of art (visual art, music, literature) that draw our minds toward virtue.

2. **Write out a timeline of the Reconquest of Spain from its beginning to the fall of Granada in 1492. Include the most important events.**

   This can be done as a class assignment, or in groups, or individually by students.

3. **(a) Write a character description of Queen Isabel from the encyclopedia or another source. Or (b) Compose for class performance a little dramatization of Columbus asking Isabel for her aid in getting the "enterprise of the Indies" under way. Who would be the characters? What could Columbus say that would persuade the queen to invest so much money in this gamble of an exploration?**

   This can be done as a class assignment, or in groups, or individually by students.

4. **Make a wall map of the Old World of Europe and the New World of America. Show the lands that Spain, Russia, and the Ottoman Empire came to own. Why would the Ottoman Empire have been a threat to Christian Europe? To Spanish territories? To Russian territories?**

   This can be done as a class assignment, or in groups, or individually by students.

Chapter 16   The Birth of a New World   **173**

Sample Quiz for Pages 413–422

Please answer the following in complete sentences.

1. What was reborn in the Renaissance?
2. What do we call the philosophy of the Renaissance?
3. In what country did the Renaissance begin?
4. What city was the first great center of the Renaissance? What family patronized Renaissance artists, writers, and thinkers in this city?
5. Who was the first pope to patronize Renaissance writers, artists, and thinkers?
6. What artistic device did Renaissance artists use that medieval artists did not use?

Answer key to Sample Quiz I

Students' answers, of course, should only approximate the following.

1. *The creativity and spirit of ancient Greece and Rome* were thought to be reborn in the Renaissance.
2. We call the philosophy of the Renaissance *Humanism*.
3. The Renaissance began in *Italy*.
4. The first great center of the Renaissance was *Florence*. There, *the Medici family* patronized Renaissance artists, writers, and thinkers.
5. The first pope to patronize Renaissance writers, artists, and thinkers was *Nicholas V*.
6. The artistic device used by Renaissance, but not medieval artists, was *perspective*.

Sample Quiz for Pages 422–438

Please answer the following in complete sentences.

1. What is the name of the council where representatives of the Church of Constantinople and the Church of Rome signed a declaration of union acknowledging the pope as head of the Church?
2. In what year did Constantinople fall to the Ottoman Turks? Who was the Ottoman sultan who conquered Constantinople?
3. Who was the Grand Prince of Muscovy who called himself the heir to the Byzantine Empire? What title did he give himself?
4. Who is the inventor of the printing press? What was the first full-length book he printed?
5. The conquest of what city ended the Reconquest of Spain? In what year was the city conquered?
6. What was Christopher Columbus looking for when he set sail westward across the Atlantic Ocean? What did he really discover?

Answer key to Sample Quiz II

Students' answers, of course, should only approximate the following.

1. The council where the Churches of Rome and Constantinople signed a declaration of union was *the Council of Florence.*

2. Constantinople fell to the Ottoman Turks in *1453.* The Ottoman conqueror of Constantinople was *Mahomet II.*

3. The grand prince of Muscovy who called himself the heir of the Byzantine Empire was *Ivan III.* He gave himself the title *tsar.*

4. The inventor of the printing press was *Johannes Gutenberg.* The first book he printed was *the Bible.*

5. The conquest *of Granada* ended the Reconquest. Granada was conquered in *1491.*

6. In sailing westward over the Atlantic, Christopher Columbus was looking *for a direct trade route to India and China.* What he really discovered was *North and South America.*

Sample Test

1. What was the Renaissance? How did Renaissance ideals differ from medieval ideals?

2. Why did the Renaissance occur first in Italy?

3. Who was the first pope to promote the Renaissance? What was his goal for Rome? What is perhaps his greatest cultural achievement?

4. At what council did representatives of the Churches of Rome and Constantinople agree to reunite under the pope as head of the Church? When did this council occur? Why did it finally fail to bring unity to the churches?

5. How did Mongol rule change Russia's political and cultural life?

6. How did the invention of the printing press change civilization?

7. Identify the following:

   a) The name for the philosophy of the Renaissance

   b) The author of *The Prince,* a work that claimed that rulers should make decisions based only on what benefits themselves

   c) The Florentine family that patronized Renaissance artists, writers, and thinkers

   d) The artistic device in painting in which figures are made to appear farther away than other figures

   e) The inventor of the printing press

   f) The king of Aragon and queen of Castile and León who completed the Reconquest of Spain and sent Columbus on his voyage to the "Indies"

   g) The Muslim Turk conqueror of Constantinople

   h) The year Constantinople fell to the Ottoman Turks

   i) The Portuguese captain who found a trade route to India by sailing around the southern tip of Africa

Answer key to Sample Test

Students' answers, of course, should only approximate the following.

1. The Renaissance refers to *the time when Europeans developed a renewed respect for the literature, art, and architecture of ancient Greece and Rome.*

    In the Middle Ages, God and the worship of God was seen to stand at the center of human life and society. Life was seen as reflecting God and his will, as we learn of it through the Church. Everything was to be done for God's glory and to fulfill the purpose of human life, which is union with God. *The Church stood at the center of life.*

    In the Renaissance, people *began to see man, not God, as the center of the world. Human ideals, not the ideals of divine revelation or the Church,* were thought to guide the life of individuals and human society.

2. The Renaissance occurred first in Italy *because it had more visible reminders of classical civilization* than did any other European land.

3. The first pope to support the Renaissance was *Nicholas V.* He *wanted to make Rome the center of Renaissance art and literature.* Nicholas's greatest cultural achievement is, perhaps, *the founding of the Vatican Library.*

4. Representatives of the Churches of Rome and Constantinople agreed to reunite at *the Council of Florence,* held in *1439.* The union failed *because the Greek bishops who had agreed to it ended up rejecting it,* under pressure of their people, the priests, and the monks.

5. Before the Mongol conquest, Kievan *Russia had mild laws and local governments in which common people could participate.* After the Mongol conquest, *Russian rulers began to imitate the khans' harsh and cruel rule.*

6. The printing press changed civilization *by making printed materials—books and pamphlets—available to ordinary people.* Unlike hand-copied works, printed works could be printed and reprinted in large numbers.

7. *Answers:*

    a) Humanism

    b) Niccolò Macchiavelli

    c) Medici

    d) perspective

    e) Johannes Gutenberg

    f) Fernando and Isabel

    g) Mahomet II

    h) 1453

    i) Vasco da Gama

CHAPTER 17: The Protestant Reformation

Chapter Overview

- In 1507 Pope Julius II issued a jubilee indulgence to fund the rebuilding of St. Peter's Basilica in the Vatican.

- Martin Luther nailed his Ninety-five Theses on the door of the Castle Church in Wittenberg on the eve of All Saints Day, 1517, the traditional beginning of the Protestant Reformation.

- Luther debated the Catholic theologian, Johannes Eck, in 1519. During this debate, Luther discovered that he agreed with John Hus on many points and declared that the pope as well as the ecumenical councils could be in error.

- In 1520 Pope Leo X issued the bull, *Exsurge Domine*, condemning Martin Luther's teachings and threatening to excommunicate him if he did not recant. On December 10, 1520, Luther answered the pope's challenge by publicly burning the bull.

- Luther appeared before the Imperial Diet in Worms in 1521, defending himself and his teachings before the Emperor Charles V and the assembled princes. The diet condemned Luther in the Edict of Worms.

- Luther's reform early on splintered into several different groups. Among these were the followers of the Swiss reformer Ulrich Zwingli, the French reformer John Calvin, and the Anabaptists.

- John Calvin came out with his *Institutes of the Christian Religion* in 1536. Calvin and his teachings became the foundations of the Reformed tradition, one of the great branches of Protestantism besides Lutheranism.

- The Ottoman Turks again became a danger to Christendom under their new sultan, Suleiman I. In 1521, Suleiman took the important fortress city of Belgrade; the following year, he took the island of Rhodes in the eastern Mediterranean.

- War between Emperor Charles V and King Francis I of France lasted on and off from 1521 to 1544. Francis allied himself with the German Protestant princes, Pope Clement VII, and the Ottoman Turks against the emperor. Charles was ultimately successful against Francis.

- Charles V's troops in Italy mutinied in the spring of 1527 and marched on Rome. While Pope Clement VII was holed up in Castel Sant'Angelo, the imperial troops pillaged Rome.

- In 1529, the Turks under Suleiman I laid siege to Vienna. After an assault of three weeks, the Turks withdrew.

- At an Imperial Diet held in Augsburg in 1530, the German Lutheran princes presented a confession of faith, called the Augsburg Confession, to the emperor. Charles V pledged to enforce the Edict of Worms against the Protestants; but needing the help of the Lutheran princes against Suleiman, Charles proclaimed the Peace of Nuremberg by which he suspended all laws against the Lutherans.

- Pope Paul III called for a meeting in 1537 of an ecumenical council at Trent. Because of Francis I's continued plots against Charles V, however, the council was not able to meet until 1545.

- War between the Lutheran princes of Germany and the emperor began in 1546. It continued until 1555, when an Imperial Diet proclaimed the "Religious Peace of Augsburg." The Peace gave every prince the right to choose what religion he and his subjects would follow in his territory.

- When his wife, Catherine of Aragon, did not give birth to any sons, England's King Henry VIII wanted his marriage to her annulled. When, after several years, the pope rendered no decision about the annulment, Henry took matters into his own hands. His newly appointed archbishop of Canterbury, Thomas Cranmer, annulled Henry's marriage to Catherine and blessed his marriage to Anne Boleyn.

- Parliament decreed that Henry VIII was head of the Church of England. Anyone who refused to acknowledge that the king was supreme over the English Church was accused of treason. Bishop St. John Fisher and St. Thomas More were executed for remaining faithful to the pope.

- Beginning in 1536, King Henry VIII ordered the dissolution of the monasteries in England. The wealth from the monasteries went to the king and his supporters, forming a new class of powerful and wealthy men.

- Under Queen Mary I, the Church of England was restored to communion with the pope. However, Mary's hundreds of executions of Protestants made her unpopular and brought the Catholic Church into disrepute.

- Queen Elizabeth I continued the Protestantizing of the Church of England, which had begun during the reign of her half-brother, Edward VI.

- Elizabeth required all her subjects to attend Church of England services. At first she was relatively gentle toward Catholics; but after Pope Pius V excommunicated Elizabeth, she began a bitter persecution of Catholics, in which thousands died.

Chapter Goals

Students need to understand the Protestant Reformation as one of the great watershed events of Western Europe, changing forever the character of European society (and, indeed, the world) and mortally wounding the civilization we have called Christendom. Yet, students must understand how the roots of the Reformation go back to the 14th century—to the events at Anagni, the "Babylonian Captivity" of the papacy at Avignon (and the abuses that arose during that period), and the subsequent Great Schism. The Protestant Reformation occurred because the Church had come to need reform in all areas of her life, and no one was undertaking a meaningful reform.

In treating Martin Luther, teachers must be careful of the temptation to demonize him. While the movement he initiated was destructive of the Catholic Faith and the unity of Christendom, Luther himself was a complex character inspired in large part by what he believed to be the truth. One can disagree with what a man does or believes without descending to simplistic evaluations of his character.

Students should understand that, despite the Reformation, Europe continued to suffer from fratricidal political struggles (such as that between Francis I and Charles V) and faced the threat posed by the Ottoman Turks. By their best lights, Europeans deemed the Turks a very real threat to all of Europe. Yet, for short-term political goods, Christian rulers were willing to ally with the very enemy that threatened them with destruction. This is a good lesson in the short-sighted foolishness of human beings.

What Students Should Know

1. **What the ills afflicting the Church before the Reformation were**

    The ills afflicting the Church were:

    a) greater attention to politics and wealth among the popes and bishops rather than the spiritual good of the Church

    b) granting benefices to those who could pay the most money for them; benefices, thus, going, not to the holiest or most learned men, but to the wealthiest

    c) ignorance and immorality among the lower clergy; laxity among friars and monks

    d) granting more than one benefice to one man, or a benefice in a country where the grantee did not live

    c) simony and nepotism

    d) the inability of the Church to reform itself, either through the popes or councils

2. **What the "spark" was that set off the Reformation in Germany. How Martin Luther responded to it**

    The preaching of an indulgence (ostensibly) to help pay for the building of St. Peter's Basilica in Rome was what set off the Reformation. Pope Leo X approved the preaching of the indulgence, part of the money from which would help Archbishop Albert of Mainz pay off his debt to the curia in Rome. The indulgence promised the remission of penalties for sins to those who donated money to the building of the basilica. The Augustinian priest, Martin Luther, a theologian at the University of Wittenberg in Saxony, disagreed with how the indulgence was being presented. Further, he had begun to doubt that the pope even had the power to issue indulgences. On the Feast of All Saints, October 31, 1517 Luther posted his Ninety-Five Theses on indulgences on the door of the Castle Church in Wittenberg. The theses were presented as topics for debate among scholars. But Luther took the further step of having them translated from Latin into German and then printing them and having them distributed throughout Germany. The theses became popular among Germans of all classes.

3. **How Luther went from protesting against indulgences to denying the authority of the Church**

    In 1518, in a meeting with Cardinal Cajetan, Luther appealed to the authority of a general council, thus stating that a council had more authority than the pope. In 1519, in a debate with Johannes Eck, Luther came to the conclusion that not only the pope, but councils could be in error.

4. **What Luther taught**

    a) *sola fide*: that God's grace comes to man by faith alone

    b) *sola gratia*: that, since man's nature has been wholly corrupted by original sin, salvation comes to man by God's grace alone, without any works on man's part

    c) *sola scriptura*: that God's revelation comes to man by scripture alone

    d) that the Mass is not a sacrifice, but a banquet; that the bread and wine do not become the Body and Blood of Christ (transubstantiation), but the Body and Blood of Christ are present in, with, and under the bread and wine

e) works, such as pilgrimages, the use of sacramentals, and private devotions do not bring grace to the soul, and that monastic life is opposed to the Gospel

5. How the printing press aided Luther

To disseminate his Ninety-Five Theses and tracts he wrote subsequently, Luther used the printing press. Instead of just spreading the tracts among a relative few, the printing press allowed Luther to publish his writings all over Germany. Because of this, many Germans read Luther and began to see in him the long-awaited reformer of the Church.

6. How the Church and the empire dealt with Luther

Though news of Luther's attacks on indulgences and the authority of the pope reached Rome not long after the posting of the Ninety-five Theses, Rome moved slowly against Luther. It was not until the summer of 1520 that Rome took any action against Luther by issuing a bull of excommunication, *Exsurge Domine*. The bull gave Luther 60 days after the date he received the bull to recant. Luther, instead, burned the bull on December 10, 1520, and so was formally executed.

By excommunicating Luther, the pope turned him over to the temporal arm for punishment. But the new emperor, Charles V, was persuaded by Frederick of Saxony to allow Luther to defend himself at the imperial diet, to be held at Worms. Going to Worms under safe conduct, Luther appeared before the diet and the emperor in April 1521 and declared he would not recant. The next day, Charles V condemned Luther; on May 8, the diet issued the Edict of Worms, which condemned Luther's heresy and declared him an outlaw under sentence of death. But Luther escaped death on account of the safe conduct and because, on his return journey, he was taken to the Wartburg.

7. Why Luther's followers became known as Protestants; what "Protestant" means

Luther's followers received the name "Protestant" because of the 1529 *Protest of Speier*, which spoke out against a German diet's condemnation of Luther's teachings and in favor of Luther's teachings. In the 16th century, *to protest* had the sense of "to witness for" something rather than to speak out against something.

8. Who the radical reformers were and what they stood for

Luther's idea that every believer could interpret the Bible for himself without the guidance of tradition or the Church inspired others to do that very thing—interpret the Bible for themselves. This often led other reformers to come to different conclusions from Luther and so enter into direct conflict with him. Compared to these reformers, Luther was quite traditional, even though, initially, he approved of the reforms carried out by the radicals.

An important radical reformer was Ulrich Zwingli, preacher at the cathedral in Zürich, Switzerland. More radical than Zwingli were the Anabaptists. Their name means "rebaptizer," since they rejected infant baptism and insisted that everyone who had been baptized as an infant had to be baptized again as an adult. The Anabaptists differed among themselves and had no unified church structure. Some were communistic; some were violent, while others were peaceful.

9. What John Calvin taught and what his influence was on Europe

Like Luther, Calvin taught *sola gratia, sola scriptura* and *sola fide*, and that human nature had been totally corrupted by Original Sin. Unlike Luther, however, Calvin said Baptism and Communion are not sacraments, and he denied the Real Presence in the Eucharist. Calvin taught that God predestines some men to go to heaven and others to go to hell.

Calvin and his theological work, the *Institutes of the Christian Religion*, shaped and formed one of the great divisions of Protestantism besides Lutheranism. Calvin's influence and teachings formed Protestant thought in England, France, Holland, and Scotland. In Scotland, the Calvinist church was called Presbyterian because Calvin taught that the church is not to be ruled by bishops but by councils of elders or "presbyters."

10. Who Charles V was and why he was unable to deal effectively with the German Protestant princes

As Roman emperor and king of Spain (and all its New World possessions), Charles V was perhaps the most powerful man of his day. Yet, despite his power, Charles could not stop the Protestant princes from establishing Lutheranism in their domains.

One reason Charles could not stop the Protestant princes was the actions of King Francis I of France. Francis's goal was to weaken Charles's power, so he allied himself with the German Protestant princes joined in the Schmalkaldic League against the emperor. Francis fought a series of wars against Charles, keeping the emperor so occupied that he had to turn his attention away from Germany.

Francis was allied with Suleiman the Magnificent, the Turkish Sultan. Unable to rely on Francis I for aid against Suleiman's invasions, Charles had to make peace with the German princes and give them temporary guarantees of religious freedom.

Finally, in a war fought from 1546–1547, Charles was able to humble the Schmalkaldic League, capturing and imprisoning one of the most powerful of the Lutheran princes. Yet, in 1551, King Henry II of France brought this all to naught by invading imperial territory. To deal with Henry, Charles was forced to sign a treaty with the Lutheran princes.

11. To identify the following:

a) *The Augsburg Confession*: a statement of belief drawn up by Lutheran theologians for the Diet of Augsburg and the emperor in 1530

b) *Peace of Nuremberg*: Emperor Charles V's suspension of laws against the Protestants in return for their aid against Suleiman

12. What the Religious Peace of Augsburg was and its significance

The Religious Peace of Augsburg, proclaimed at the Imperial Diet of Augsburg in 1555, laid down the principle, *cuius regio, eius religio* ("whose region, his religion.") Under the peace, each prince would determine what religion the people in his lands would follow. The Peace made the religious division of Germany permanent, ending all hope of reconciliation between Lutherans and Catholics.

13. Why King Henry VIII led the English Church into schism

Henry had married Catherine of Aragon, the daughter of Fernando and Isabel of Spain. Though this was a powerful alliance, Henry derived no male offspring from this marriage. Claiming their marriage was invalid because Catherine had been married to his brother, Henry asked the pope for an annulment. From 1526–1532, Pope Clement VII basically took no action on the annulment request. Finally, having appointed Thomas Cranmer archbishop of Canterbury, Henry took matters into his own hands. In 1533, Cranmer proclaimed Henry's marriage to Catherine null and void and blessed his marriage to Anne Boleyn.

In response to these acts, Pope Clement VII excommunicated Henry, and Henry responded by declaring the king, not the pope, the head of the Church of England. Nearly all the English clergy followed the king into schism.

14. **What the effects of the dissolution of the monasteries were**

    Henry took control of the lands and wealth of the monasteries dissolved by him, but then he distributed them among his favorites, thus creating a new and powerful class of wealthy men. The poor who were dependent on the monasteries for livelihood formed a new class of beggars.

15. **What the Church of England was like under Henry VIII and how it changed**

    Except for the end of monasticism in England, the Church of England changed little after Henry VIII led it into schism. Mass continued to be said in Latin, communion was given only under one species, and priests did not marry.

    During the reign of Edward VI, however, Protestants took control of the Church of England. Archbishop Cranmer composed the *Book of Common Prayer*, which replaced the Latin liturgy with an English liturgy all throughout England. The Church of England adopted a confession of faith, based on the theology of John Calvin, and drew up new rites for consecrating bishops, priests, and all members of the clergy. In sum, under Edward, the Church of England went from being merely schismatic to being fully Protestant.

16. **What Queen Mary of England tried to do and why she failed**

    Queen Mary tried to bring England back into communion with the Catholic Church. During her five-year reign, she restored the Mass and Catholic customs and suppressed all the Protestant changes made under Edward VI.

    Mary, however, made the mistake of persecuting the Protestants in her kingdom, of whom 277 were executed. If she had treated them as traitors to her throne, public opinion might not have turned against her. But in executing them for their religion, Mary made these Protestants heroes and martyrs in the eyes of Englishmen.

17. **What Queen Elizabeth I's religious policy was**

    Queen Elizabeth brought the Church of England again into schism, restoring its Protestant doctrine and worship. Under her, Parliament passed the Act of Uniformity, which ordered every English subject to attend Church of England services or pay a fine.

    At first, Elizabeth was relatively gentle towards Catholics. But then, in 1570, Pope Pius V excommunicated her, declaring her subjects were not bound to obey her. After that, Elizabeth became a bitter persecutor of Catholics, particularly priests.

18. **To identify the following:**

    a) *John Knox*: follower of John Calvin who established the Presbyterian Church in Scotland

    b) *Mary Queen of Scots*: The Catholic queen of Scotland who, threatened in Scotland, fled to England. In 1569, Queen Elizabeth had Mary arrested because Elizabeth saw her as a rival to the English throne. Mary was executed by beheading in 1587.

    c) *Spanish Armada*: The large fleet of ships King Philip II sent to invade England in 1588. The English fleet forced the armada to withdraw. Many of its ships were wrecked in storms.

    d) *Douai-Reims Bible*: a translation of the Bible from Latin into English, prepared by priests at the English seminary in Douai, Belgium (later at Reims, France)

Questions for Review

1. **What was Luther objecting to in the Ninety-five Theses?**

   Luther was objecting to the way indulgences were being preached in his time. He thought the way they were being preached led people away from a true understanding of the forgiveness of sins offered by Christ.

2. **What was the Edict of Worms?**

   The Edict of Worms was Emperor Charles V and the Diet of Worms' condemnation of Luther as a heretic. It declared him an outlaw under sentence of death.

   Why was Emperor Charles V not able to enforce it?

   The emperor was unable to enforce the Edict of Worms because, by order of Elector Frederick of Saxony, Luther was taken and hidden in Wartburg Castle.

3. **What did Luther mean by *sola fide*?**

   By *sola fide*, Luther meant that salvation comes by faith only and not by any good works.

   What did he mean by *sola scriptura* and *sola gratia*?

   Sola scriptura is Luther's teaching that Scripture alone (not tradition or the Church) is the source of divine revelation. *Sola gratia* means that only by God's grace can one be saved.

4. **What is Calvinism?**

   Calvinism refers to the religious doctrines and practices instituted by the French reformer, John Calvin.

   How does it differ from Lutheranism?

   Calvinism differs from Lutheranism in that, while Luther taught that Baptism and the Eucharist are sacraments, Calvin taught that they are not. Luther denied transubstantiation but believed that the Body and Blood of Christ are present in, with, and under the bread and wine. Calvin taught that the bread and wine only represent Christ's Body and Blood.

   What did Calvin mean by predestination?

   By predestination, Calvin meant that God has chosen from before all time those who will go to heaven and those who will go to hell.

Some Key Terms at a Glance

indulgence: a full or partial remittance by the Church of the temporal punishment for sins (such as one suffers in Purgatory)

Protestant: one who "witnesses" (protests) to the complaints against the Church; one of the reforming theologians of the 16th century or a follower of the reformers

sola fide, sola gratia: Luther's doctrine that only by God's Grace, through faith alone, may one be saved

sola scriptura: Luther's teaching that divine revelation comes through the Scriptures alone

annulment: a decree by the Church court that a marriage is invalid; that is, has never existed. It differs from a divorce, which is the splitting of a valid and existing marriage.

uniformity: the legal demand that all the citizens of a country adhere to the official religion

5. **Why did Henry want a divorce from Catherine?**

   Henry claimed that his marriage to Catherine had been invalid because she had been his brother Arthur's wife. Catherine had only given birth to a daughter, and Henry wanted a male heir, which he thought he could get if he could marry another woman. Later, Henry fell in love with Anne Boleyn and, in order to marry her, had to obtain a divorce from Catherine.

   Why could he not get an annulment from the pope?

   The pope would not grant an annulment to Henry because the king had received a dispensation to marry his brother's wife, making his marriage valid. Pope Clement VII also feared he would anger Emperor Charles V if he gave in to Henry's demand, for Catherine was Charles's aunt.

   What was his solution?

   Henry's solution was to declare the Church of England independent of the pope and himself as its head. In this situation, the archbishop of Canterbury annulled Henry's marriage without consulting the pope.

6. **Who was Henry VIII's heir?**

   Henry VIII's heir was King Edward VI.

   What important English book was written during his reign?

   Under his reign, the *Book of Common Prayer* was written.

7. **What was the effect of the dissolution of the monasteries of England?**

   Because monastery lands went to the king, who gave much of the property to Thomas Cromwell and his friends, the dissolution of the monasteries created a new and powerful class of wealthy men. Since the monasteries were a source of livelihood for many poor, the loss of the monasteries created a new class of beggars.

8. **What did the Peace of Augsburg accomplish?**

   The Peace of Augsburg gave every prince in the empire the right to determine what religion (Catholic or Lutheran) his lands would follow. If someone did not want to follow the religion of his lord, he would have to leave.

   How did it perpetuate the religious division in Germany?

   The Peace made the religious divisions permanent because it signified that all hope of reconciliation between Lutherans and Catholics was ended.

9. **What did King Philip II of Spain hope to accomplish with the Spanish Armada?**

   King Philip II hoped to invade and conquer England.

10. **Why did Pope Pius V's excommunication of Elizabeth turn her against her Catholic subjects?**

    The excommunication turned Elizabeth against her Catholic subjects because the pope said her subjects were not bound to obey her—which, in the queen's eyes, made them possible traitors.

11. **What poets and great men made Elizabeth's reign famous in English history?**

    Men like William Shakespeare, Ben Jonson, Edmund Spenser, and Sir Walter Raleigh made Elizabeth's reign famous in English history.

184 Chapter 17 The Protestant Revolution

Ideas in Action

1. Make a map showing the divisions of Europe between Protestant and Catholic after the Lutheran revolt.

   This can be an in-class assignment or assigned as homework to groups or individual students.

2. Read a passage from the Douai-Reims Bible and then read the same one from the King James Bible. What differences, if any, do you spot?

   This can be an in-class assignment, where students discuss selected passages together, or the teacher may assign various passages to different students or groups of students who would, then, report their findings to the class.

3. Discuss in class the splintering effect of Luther's revolt on the body of Christendom.

4. Discuss with your teacher and the class: "How does the Protestant Reformation still affect us even today?"

Sample Quiz for Pages 443–462

Please answer the following in complete sentences.

1. Name one problem that afflicted the Church before the Reformation.

2. What important event occurred on October 31, 1517? (It is said to be the beginning of the Protestant Reformation.)

3. What did Martin Luther mean by *sola fide*?

4. Who issued the Edict of Worms? What did it say?

5. What did "Protestant" mean in the 16th century?

6. Please identify:

   a) The religious group of those who believed that those baptized as infants had to be rebaptized as adults

   b) The author of the *Institutes of the Christian Religion*

   c) The emperor who condemned Martin Luther

   d) The man who led the Reformation in the Swiss city of Zürich

Answer key to Sample Quiz I

Students' answers, of course, should only approximate the following.

1. *Possible answers*:

   a) greater attention to politics and wealth rather than the spiritual good of the Church among the popes and bishops

   b) granting benefices to those who could pay the most money for them; benefices, thus, going, not to the holiest or most learned men, but to the wealthiest

   c) ignorance and immorality among the lower clergy; laxity among friars and monks

   d) granting more than one benefice to one man, or a benefice in a country where the grantee did not live

   e) simony

   f) nepotism

   g) the inability of the Church to reform itself, either through the popes or councils

2. *Martin Luther's posting of the 95 Theses* on the door of the Castle Church in Wittenberg occurred on October 31, 1517.

3. By *sola fide* Martin Luther meant that *people are saved by faith alone*, without having to perform good works.

4. The Edict of Worms was a decree *from Emperor Charles V and the Diet of Worms. It proclaimed Luther a heretic and an outlaw under sentence of death.*

5. In the 16th century, Protestant signified *someone who witnessed* for *something*.

6. *Answers*:

   a) the Anabaptists

   b) John Calvin

   c) Charles V

   d) Ulrich Zwingli

Sample Quiz for Pages 463–477

Please answer the following in complete sentences.

1. What two political enemies kept Charles V from dealing effectively with the Protestant princes in Germany?

2. What right did the Peace of Augsburg grant to the princes of the empire?

3. What did the Act of Supremacy declare about the king and the Church in England?

4. How did Queen Elizabeth treat Catholics in her kingdom?

5. Why is Queen Mary remembered as "Bloody Mary"?

6. *Please identify*:

   a) The archbishop of Canterbury who wrote the *Book of Common Prayer*

   b) Henry VIII's first wife, daughter to King Fernando of Aragon and Queen Isabel of Castile

   c) The queen executed by Elizabeth I

   d) The invasion fleet sent by King Philip II of Spain to invade England

   e) The translation of the Bible into English, done at the English seminary in Belgium and, then, France

Answer key to Sample Quiz II

Students' answers, of course, should only approximate the following.

1. The two political leaders who kept Charles V from dealing effectively with the Protestant princes in Germany were *the king of France [Francis I]* and *the Ottoman Turk sultan, Suleiman I, the Magnificent.*

2. The Peace of Augsburg gave the German princes the right *to choose what religion people in their regions would follow* and *to expel all those who would not follow the state religion.*

3. The Act of Supremacy declared *that the Church in England was independent of Rome* and *the king was supreme over the Church of England.*

4. *At first, Elizabeth was relatively kind to Catholics. But after Pope Pius V excommunicated the queen, Elizabeth became a bitter persecutor of Catholics.*

5. Queen Mary is called "Bloody Mary" *because she executed 277 Protestants during her reign.*

6. *Answers:*

   a) Thomas Cranmer

   b) Catherine of Aragon

   c) Mary, Queen of Scots

   d) Spanish Armada

   e) Douai-Reims Bible

Sample Test

1. Name three evils in the Church that led to the Protestant Reformation.

2. How were Martin Luther and John Calvin's teachings alike? Where did they differ?

3. Why have Calvin's teaching and influence been so important?

4. Why was Charles V unable to deal effectively with the Protestants in Germany?

5. What powers did the Religious Peace of Augsburg give to princes in the empire? What effect did it have on Germany?

6. Why did Henry VIII decide to take the Church of England into schism?

7. Compare and contrast what the Church of England was like under Henry VIII with how it came to be under Edward VI and Elizabeth I.

8. Identify the following:

   a) The Swiss preacher who led the Reformation in Zürich

   b) The statement of belief drawn up by Lutheran theologians in 1530

   c) The English prayer book composed by Thomas Cranmer

   d) The English queen who for a short time restored the Church of England to the Catholic Church

   e) The fleet King Philip II of Spain sent to invade England

Answer key to Sample Test

Students' answers, of course, should only approximate the following.

1. *Possible answers*:

    a) greater attention to politics and wealth rather than the spiritual good of the Church among the popes and bishops

    b) granting benefices to those who could pay the most money for them; benefices, thus, going, not to the holiest or most learned men, but to the wealthiest

    c) ignorance and immorality among the lower clergy

    d) laxity among friars and monks

    e) granting more than one benefice to one man, or a benefice in a country where the grantee did not live

    f) simony

    g) nepotism

    h) the inability of the Church to reform itself, either through the popes or councils

2. *Both Calvin and Luther* taught that people *are saved by grace alone (sola gratia) through faith alone (sola fide)*. Both taught *that Scripture alone (sola scriptura) is the source of divine revelation.*

    But *Calvin and Luther differed over the sacraments. While Luther taught that Baptism and the Eucharist are sacraments, Calvin taught that they are not.* Luther denied transubstantiation but believed that the Body and Blood of Christ are present in, with, and under the bread and wine. Calvin taught that the bread and *wine only represent Christ's Body and Blood.*

3. Calvin's teaching and influence have been so important *because they formed Protestant thought in many countries*—England, France, Holland, and Scotland. *Calvinism forms one of the great divisions of Protestantism.*

4. Charles V was unable to deal effectively with the Protestants in Germany *because he faced continual wars with the Turks and with the king of France. The king of France allied himself both with the Turks and the Protestant German princes.*

5. The Religious Peace of Augsburg gave princes in the empire the *right to decide what religion their domains would follow and to expel from their domains all who would refuse to follow that religion.*

    The Peace's effect on Germany was *that it made the religious divisions of Germany permanent.*

6. Henry VIII took the Church of England into schism *because he wanted his first marriage to Catherine of Aragon annulled and the pope would not grant him the annulment.*

7. Except for the dissolution of the monasteries, *little changed externally in the Church of England as long as Henry VIII lived.* Mass was still said in Latin, for instance, and the teachings were the same. *The Church of England was schismatic, but not heretical.*

    Under Edward VI and Elizabeth I, however, *the Church of England became a thoroughly Protestant body*, in its liturgy and beliefs.

8. *Answers*:

    a) Ulrich Zwingli

    b) Augsburg Confession

    c) *Book of Common Prayer*

    d) Mary

    e) Spanish Armada

CHAPTER 18: Catholic Renewal and Religious War

Chapter Overview

- The Council of Trent met on and off from 1545 to 1563. The council addressed both doctrinal issues and Church reform.

- The Council of Trent began a movement of Church reform and renewal that has been called the Counter-Reformation, or, better, the Catholic Reformation.

- Reform of the Church began before, and continued during and after, the council. The reform was carried through by the pope, bishops, and by religious orders, particularly the Society of Jesus.

- Ignatius de Loyola had dreamed only of military glory; but, after being injured in battle, he began to dream of serving Christ. At the University of Paris, he inspired other young men to follow his example. In Rome, they offered their services to the pope and formed a new religious order called the Society of Jesus, or the Jesuits. The Jesuits were an important force in carrying the Catholic Reformation forward.

- By his preaching, writing, and work in education—but most of all by his charity—St. Peter Canisius saved Catholic Germany from Protestantism and brought many Protestant Germans back into the Church.

- By 1571, the Ottoman sultan Selim II had conquered the island of Cyprus and launched a large fleet for an invasion of Italy. A Christian fleet under Don Juan of Austria defeated the Turkish fleet at the Battle of Lepanto on October 7, 1571.

- Religious civil war between Calvinists (called Huguenots) and Catholics troubled France from 1547 to 1597. In 1597, the first Bourbon king of France, Henry IV, issued the Edict of Nantes, granting religious and political liberty to the Huguenots. The Huguenots continued to threaten the unity of France until 1629, when, after the capture of La Rochelle, King Louis XIII and Cardinal Richelieu signed the Peace of Alais with the Huguenots. In the Peace of Alais, Louis XIII and Richelieu gave the Huguenots full religious liberty but ended their political and military power.

- The Protestant nobles of Bohemia did not want Ferdinand von Habsburg as their king. Choosing, instead, the Calvinist Frederick, elector of the Palatinate, the nobles revolted against Ferdinand, who in 1619 became the German emperor. With the aid of King Maximilian of Bavaria and the army of the Catholic League, Ferdinand II defeated Frederick and the Bohemians at the Battle of White Mountain in 1620. The Bohemian revolt finally ended in 1623.

- With the encouragement of England and France, King Christian IV of Denmark invaded Germany in 1625, joining forces with the Protestant German princes against the emperor and the Catholic League. Albrecht von Wallenstein's mercenary army and the Catholic League army under Tilly defeated the Protestant and Danish forces. In 1626, Christian IV withdrew from the war.

- After the defeat of Christian IV and his Protestant allies, Emperor Ferdinand issued the Edict of Restitution, which said that the Protestant princes had to return all the lands they had seized from the Church since 1555. The edict weakened the emperor's cause, for it turned many of the Protestant princes who had once supported him against him.

- In 1631, King Gustavus II Adolphus of Sweden began his war of conquest in Germany. In 1632 he defeated Count Tilly's Catholic League forces, but Gustavus himself was defeated by Wallenstein at the Battle of Lützen. The Swedish king died in this battle. In 1634, the combined imperial and Catholic League forces defeated the Swedes at Nördlingen.

- In 1635, France under Cardinal Richelieu declared war on the Habsburg emperor and his cousin, King Philip IV of Spain. At first the Spanish scored victories against the French, but gradually Spain lost its advantage. Aided by rebellions in Spain and Naples, the French began defeating Spanish armies. French forces began pouring into Germany to aid the Protestant princes and the Swedes. By 1647 the entire empire, except for the Habsburg lands, was under the control of the Swedes and the French.

- The Peace of Westphalia, signed November 3, 1648, made the German princes practically independent of the emperor. More importantly, however, the Peace made the religious division of Christendom into Protestant and Catholic camps permanent.

- The war between France and Spain continued until 1659. At war's end, the Spanish power had been crushed. France became the most powerful nation in Europe.

Chapter Goals

The first part of this chapter details the measures the Catholic Church took to meet the Protestant challenge and to reform herself. Though the period in question is sometimes called the "Counter-Reformation," it is more properly understood as the Catholic Reformation. Though the Council of Trent enacted reforms and defined doctrines in response to the Protestant reformers, its activity was not primarily negative, but reconstructive. It was the Church's long-awaited, and too long-delayed, reform.

Students should understand what the Church did in the Counter-Reformation. In reforming herself, she not only corrected abuses and errors but was renewed in her life. This renewal was reflected in a renaissance of the Faith in Catholic regions, the return of some Protestants to the Church, and in a new and vibrant missionary activity outside the confines, not only of Europe, but of the Western Hemisphere itself.

Students must understand how religious controversy so easily resolved into hatred and war. The people of this period took religion seriously; religion still was considered the most important good that human beings could possess. Heresy was not just a personal opinion that differed from another opinion—it could lead to the overthrow of Christian society and the eternal damnation of souls. People of the 16th and early 17th centuries looked upon heresy as we might the poisoning of a city's water system. Indeed, though, like us, they would have seen the latter as a great evil, it would pale for them in comparison to the poisoning of the mind through false teaching.

Yet, students must understand that the religious wars in France and Germany were not merely religious; as the case of Cardinal Richelieu demonstrates, lust for power played a large part. If the Thirty Years' War began as a religious war, it ended as mostly a political struggle, with Catholics supporting the Protestant side, and Protestants, the Catholic side. More than anything else, the Thirty Years' War represents the destruction of that unified civilization we have called Christendom in this book.

What Students Should Know

1. **How long the Council of Trent lasted; when it began and when it ended**

   The Council of Trent met on and off for 18 years, from December 1545 to December 1563.

2. **What the Council of Trent accomplished and whether it was successful in its goals**

   The Council of Trent promulgated decrees that addressed challenges laid down by Protestant reformers. It sought to clarify doctrinal problems and to correct abuses in the Church.

   In one way, the council was a failure: it did not reconcile the Protestants to the Church nor were its reforms implemented in some parts of Europe for many years. Yet, it another way it was a triumph because it clearly spelled out Catholic teaching on several points the Protestants had challenged and it set in motion a true reform of the Church's life.

3. **Be able to define:**

   a) *Ultramontane*: the name given to those who favored strong papal control over national churches

   b) *Gallican*: from *Gallicanism,* a position held by many French churchmen that the French Church should be in most respects independent of the pope while remaining in communion with him

   c) *Counter-Reformation*: the period of Church renewal after the Council of Trent—not to be characterized primarily as a struggle against the Protestant Reformation but as a reform and renewal of Catholic life

   d) *Holy Office or "Inquisition"*: the congregation of the curia that issued doctrinal decrees and condemned heretical teachings. Its purpose was to protect the purity of the Catholic Faith.

   c) *Index of Forbidden Books*: the list of those books the Church considered dangerous to the Catholic Faith and forbade Catholics to read

4. **In what the reform of the liturgy consisted**

   Though the Council of Trent ordered a reform of the Roman liturgy, it was not carried out by the council but by Pope Pius V. The reform established a uniform, Latin liturgy (the Roman Rite) for the entire Church, to root out changes and abuses that had crept into the liturgy. Some dioceses and orders, however, were allowed to continue using a few of the most ancient Latin rites of the Mass. The reformed rite is often called the Tridentine or Extraordinary Rite today.

5. **What was the character of the order founded by St. Ignatius of Loyola and what work it did**

   St. Ignatius of Loyola founded his order on the model of an army. At its head was the superior general, to whom every member vowed absolute, unquestioning obedience. The superior was subject to no one but the pope, who stood like a king in relation to the Jesuit "army." Jesuits took a special vow, to go wherever the pope sent them. They could easily go wherever they were sent because, unlike other religious orders, they were not required to live in community. Thus, the Jesuits were an effective instrument to realize the Counter-Reformation.

In Catholic lands, Jesuits taught Catholic doctrine and strove to inspire the faithful with love for Christ and His Church. In many places they founded schools and colleges or staffed existing institutions. Jesuits risked death and won martyrdom by going to England and Scotland to minister secretly to Catholics there. They ministered to enslaved Christians in Muslim lands. They served as missionaries in Africa, the Americas, and Asia.

6. **What the Battle of Lepanto was and why it was important**

Fought on October 7, 1571, the Battle of Lepanto was a sea battle between a Christian and Turkish fleet. The Turkish fleet had gathered for an invasion of Italy. To stop the invasion, Pope Pius V called on Christian nations to form the Holy League. The Christian fleet, under Don Juan of Austria, defeated the Turkish fleet, thus halting the invasion of Europe. Thereafter, the Turkish fleet was no longer as great a threat to Europe as it had been.

7. **What were the causes of the religious wars in France. How they ended**

Though most people in France in the 16th century were Catholic, there was a large minority of Calvinists there. These Huguenots, as they were called, increased in numbers and in power, for they attracted some members of the nobility. The Huguenots were thus a strong political power. Opposing the Huguenot lords was a league of Catholics, led by the family of the duke of Guise. Violence between the Guises and the Huguenots in 1561 and 1562 led to an open civil war in France.

Catherine de Medici, the powerful queen mother of the last Valois kings of France, sometimes supported the Catholic, sometimes the Protestant side in the civil war. Her sons followed this vacillating policy. In 1572, she ordered a mass killing of the Huguenot leaders on the Feast of St. Bartholomew, August 24, 1572. The massacre, beginning in Paris, spread to other parts of France. Thousands were killed.

The assassination of King Henry III left the Huguenot leader, Henry de Bourbon, the heir to the French throne. The new king, Henry IV, fought a four-year war with the Catholic League. Finally, becoming Catholic in 1593, Henry IV was able to make peace with the Catholic nobility and so establish his house—the House of Bourbon—on the French throne.

The Huguenots, however, still remained powerful and threatened to establish an independent republic in the heart of France. To prevent this, in 1589 Henry IV issued the Edict of Nantes, which granted Protestants the freedom to hold their religious beliefs and the right to worship in certain places. The edict granted Protestants equal rights with Catholics in holding public offices and conceded them the right to protect themselves with arms and fortresses.

8. **Who Armand-Jean du Plessis de Richelieu was and what his goals were**

Richelieu was a French Catholic bishop and cardinal, as well as the prime minister of France under King Louis XIII. Richelieu, who thought the king should be supreme over even the Church, worked to make the king supreme in France. To do this, he ended the political power of the Huguenots by conquering their fortress of La Rochelle and bringing them to sign the Peace of Alais in 1629. The Peace granted the Huguenots religious freedom but forced them to give up their political and military power.

Richelieu's second major goal was to make the king and France supreme in Europe. To do this, he had to crush the power of the Habsburgs—a goal he accomplished ultimately by waging war.

9. **What were the causes of the Thirty Years' War**

Control of the kingdom of Bohemia was necessary to secure the imperial throne of Germany. Seven electors determined who would be emperor; besides the king of Bohemia, three of these electors were Protestant and three were Catholic. If a Protestant secured the throne of Bohemia, it could happen that a Protestant could become emperor. Thus, in order to become emperor, Ferdinand von Habsburg (the nephew of the reigning Emperor Matthias) needed to become king of Bohemia.

The Protestant nobles of Bohemia did not want Ferdinand von Habsburg as their king. And though they at first voted to make him king, they later changed their minds and chose, instead, the Calvinist Frederick, elector of the Palatinate. The Protestant Bohemian nobles revolted against Ferdinand, who in 1619 became the German emperor. This was the beginning of the Thirty Years' War.

10. **What were the phases of the Thirty Years' War and what happened in each phase**

The Bohemian Phase: With the aid of King Maximilian of Bavaria and the army of the Catholic League, Ferdinand II defeated Frederick and the Bohemians at the Battle of White Mountain in 1620. Fighting occurred also in the Rhine Valley and northern Germany. The Bohemian revolt finally ended in 1623.

The Danish Phase: Cardinal Richelieu wanted to use the war that had begun in Bohemia as a means to weaken the Habsburg power and thus advance the power of France. Along with England, Richelieu induced King Christian IV of Denmark to invade Germany in 1625, and join forces with the Protestant German princes against the emperor and the Catholic League. But an imperial mercenary force and the Catholic League army defeated the Protestant and Danish forces. In 1626, Christian IV withdrew from the war.

Edict of Restitution: After the defeat of Christian IV and his Protestant allies, Emperor Ferdinand issued the Edict of Restitution. The Edict said that the Protestant princes had to return all the lands they had seized from the Church since 1555. The edict weakened the emperor's cause, for it turned many of the Protestant princes who had once supported him against him.

The Swedish Phase: Cardinal Richelieu again intervened and convinced Sweden's King Gustavus II Adolphus, a Lutheran, to enter the war on the Protestant side. In 1631, King Gustavus II Adolphus of Sweden began his war of conquest in Germany. In 1632 he defeated the Catholic League forces, but was himself defeated by imperial forces at the Battle of Lützen. The Swedish king died in this battle. In 1634, the combined imperial and Catholic League forces defeated the Swedes at Nördlingen.

The French Phase: In 1635, France under Cardinal Richelieu declared war on the Habsburg emperor and his Habsburg cousin, King Philip IV of Spain. At first the Spanish scored victories against the French, but gradually Spain lost its advantage. Aided by rebellions in Spain and Naples, the French began defeating Spanish armies. French forces began pouring into Germany to aid the Protestant princes and the Swedes. By 1647, the entire empire, except for the lands under direct Habsburg control, was under the control of the Swedes and the French. The war against the empire ended with the Peace of Westphalia in 1648.

Abandoned by the German Habsburg emperor, Spain continued to resist France until 1659. At the war's end, the Spanish power had been crushed. France became the most powerful nation in Europe.

The war left Germany a wasteland. Whole provinces had been rendered uninhabitable, and almost half the population of Germany had been killed. It would take Germany nearly 150 years to recover the level of prosperity she had enjoyed before the war.

11. **What the Peace of Westphalia was and what its effects were**

The Peace of Westphalia, signed November 3, 1648, made the German princes practically independent of the emperor. Under the peace, the empire for the first time had to recognize Calvinism, alongside Lutheranism and the Catholic Church, as an official religion. The peace declared that all states that were Catholic or Protestant as of 1624 would remain Catholic or Protestant. The Peace of Westphalia made the religious division of Christendom into Protestant and Catholic camps permanent.

Questions for Review

1. **When did the Council of Trent begin? When did it end?**

The Council of Trent began in December 1545 and ended in December 1563.

How many years were there between Luther's posting of the *Ninety-five Theses* and the close of the council?

There were 46 years between Luther's posting of the *Ninety-five Theses* and the close of the council.

Some Key Terms at a Glance

Counter-Reformation: the common name for the Catholic Renewal and Reform of the 16th and 17th centuries

Ultramontane: the name given to those who favored strong papal control over national churches (from *ultra*, meaning "beyond" or "on the other side," and *mons, montes*, meaning "mountains"—"on the other side of the mountains" or the Alps)

Holy Office: the "Inquisition," a congregation of the curia that issued doctrinal decrees and condemned heretical teachings. Its purpose was to protect the purity of the Catholic Faith.

Index of Forbidden Books (*Index librorum prohibitorum*): the list of those books the Church considered dangerous to the Catholic Faith and forbade Catholics to read

catechism: an explanation of the doctrines of the Faith

Tridentine Rite: a name given to the reform of the Roman rite carried out under Pope Pius V after the Council of Trent

Society of Jesus: the order founded by St. Ignatius of Loyola, whose members are called Jesuits

Huguenots: French Calvinists

Edict of Nantes: issued by King Henry IV of France in 1597, the Edict gave the Huguenots freedom of religion and worship, and granted them political and military power. It was later modified by the Peace of Alais, which assured the Huguenots freedom of religion and worship but removed their political and military power.

Peace of Westphalia: the 1648 treaty ending the Thirty Years' War; the Peace made the religious division of Germany permanent and indicated that any hope of reuniting Christendom had been openly abandoned.

2. **What sort of questions did Trent consider?**

   The council considered doctrinal questions and the correction of abuses.

3. **What doctrines did the Council of Trent affirm?**

   Doctrines affirmed by the Council of Trent

   a) The equal authority of Scripture and Tradition

   b) Man is not totally depraved.

   c) Not faith alone, but faith, hope, and charity are necessary for salvation. All are gifts of God's Grace.

   d) The Eucharist is truly the Body, Blood, Soul, and Divinity of Christ.

   e) There are seven, and only seven, Sacraments.

   f) All the books found in the Latin Vulgate are inspired.

   g) The pope is the head of the Church.

   What reforms did it call for?

   Reforms called for by the council

   a) Bishops must be fit for their office.

   b) Priests must be worthy of their calling.

   c) The liturgy must be reformed.

   d) Abuses (such as simony and offering money for indulgences) must be suppressed.

4. **How did the order founded by St. Ignatius de Loyola help the cause of Catholic reform?**

   a) Jesuits worked in Catholic countries, such as Spain and Portugal, teaching Catholic doctrine and striving to inspire the faithful with love for Christ and His Church.

   b) They founded schools and colleges or staffed existing institutions of learning.

   c) They braved torture and death to minister to Catholics in England and Scotland and other parts of Protestant Europe.

   d) They served as missionaries in foreign lands.

5. **Who fought at Lepanto?**

   A Christian fleet, captained by Don Juan of Austria, and a Turkish fleet, fought at Lepanto.

   Why was it an important battle?

   Lepanto was an important battle because it halted a Turkish invasion of Europe and reduced the future threat of the Turkish fleet.

6. **What was the Edict of Nantes?**

   The Edict of Nantes was an agreement between King Henry IV of France and the Huguenots.

   What did it give the Huguenots?

   The edict granted the Huguenots the freedom to hold their religious beliefs and the right to worship in the places they had been worshipping up to 1597, as well as at other specified locations. Huguenots were granted equal rights with Catholics in holding public offices and received 100 fortresses for a period of eight years.

   How was it later changed?

   The edict was later changed by the Peace of Alais, which granted the Huguenots full religious liberty but forbade them to control towns or fortresses or hold public offices. It basically ended Huguenot political power.

7. **Who was Cardinal Richelieu?**

   Cardinal Richelieu was a Catholic bishop, a member of the Roman curia, and the first minister of France.

   What were his goals for France?

   His goals were to make the king all-powerful in France and France the most powerful nation in Europe.

Why did he support the Protestant side in the Thirty Years' War?

To make France the most powerful nation in Europe, Richelieu had to weaken the power of the Habsburgs—which is why he supported the Protestant side in the Thirty Years' War.

8. **Was Emperor Ferdinand II's issuing of the Edict of Restitution wise or foolish? Why?**

The issuing of the Edict of Restitution was foolish because it threatened the economic and social order of Germany, exposing Protestant landholders to financial ruin. Protestant princes thus opposed the edict, and some of them who had supported Ferdinand now turned against him.

9. **How did the Peace of Westphalia affect the German Roman Empire?**

The Peace of Westphalia made the German states practically independent of the emperor, and the empire became an empire in name only. By recognizing Calvinism alongside Lutheranism and stating that all states that had been Protestant or Catholic in 1624 would remain so, the peace made the religious division of Germany permanent.

How did it affect Christendom?

The peace also made the religious division of Europe permanent and signified that any hope of reuniting Christendom had been openly abandoned.

Ideas in Action

1. Find a copy of the *Catechism of the Council of Trent* in English. Read a short portion of it—for instance, on Transubstantiation or Baptism or one of the other Sacraments. Read a similar section from the modern *Catechism of the Catholic Church*. How are they alike? How do they differ?

2. Read G. K. Chesterton's poem, "Lepanto." What can be learned from this poem about the battle?

3. Discuss what sort of books might be put on an *Index* today. Why? Should Catholics be forbidden to read certain books? Why or why not?

4. Make a list of modern Protestant and Catholic countries. Are they the same countries that were Catholic or Protestant in the 17th century? (For non-European countries, indicate what European countries founded them.)

Sample Quiz for Pages 483–501

Please answer the following in complete sentences.

1. What were the two goals of the Council of Trent?

2. What was the name of the religious order founded by St. Ignatius of Loyola? What did people come to call the members of this order?

3. What is the name of the sea battle where the Christian forces under Don Juan of Austria destroyed the Turkish fleet? In what year did this battle occur?

4. Please identify:

   a) The name given to those who favored strong papal control over the Church

   b) The congregation of the Roman curia whose purpose was to protect the purity of the Faith

   c) The name for the Calvinists in France

   d) The name given to those French churchmen who believed that the French Church should be in most respects independent of the pope while remaining in communion with him

Answer key to Sample Quiz I

Students' answers, of course, should only approximate the following.

1. The two goals of the Council of Trent were:

   a) to clarify doctrinal problems

   b) to correct abuses in the Church

2. The name of the religious order founded by St. Ignatius of Loyola was *the Society of Jesus*. People came to call the members of this order, *Jesuits*.

3. The battle where the Christians defeated the Turkish fleet was *the Battle of Lepanto*, fought in *1571*.

4. Answers:

   a) Ultramontane

   b) Holy Office or "Inquisition"

   c) Huguenots

   d) Gallican

Sample Quiz for Pages 501–514

Please answer the following in complete sentences.

1. What were Cardinal Richelieu's two goals for France?

2. In what kingdom did the Thirty Years' War begin?

3. What did the Emperor Ferdinand demand of the German Protestants in the Edict of Restoration?

4. Who was the king of Sweden who led the Protestant side in the Thirty Years' War?

Answer key to Sample Quiz II

Students' answers, of course, should only approximate the following.

1. Cardinal Richelieu's two goals for France were:

    a) to make the king supreme in France

    b) to make France supreme in Europe

2. The Thirty Years' War began in *the kingdom of Bohemia.*

3. In the Edict of Restitution, Emperor Ferdinand *demanded that the German Protestants return all the lands they had seized from the Church since 1555.*

4. The king of Sweden who led the Protestant side in the Thirty Years' War was *Gustavus Adolphus.*

Sample Test

1. In what way did the Council of Trent succeed? In what way did it fail?

2. Why was the Society of Jesus well suited to carry on the Catholic reform following the Council of Trent?

3. Why was the victory at Lepanto so important to European history

4. Why were the Huguenots a threat to Catholic France in the 16th century? What was the Edict of Nantes? When was it issued? What did it grant the Huguenots?

5. Who was Armand-Jean du Plessis de Richelieu? What were his two main goals? What did he do to realize each of these goals?

6. What was the Peace of Westphalia? When was it signed? What was its effect on the religious division of Europe?

7. Please identify:

    a) The name given to those who favored strong papal control over national churches

    b) The name given to those who held that the French Church should be in most respects independent of the pope while remaining in communion with him

    c) The list of books the Church considered dangerous to the Catholic Faith

    d) Henry de Bourbon

    e) Ferdinand II

    f) The king of Sweden who fought for the Protestant side in the Thirty Years' War

Answer key to Sample Test

Students' answers, of course, should only approximate the following.

1. The Council of Trent succeeded *because it clarified the teachings of the Church on a number of important points* and *corrected abuses in the Church.* It failed insofar *as it was unable to reconcile the Protestants to the Church.*

2. The Society of Jesus was well suited to carry on the Catholic reform *because the Jesuits took a special vow to go wherever the pope sent them. They could easily go wherever they were sent because, unlike other religious orders, they were not required to live in community. Thus they were an effective instrument to realize the Catholic Reformation.*

3. The victory at Lepanto was important to European history *because it stopped a Turkish invasion of Italy and greatly weakened the Turkish sea power, rendering it no longer as great a threat to Europe as it had been.*

4. The Huguenots were a great threat to *France because they formed a strong political power that could oppose the king.* The Edict of Nantes, issued *in 1589, was an agreement between the king of France and the Huguenots which gave the Huguenots religious freedom, the right to worship in certain places, equal rights with Catholics in holding public offices, and the right to protect themselves with arms and fortresses.*

5. Richelieu was *a Catholic bishop, a cardinal, and the first minister of France.* His two major goals were *to make the king of France supreme in France and France the most powerful nation in Europe.* To realize the first goal *he defeated the Huguenots in a war, forcing them to give up their political and military power.* To realize the second goal, *he supported the Protestant side in the Thirty Years' War, in order to break the power of the Habsburgs.*

6. The Peace of Westphalia was *the treaty ending the Thirty Years' War,* signed in *1648.* It made *the religious division of Europe permanent.*

7. *Answers:*

   a) Ultramontane

   b) Gallican

   c) Index of Forbidden Books

   d) the leader of the Huguenots who became king of France as Henry IV

   e) German emperor who led the Catholic side in the Thirty Years' War

   f) King Gustavus II Adolphus

CHAPTER 19: Europe Before the Flood

Chapter Overview

- King James I held to the doctrine of the divine right of kings, which said that kings are established on their thrones by God and so have absolute power in their kingdoms. James's attempts to achieve absolute power in England brought him into conflict with Parliament.

- King Charles I, like his father, James I, believed in the divine right of kings. In 1628, Parliament forced Charles to sign the Petition of Right, which said the king could not levy taxes without Parliament's consent. Because of its continued opposition to him, Charles dissolved Parliament in 1629.

- For 11 years Charles ruled without summoning Parliament. He raised the money he needed by collecting fines for the violation of old laws he revived and by collecting "ship money."

- Charles I's attempts to force bishops and the Anglican prayer book on the Presbyterian Church of Scotland led to a revolt of the Scottish Covenanters. In 1639, Charles was forced to sign the Peace of Berwick with the Covenanters.

- To subdue the Covenanters, Charles was forced to summon Parliament in 1639. He soon dissolved this Parliament (the Short Parliament); but when the Covenanters crossed into England in 1640, Charles summoned Parliament again (the Long Parliament). The Long Parliament forced the king to abandon several of his rights, including the power to dissolve Parliament itself. After Charles failed to arrest five of Parliament's leaders, the House of Commons rebelled against him. The king and his family fled London.

- From 1642 to 1649, the king's forces fought the forces of Parliament and the Covenanters in what is called the Great Rebellion. Under Oliver Cromwell, Parliament's army won the Battle of Naseby in 1645. Charles surrendered to Parliament, but in 1647 he escaped. At the Battle of Preston in 1649, Cromwell's army defeated the royalist forces, and Charles again surrendered to Parliament.

- Parliament set up a court to try King Charles. The court accused the king of being a tyrant, traitor, murderer, and public enemy and condemned him to death. Charles I was executed by beheading on January 30, 1649.

- After the death of Charles I, Cromwell and Parliament set up the Protectorate. But after twice dissolving Parliament, Cromwell ruled England, Scotland, and Ireland from 1655 to 1658 as dictator. When Cromwell died, the army forced the restoration of the Long Parliament.

- Charles II was restored to the English throne in 1661. In trying to keep his throne for himself and the Stuart family, King Charles II compromised with Parliament, giving in to its demands. He refused, however, to accept Parliament's demand

- that he divorce his Catholic wife and marry a Protestant; and he would not sign the Act of Exclusion that would have barred his brother James, who was Catholic, from the throne.

- English Protestants feared that King James II would overthrow the Protestant religion in England. Their fears increased when the king's second wife gave birth to a son, who was baptized Catholic. Parliament invited William of Orange and his wife, Mary Stuart, to England to take the throne. Abandoned by his own general, James II fled England in 1688. Parliament made William and Mary king and queen of England.

- Under King William and Queen Mary, then Queen Anne, and then the Hanoverian kings, Parliament increased its control of the English government. In 1707, Parliament forced the Scottish Parliament to accept the Act of Union, forming one kingdom of Great Britain.

- Louis XIV became king of France when he was only four-and-a-half years old. During the first years of his reign, the young king was guided by Cardinal Jules Mazarin. When Mazarin died in 1661, Louis announced that he would rule France without a prime minister.

- King Louis XIV held to the doctrine of the divine right of kings. Louis centralized French government under his authority, using a bureaucracy that oversaw all aspects of life in France. The king lived lavishly and luxuriously, encouraging the arts of dancing, theater, music, and literature.

- King Louis XIV worked to make France a powerful mercantile nation. He encouraged the growth of France's American settlements and extended French territory down the Mississippi. The king built up the French army until it was 400,000 strong, and he armed its troops with the best and most modern weapons.

- Louis fought a series of wars to expand the borders of France and to weaken his neighbors. By 1700, he had achieved many of his goals and made France the most powerful nation in Europe. Louis's desire to extend the power of his family, the Bourbons, led to the War of the Spanish Succession. In the 1713 Peace of Utrecht, which concluded the war, Louis's grandson, Philip of Anjou, was recognized as king of Spain.

Chapter Goals

This chapter is so named because it deals with the political state of Europe before the "flood" of the French Revolution. The chapter focuses on two nations (England and France) because each represents a different tendency in the direction politics was taking in the late 17th and early 18th centuries. France was moving toward greater and greater centralization under her king, achieving a high degree of royal absolutism under King Louis XIV. England, on the other hand, was moving toward a system where a representative body (Parliament) was becoming the sovereign power.

The goal of this chapter is to give students an understanding of what was happening during this very pivotal period in European history. English parliamentarianism is the forerunner of Liberal representative government, which would be the ideal of the late 18th through the 19th and 20th centuries, and into our day. This form of government is the political manifestation of a philosophical and cultural movement, called the Enlightenment—as is, ironically enough, one form of royal absolutism. We do not deal with the Enlightenment as such in *Light to the Nations I*; we will introduce it in the next volume, *Light to the Nations II*. Thus, students should leave this chapter with a knowledge of events simply. The next volume will help them in understanding the ideas that helped form these events.

What Students Should Know

1. **What the doctrine of the divine right of kings was**

   The divine right of kings was the doctrine that God placed kings on their thrones and gave them the right to exercise absolute power in their kingdoms. According to his divine right, the king is not subject to any earthly authority, but to God alone. God has made the king the "father" of the kingdom, and his subjects are his "children," who must obey him. To resist the king is to disobey God, who gave the king his authority.

2. **Why James I and Charles I came into conflict with Parliament**

   Coming as he did from Scotland, James I did not understand the role of Parliament in England. Often in need of money, James tried to obtain it by raising it himself, when Parliament refused to vote him funds. This attempt to circumvent Parliament made its members quite angry with the king.

   James's adherence to the divine right of kings doctrine also made him an enemy of Parliament, which claimed to have traditional rights to authority in the English government. The king's devotion to episcopal government in the Church of England earned him the enmity of the Puritans in Parliament, who wanted to make the Church of England more Presbyterian.

   Charles tolerance of Catholics and his revival of old taxes to raise funds without Parliament's approval earned him the opposition of Puritans and other radicals.

3. **What events led to Charles I's execution by Parliament**

   In 1637, Charles I and William Laud tried to force the Presbyterian Church of Scotland to accept the *Book of Common Prayer* and government by bishops. To resist this Anglicanization of the Scottish church, the Scots "Covenanters" rose up in revolt, twice defeated the king's army, and forced him to sign a treaty.

   To subdue the Covenanters, Charles needed money; and to get money, he was forced to summon Parliament. When the newly assembled Parliament, dominated by Puritans, demanded more concessions of power from the king, he again dissolved it. In 1640, however, the Covenanters invaded the northern counties of England and forced the king to sign an armistice. Charles again had to summon Parliament.

   Puritans dominated this "Long Parliament," which gathered in 1640 and continued to meet for 13 years. The Long Parliament imprisoned Laud and the king's friend, the Earl of Strafford. Both were executed—Strafford by a reluctant Charles I. In 1641, when Puritans in Parliament introduced a bill to impeach Queen Henrietta Marie for treason, Charles tried to arrest the Puritan leaders. This induced the Puritans in the House of Commons to turn on the king, who fled with his family northward into Nottinghamshire.

   Thus began the Great Rebellion. Under the leadership of the "Independent" Oliver Cromwell, the Parliamentarian army was able to defeat royalist forces and force the surrender of the king. Charles, however, escaped from imprisonment and made an alliance with the Scots against Parliament. But at the Battle of Preston in 1648, Cromwell's army defeated the royalists and the king, again, surrendered.

   Parliament was divided about what to do with the king. The Presbyterian members wanted to come to an agreement with him, but the Independents wanted him executed. Finally, the Independents forcibly expelled the Presbyterian members from Parliament and formed the Rump Parliament, which brought the king to trial. Accusing Charles of treason and tyranny, the Rump Parliament ordered him executed. On January 30, 1649, Charles was beheaded.

4. **The significance of the execution of Charles I**

Even if they did not hold to the divine right of kings, Englishmen and Europeans on the whole held that a king received his right to rule from God. To kill a king was thus to strike at God's anointed.

The grounds on which the Rump Parliament defended their trial of the king were radical. He was being tried, they said, by the authority of the English people, who had elected him king. Not God, but the people were invoked as the source of the king's authority.

5. **How England, Scotland, and Ireland were ruled after the death of Charles I**

After Charles I's death, the Rump Parliament and Cromwell ruled England, Scotland, and Ireland. In 1653, however, Cromwell dissolved the Rump Parliament and set up a new parliament (Barebone's Parliament) in its stead. At last, Cromwell dissolved this Parliament.

Following the dissolving of Barebone's Parliament, Cromwell and his supporters set up the "Protectorate," with Cromwell as "Lord Protector." From 1655–1688, Cromwell ruled as dictator, claiming his authority to rule came from God. Cromwell sought to enforce Puritan religion and morality on England, Scotland, and Ireland. When he died, his son Richard could not maintain power and restored Parliament. This, the restored "Long Parliament," sent messengers to Charles II in France, inviting him to return to England and claim his throne.

6. **What the Restoration was and what the relations of Charles II and Parliament were like**

The Restoration was the recovery by the House of Stuart of the thrones of England and Scotland. To regain the throne, Charles II had to swear to respect the Magna Carta and the rights of Parliament—and not raise illegal taxes.

Charles II's goals were to stay on the throne and to keep the House of Stuart in possession of the throne. To do this, he made almost any compromise with Parliament, including rescinding his Declaration of Indulgence, which suspended Parliamentary laws against Catholics and dissenting Protestants. He resisted, however, Parliament's demand that he approve the Exclusion Act, that would have barred all Catholics from the throne.

During this period, Parliament split into two parties: the party that supported the Exclusion Act, the "Whigs," and the supporters of the Church of England and of royal power, the "Tories." When the Tories became the predominant party in Parliament, they helped Charles dissolve that body in 1681.

7. **What brought about the "Glorious Revolution**

Many English Protestants were not happy when James II became king in 1685. Not only did he believe in the divine right of kings, but he was a Catholic as well. James did several things to alienate all parties. He displeased the Tories by placing Catholics as commanding officers in a standing army he was forming. The Whigs, already in opposition to the king, were further estranged by James's religion and his issuing of the Declaration of Indulgence in 1687 and 1688, which granted freedom of religion to all religious groups in his domains. When Anglican clergymen refused to read the declaration from their pulpits, James tried to have them convicted of sedition.

8. **The "Glorious Revolution" and its significance**

Many in England found James tolerable only because the heirs to his throne were his Protestant daughters. But when the king's second wife, a Catholic, gave birth to a son, who would be raised Catholic, English Protestants feared the establishment of a Catholic, Stuart ruling house over England. Both Tories and Whigs in Parliament invited Mary, James's Protestant daughter, and her husband, Prince William of Orange, to take over the throne. Abandoned by all, James II was forced to flee England.

Parliament thereupon crowned William and Mary as king and queen of England, Scotland, and Ireland. In so doing, Parliament made it clear that it was the source of the monarchs' power and authority, thus firmly establishing parliamentary supremacy in England. The new monarchs, too, went along with parliamentary legislation drastically limiting royal power, forbidding Catholics from inheriting the throne, and granting freedom of religion to Protestant dissenters, but not Catholics.

9. **How the kingdoms of England and Scotland became the United Kingdom of Great Britain**

When James II's daughter became queen of England, Scotland, and Ireland, some feared, because she was childless, that after her death the Scottish parliament might vote to choose its own king and so separate Scotland from England. (One must remember that, at that time Scotland and England were still separate kingdoms, though ruled by the same monarch.) To prevent this, the English parliament in 1707 forced the Scottish parliament to accept the Act of Union, uniting both kingdoms under one parliament—the English parliament, increased by the addition of Scottish members. This new entity was called the United Kingdom of Great Britain.

10. **The character of Parliament under the Hanoverians**

Since George I spoke no English and had little interest in British politics, he allowed Parliament and his cabinet to govern Great Britain. Like his father, George II, who became king in 1727, cared more for Hanover than Great Britain; thus, Parliament remained the real governing power of Great Britain.

Parliament was an aristocratic, not a democratic body. Many places in England and Scotland were not represented at all, and most subjects could not by law vote for members of Parliament. So it was that Parliament came to represent the interests of the wealthy classes in Great Britain and the Protestant landholders in Ireland. Despite this, the English government came, in the 17th and 18th centuries, to serve as an example of representative government for Europeans, inspiring them to emulation. Representative governments spread with the growth of the British colonies in North America, where Britain's colonies established legislatures, like small parliaments.

11. **How Louis XIV centralized France under his power**

Working with tireless energy, Louis centralized the government by establishing a bureaucracy that oversaw all aspects of life in France. Louis whittled away the power of the nobles in their own domains. He demanded that they live at his palace for a part of every year—so he could keep an eye on them. Louis increased the glory of the French court, making it the awe and envy of Europe. He was called the "grand monarch" and the "Sun King."

12. **How some French understood the theory of the divine right of kings**

As developed by Bishop Jacques-Bénigne Bossuet, the French theory of the divine right of kings held that the king is sacred, not only because he receives his right to rule from God, but because he has been consecrated by the Church. The king is like a father, said Bossuet, and his subjects owe him the obedience and respect children pay their fathers. It is thus a blasphemy to attack the king or resist him. Subjects may do nothing to oppose the king, even if he issues unjust commands or is a tyrant. They may only pray God to change the king's heart.

Bossuet and the king also held that not only is the king's temporal power completely independent of the pope, the king has power over the Church in his domains. French bishops, they said, must act for the most part independently of Rome.

13. **What Louis XIV's international goals for France were**

Louis XIV wanted France to have every glory and power possessed by any other European power. He worked to increase France's trade and make France a powerful mercantile nation. And he tried to increase France's presence in America by sponsoring exploration by which he could claim more land for France.

Louis wanted France to be militarily the most powerful nation in Europe. To that end, he reorganized it into a complex military machine of more than 400,000 men, obtained modern weapons and had his commanders use modern strategies. Louis used this army against his neighbors. He thought to expand France to what he called its "natural boundaries" by conquering lands belonging to the German Empire and the Habsburg family. Such ambitions involved France in many wars during the reign of Louis XIV.

14. **Over what the War of the Spanish Succession was fought and what its results were**

When he married the daughter of the Habsburg king of Spain, Louis XIV agreed to abandon any claim he might have from the marriage to the throne of Spain in return for a large dowry. However, he convinced the childless king of Spain to unite Spain to France rather than to Austria by willing his kingdom to Louis's grandson, Philip of Anjou.

The Austrian Habsburg German emperor, Leopold, opposed this plan, because it betrayed the interests of the Habsburg family. Other powers, including William III of England (and the Netherlands), feared that a union of Spain and France would make the Bourbons too powerful, and these rulers along with others formed the Grand Alliance to place Leopold's son, Archduke Charles von Habsburg, on the Spanish throne.

The war ended in a compromise. In 1711, when Archduke Charles became emperor, his allies no more wanted him than Philip of Anjou to have the Spanish throne. The Peace of Utrecht (1713), besides making various territorial changes, recognized Philip as king of Spain, thus establishing the Bourbon House there; but, the treaty specified, France and Spain could never be united under a common king.

15. **The legacy of Louis XIV**

Under Louis XIV, France became the wealthiest and most powerful nation in Europe. It had a large and well-trained army. Paris was the center of art and science, and the French nobles were considered the most elegant people in the world. Indeed, the French language had become the language of the upper classes and of diplomacy throughout Europe. The Bourbon family, too, ruled a good portion of Europe as well as most of North and South America.

But Louis's construction of Versailles, his huge army and navy, and the four wars he fought in his reign were ruinously expensive. Since neither the nobility nor the high churchmen were taxed, the middle class and the peasants suffered under the ever-increasing tax burden laid on them.

Both Louis XIV and his successor, Louis XV, separated themselves from the life of the French people and so knew little of the burdens under which they suffered. The nobles lived a life of high culture and foolish pleasure, and all the while the common people suffered under heavy taxes and grinding poverty.

Some Key Terms at a Glance

divine right of kings: the doctrine that kings receive absolute power over their kingdoms from God and are subject to no earthly authority; to resist the king is to disobey God, who gave the king his authority

High Church: in Protestantism, favoring practices and ritual that are liturgical, traditional, and Catholic. Those favoring a simpler, less ritualistic worship are called *Low Church*.

Puritans: Calvinist reform party in England. They were called "Puritans" because they wanted to purify the Church of England of the traditional traces of Catholicism.

Protectorate: the name of the government of England, Scotland, and Ireland under Oliver Cromwell, who was called Lord Protector

regicide: killing a king, thought to be a great crime against God's ordinances and arrangement of political order

Tory and Whig: names for English political parties. The Tories were High Church and supporters of royal power; the Whigs, backed by Puritans and other dissenters, favored giving greater power to Parliament.

Questions for Review

1. **What is the divine right of kings?**

    The divine right of kings is a doctrine that holds that kings hold their authority from God and are not subject to any earthly authority. To resist the king is to disobey God, who gave the king his authority.

    Why was it not a successful doctrine in England?

    The doctrine was not successful in England because Parliament had come to exercise a good deal of power in the English government and so resisted the king's attempts to limit that power. England had, as well, a tradition of limited government, where the king's power was seen as limited by custom and law. The Magna Carta represented this tradition.

    Where was it successful?

    The divine right of kings doctrine was successful in France, at least throughout most of the 18th century.

2. **Why, unlike the Tudors, were the Stuart kings unable to control Parliament?**

    The Tudors had been able to control Parliament by not depending on it for money. The Stuart kings, however, were not as thrifty as the Tudors (and they could not rely on confiscated Church estates). Often in need of money, the Stuarts had to give in to Parliament's demands so that Parliament would vote them funds.

3. **What events brought about open war between King Charles I and Parliament?**

    a) Charles I's tolerance of Catholics, which angered Puritans in Parliament

    b) his dissolving of Parliament in 1629 and the revival of old taxes, such as "ship money," to raise funds

    c) Charles I's high church policies; his appointment of William Laud as archbishop of Canterbury and Laud's moves to reintroduce Catholic practices into Anglican worship

d) Charles's enforcing of laws against Puritans and Separatists while neglecting to enforce laws against Catholics

e) the Covenanter revolt and Charles's need to convene Parliament

f) Parliament's issuing of the Grand Remonstrance—a defense of Parliament and a condemnation of the king

g) Parliament's attempt to impeach Queen Henrietta Marie for treason and Charles's subsequent attempt to arrest John Pym and other Puritan leaders

h) Charles's flight from London

i) the organizing by the king and Parliament of rival armies

4. **Why was the fact that Parliament invited William and Mary to take over the throne in England so significant to the long-standing rivalry between king and Parliament?**

By inviting William and Mary to take over the throne, Parliament made it clear that it was granting the monarch the authority to rule. In this way, Parliament became the supreme authority in England.

5. **Why was Louis XIV called the Sun King?**

Louis XIV was called the Sun King because he was seen as the greatest and most glorious king in Europe.

6. **What were the ways Louis XIV tried to make France the greatest nation in Europe?**

a) He encouraged the arts.

b) He pushed further exploration in America and establishment of French colonies there as a source of wealth for the mother country.

c) He built the most powerful, best-trained army in Europe.

d) He carried on wars to expand French territory and to bring Spain under the Bourbon family.

7. **What did Louis XIV mean by** *"L'état c'est moi"* **("I am the State")?**

By saying, "I am the State," Louis XIV was asserting that he held sole power in the state.

8. **What were Louis XIV and Bossuet's ideas about the relationship between the Church and the state in France?**

Both Louis and Bossuet held that the king receives his right to rule from God and from his consecration by the Church. But the king's temporal power, they held, is completely independent of the pope and so the king has power over the Church in his domains.

9. **What were the causes of the War of the Spanish Succession?**

Louis XIV claimed the throne of Spain for his grandson, Philip of Anjou. Though the last Habsburg king of Spain had confirmed the succession of Philip, the Habsburg emperor in Austria claimed the Spanish throne for his son, Archduke Charles of Austria. Other European powers did not want Spain to fall under the Bourbon family—especially if the thrones of Spain and France were to be united under one king. These powers formed an alliance to place Archduke Charles on the Spanish throne.

How long did that war last, and who won?

The war ran from 1702–1713, eleven years. It ended in a compromise, enshrined in the Peace of Utrecht. The kingship of Spain would go to the Bourbons, but the family was never to unite the kingdoms of France and Spain under one king.

Who succeeded to the Spanish throne?

Philip of Anjou became king of Spain.

10. In what ways did Louis XIV leave France better than he found it?

Under Louis XIV, France became the wealthiest and most powerful nation in Europe and the continent's center of art and science.

In what ways did he leave it worse than he found it?

Louis XIV's building of a large army, his many wars, and the building of Versailles were ruinously expensive. Since neither the nobility nor the high churchmen were taxed, the middle class and peasants suffered under an ever-increasing burden of taxation. For the poor, the Sun King's power and glory meant greater poverty and misery.

Ideas in Action

1. Find a photograph of the bust of Louis XIV by Bernini as well as later portraits of the king by other artists. What sort of character is captured in those features? Discuss the character of Louis and how the artists portrayed that character.

2. Discuss: Did Louis XIV fulfill Cardinal Richelieu's hopes for France? Why did French culture become the model for all other European nations of the 18th century?

3. Report on French gardens of the 17th and 18th centuries, particularly those of Versailles. How are they different from English gardens or American colonial gardens of the same period? Search for pictures and descriptions of both kinds of gardening. Report to class.

4. Draw a map of North and South America, using different colors to indicate what parts of those continents belonged to the Spanish, the English, the French, and the Portuguese.

Sample Quiz for Pages 521–538

Please answer the following in complete sentences.

1. What is the name of the doctrine that holds that God has placed kings on their thrones and given them the right to exercise absolute power in their kingdoms?

2. Please give two reasons Parliament was opposed to James I and Charles I.

3. What role did Oliver Cromwell play in England after the execution of Charles I?

4. Give two reasons why English Protestants were not happy with King James II? What happened to him?

Answer key to Sample Quiz I

Students' answers, of course, should only approximate the following.

1. The name for the doctrine is *the divine right of kings*.

2. *Possible answers:*

   a) Both monarchs held to the doctrine of the divine right of kings.

   b) Both monarchs attempted to circumvent the power and authority of Parliament.

   c) Both monarchs were devoted to episcopal government in the Church of England.

   d) Charles I wanted to tolerate Catholics.

3. After the execution of Charles I, Cromwell *became Lord Protector, exercising the powers of dictator* over England and Scotland.

4. *Possible answers:*

   a) James II believed in the divine right of kings.

   b) James II was a Catholic.

   c) He issued the Declaration of Indulgence for Catholics and dissenters.

   d) He placed Catholics as commanders in the army.

   e) The threat that, because James had a Catholic son, he was establishing a Catholic dynasty over England

   What happened to James II?

   To prevent England being ruled by a Catholic, *Parliament invited James's daughter Mary and her husband, William of Orange, to take over the throne. Abandoned by everyone, James was forced to flee England* in what has been called the "Glorious Revolution."

Sample Quiz for Pages 538–551

Please answer the following in complete sentences.

1. What was the union of England and Scotland under one parliament called?

2. Who had more power in England, the king or Parliament, after the Glorious Revolution? Why?

3. Why is the king sacred, according to Bossuet's divine right of kings theory?

4. Name one of Louis XIV's international goals for France.

5. Give one reason why there was suffering in France during the reigns of Louis XIV and Louis XV.

Answer key to Sample Quiz II

Students' answers, of course, should only approximate the following.

1. The union of England and Scotland was called the *United Kingdom of Great Britain.*

2. *Parliament had more power in England after the Glorious Revolution* because it had invited William and Mary to take the throne as king and queen. *The monarchs were thus seen as deriving their authority from Parliament.*

3. According to Bossuet, the king is sacred *because he receives his right to rule from God and is consecrated by the Church.*

4. *Possible answers*:

    a) Louis XIV worked to increase France's trade and make it a powerful mercantile nation.

    b) He tried to increase France's presence in America by sponsoring exploration by which he could claim more land for France.

    c) Louis wanted France to be militarily the most powerful nation in Europe.

    d) Louis tried to expand France to what he called its "natural boundaries" by conquering lands belonging to the German Empire and the Habsburg family.

5. *Possible Answers:*

    a) Louis XIV's building of a large army

    b) The monarchs' many wars

    c) The building of Versailles

    d) Since neither the nobility nor the high churchmen were taxed, the middle class and peasants suffered under an ever-increasing burden of taxation.

Sample Test

1. Describe the doctrine of the divine right of kings as the Stuarts held it. How was Bossuet's doctrine of the divine right of kings like the Stuart doctrine? How did they differ?

2. Why was the execution of Charles I so important and significant an event in the history of Europe?

3. How did the Glorious Revolution show that Parliament had become supreme over the king in England?

4. Why were the peasants and middle class in France unhappy during the reign of Louis XIV?

5. Before the Act of Union, England and Scotland shared the same king but were separate kingdoms. How did the Act of Union make them more united? What is the name for the union of England and Scotland?

6. Identify the following:

    a) The first Stuart king of England

    b) The religious group in England who, as members of Parliament, opposed the Stuart kings

    c) The head of Parliament's army during the Great Rebellion. He became the dictator of England and Scotland after the execution of Charles I.

    d) The war that ended with a Bourbon rather than a Habsburg as king over Spain

Answer key to Sample Test

Students' answers, of course, should only approximate the following.

1. The divine right of kings doctrine as held by the Stuarts *declared that kings hold their authority from God and are not subject to any earthly authority. To resist the king is to disobey God, who gave him his authority.*

    Bossuet basically agreed with the Stuart divine right of kings doctrine, but he added the notion that the king is sacred both by the fact that he receives his right to rule from God and because he is consecrated by the Church.

2. The execution of Charles I was significant because the Rump Parliament said the king was being tried by the authority of the English people, who had elected him king. *The Rump thus claimed the king did not receive his authority to rule from God, but from the people.*

3. In the Glorious Revolution, Parliament invited William and Mary to take over the throne from James II. In doing so, and in crowning William and Mary king and queen, *Parliament made it clear that it was the source of a monarch's power and authority, which meant it was supreme over the monarch.*

4. The peasants and middle class in France were unhappy during the reign of Louis XIV *because they had to pay burdensome taxes* so Louis could finance his building of Versailles, his army and navy, and his wars.

5. The Act of Union made England and Scotland more united *by abolishing the Scottish parliament and joining both countries under the English parliament.* The name for the union of England and Scotland was *the United Kingdom of Great Britain.*

6. *Answers*:

    a) James I

    b) the Puritans

    c) Oliver Cromwell

    d) War of the Spanish Succession

Resources

Supplemental Reading List

General
Golden Legend of Young Saints—Henri Daniel-Rops (Sophia Press)
Young People's Book of Saints—Hugh Ross Williamson (Sophia Press)
Christians Courageous—the Rev. Aloysius Roche (Sophia Press)
The Book of Saints & Heroes—Andrew Lang (Sophia Press)

Chapter 1: A Light to the Nations
The First Christians—Marigold Hunt (Sophia Press)
St. Paul, Missionary to the Gentiles—Mary Fabyan Windeatt
Abigail & the Widow Mary—Noel Trimming (out of print/check library)
The Face of the Nazarene—Noel Trimming (out of print/check library)
The Vinegar Boy—Alberta Hawse
The Bronze Bow—Elizabeth George Speare

Advanced readers/high school level:
The Book of Life—Henri Daniel-Rops (Sophia Press)
The Glorious Folly: A Novel of the Times of St. Paul—Louis de Wohl (out of print/check library)
The Spear—Louis de Wohl
Ben Hur—Lew Wallace

Chapter 2: Emperors and Madmen
Augustus Caesar's World—Genevieve Foster
The White Isle—Caroline Dale Snedeker
Between the Forest & the Hills—Ann Lawrence

Advanced readers/high school level:
Eagle of the Ninth (first in a series)—Rosemary Sutcliff
  The Silver Branch (second in the series)
  The Lantern Bearers (third in a series)
The Ides of April—Mary Ray
Beyond the Desert Gate (sequel to *The Ides of April*)
The Last Days of Pompeii—Sir Edward George Bulwer-Lytton

Chapter 3: The Blood of Martyrs
Junia: The Fictional Life & Death of an Early Christian—Michael Giesler
Marcus—Michael Giesler
Grain of Wheat—Michael Giesler

Advanced readers/high school level:
Fabiola—Nicholas Cardinal Wiseman

Chapter 4: The Christian Empire
Noble Lady: The Life of St. Helen—Daughters of St. Paul

Advanced readers/high school level:
The Living Wood: Saint Helena & the Emperor Constantine—Louis de Wohl
The Restless Flame: A Novel of St. Augustine—Louis de Wohl

Chapter 5: Germanic Kingdoms in the West
The White Stag (Attila the Hun)—Kate Seredy
Beowulf the Warrior—Ian Serraillier
D'Aulaires' Book of Norse Myths—Ingri D'Aulaire

Advanced readers/high school level:
Throne of the World—Louis de Wohl
Beowulf
The Legend of Sigurd & Gudrun, J.R.R. Tolkein
Myths of the Norsemen, From the Eddas & Sagas—H. A. Guerber

Chapter 6: Founders of Christendom (500–700)
Hero of the Hills (St. Benedict)—Mary Fabyan Windeatt
Brendan the Navigator—Jean Fritz
Fingal's Quest—Madeleine Polland
Augustine Came to Kent (St. Augustine of Canterbury)—Barbara Willard

Advanced readers/ high school level:
Citadel of God: A Novel of St. Benedict—Louis de Wohl
The Shining Company—Rosemary Sutcliff
Belisarius: The First Shall be Last—Paolo Belzoni

Chapter 8: The Defense and Building of Christendom
The Ballad of the White Horse—G.K. Chesterton
Son of Charlemagne—Barbara Willard
The Vikings—Elizabeth Janeway (Landmark Book)
Leif Eriksson—Katherine B. Shippen
Voyage to Coromandel—Margaret Leighton
Beorn the Proud—Madeleine Polland
The Story of Rolf & the Viking Bow—Allen French (book, audio)
Viking Dawn (first in series)—Henry Treece
  Road to Miklagard (second in series)
  Viking Sunset (third in series)
Horned Helmet—Henry Treece

Chapter 9: The Achievements of Feudalism *and* Chapter 10: The Medieval Reformation (late 900–1100)
The Little Duke—Charlotte Yonge
Castle—David MacCaulay
Otto of the Silver Hand—Howard Pyle
The Red Keep—Allen French
If All the Swords in England—Barbara Willard
The Hidden Treasure of Glaston—Eleanore M. Jewett & Frederick T. Chapman
The Sword of Clontarf (Ireland and Brian Boru)—Charles A. Brady
Myths & Legends of the Middle Ages—H. A. Guerber (Dover)

Advanced readers/high school level:
Blood Feud—Rosemary Sutcliff

Chapter 11: The New Nations: Spain, England, and France
El Cid: God's Own Champion—James Fitzhenry
In the Days of William the Conqueror—Elizabeth Tappan
The Golden Warrior (William the Conqueror)—Hope Muntz
The Bayeux Tapestry—Norman Denny
The Striped Ships (Norman Invasion)—Eloise Jarvis McGraw
The Adventures of Robin Hood—Roger Lancelyn Green
The Magna Charta—James Daugherty

Advanced readers/high school level
Ivanhoe—Sir Walter Scott

Chapter 12: The Crusades
The Blue Gonfalon—Margaret Ann Hubbard
Big John's Secret—Eleanor M. Jewett
Crusader King: A Novel of King Baldwin IV & the Crusades—Susan Peek
Sing Morning Star (King Baldwin)—Elizabeth Bleecker Meigs
The Crusade & the Cup—Elizabeth Bleecker Meigs
St. Louis & the Last Crusade—Margaret Anne Hubbard

Chapter 13: The Great Century
Cathedral—David MacCaulay
Francis & Clare, Saints of Assisi—Helen Walker Homan
St. Dominic & the Rosary—Catherine Bebee
St. Thomas Aquinas—Mary Fabyan Windeatt
St. Thomas Aquinas & the Preaching Beggars—Brendan Larnen
Saint Thomas Aquinas—Raissa Maritain (Sophia Press)
St. Anthony & the Christ Child—Helen Walker Homan
St. Elizabeth's Three Crowns—Blanche Thompson
Adam of the Road—Elizabeth Janet Gray
The Lost Baron—Allen French
Red Falcons of Tremoine—Hendry Peart
He Went with Marco Polo—Louise Andrews Kent
Saint Fernando III—James Fitzhenry

Advanced readers/high school level:
The Joyful Beggar: A Novel of St. Francis Assisi—Louise de Wohl
A Quiet Light: A Novel of St. Thomas Aquinas—Louise de Wohl

Chapter 14: Decline and Decay of the Middle Ages
St. Catherine of Siena—F.A. Forbes
The Writing on the Hearth—Cynthia Harnett
The Sign of the Green Falcon—Cynthia Harnett
The Merchant's Mark—Cynthia Harnett
The Cargo of the Madalena—Cynthia Harnett
The Door in the Wall—Marguerite de Angeli
Crown of the World (Book I, Knight of the Temple)—Nathan Sadasivan

Advanced readers/high school level:
Lay Siege to Heaven: A Novel of St. Catherine of Siena—Louis de Wohl

Chapter 15: Two Centuries of Conflict
The Black Arrow—Robert Louis Stevenson
The Lark & the Laurel—Barbara Willard
Men of Iron—Howard Pyle
The Trumpeter of Krakow—Paul Murray Kendall
Joan of Arc, the Girl Soldier—Louise de Wohl
Boy Knight of Reims—Eloise Lownsberry
Candle in the Sky (Joan of Arc)—Elizabeth Bleecker Meigs

Advanced readers/high school level:
Henry V—William Shakespeare

Chapter 16: The Birth of a New World
St. Thomas More of London—Elizabeth Ince
He Went With Christopher Columbus—Louise Andrews Kent

Chapter 17: The Protestant Reformation
Red Hugh: Prince of Donegal—Robert Reilly
Crossbow & Crucifixes—Henry Garnett

Advanced readers/high school level:
The King's Achievement—Msgr. Robert Hugh Benson
Come Rack! Come Rope!—Msgr. Robert Hugh Benson
The Martyrdom of Father Campion & His Companions—William Cardinal Allen
Kenilworth—Sir Walter Scott

Chapter 18: Catholic Renewal and Religious War
The Blood Red Crescent—Henry Garnett
Angels in Iron—Nicholas C. Prata

Chapter 19: Europe Before the Flood
Outlaws of Ravenhurst (Scottish Catholics)—M. Imelda Wallace
Kidnapped (Jacobites)—Robert Louis Stevenson
David Balfour (Jacobites)—Robert Louis Stevenson

Advanced readers/high school
Lorna Doone—R.D. Blackmore
Waverly: or, 'Tis Sixty Years Since—Sir Walter Scott
Rob Roy—Sir Walter Scott

II. Suggested Recordings
Introduction
Music from the Ancient Near East
Music of the Ancient Sumerians, Egyptians, & Greeks, Ensemble de Organographia. 1999. (CD)

Ancient Greek Music
The website for the Commission for Ancient Literature of the Austrian Academy of Sciences provides examples of reconstructions of ancient Greek music, played on original instruments. See: http://www.oeaw.ac.at/kal/agm/

Music of the Ancient Greeks, Ensemble de Organographia. (CD)

Musique de la Grèce antique. Gregorio Paniagua and Atrium Musicae de Madrid. Harmonia Mundia. 1979. (CD)

Music of Ancient Greece. Christodoulos Halaris. Includes 80 pp. Booklet. (CD)

Musiques de l'Antiquité Grecque. Annie Bélis and the Kérylos ensemble. 1996. (CD)

Chapters 1–3
Ancient Roman Music
Music from Ancient Rome, Vol 1. Performed by Synaulia. Amiata. 1997. (CD)

Music from Ancient Rome, Vol 2. Performed by Synaulia. Amiata. 2003. (CD)

Ancient Jewish Music
Ancient Echoes, Music from the Time of Jesus and Jerusalem's Second Temple. Performed by SAVAE, the San Antonio Vocal Arts Ensemble. (CD)

Ancient Christian Chant
Syrian Liturgy, St. Mark's Syrian Orthodox Monastery. Holy Land Records. 1999. (CD)

Chapter 4
Byzantine Chant
Christ Is Born: Ancient Hymns of Nativity & Theophany. All Saints of America Mission. St Romanos Press. 2008. (CD) Sung in English.

The Divine Liturgies—Vol. 1. Athonite Fathers of St. Anthony's Monastery. 2006. (CD) Sung in English.

Nektarios of Pentapolis. Byzantine Choir of Odigitria. 2002. (CD) Sung in English.

O Taste and See—Hymns From the Presanctified Liturgy. Byzantine Choir of Odigitria. 2006. (CD) Sung in English.

Old Roman and Ambrosian (Milanese) Chant
Incarnatio Verbi: Chant of the Church of Rome (6th–13th Century). Marcel Peres; Ensemble Organum. Zigzag. 2009. (CD) Sung in Latin.

Chants of the Roman Church-Byzantine Period. Marcel Peres, Ensemble Organum. Harmonia Mundi. 1986 (CD) Sung in Latin.

Ambrosian Liturgical Chants. Schola Hungarica. Hungaroton. 1987. (CD) Sung in Latin.

Ambrosian Chant. In Dulci Jubilo. A. Turco. Naxos. 1995. (CD) Sung in Latin.

Chapter 5–9
Byzantine Chant
Kontakion on the Nativity of Christ. Cappella Romana. 2008. (CD) Sung in English.

Arab Islamic Music
The Music of Islam Sampler. Celestial Harmonies Series. (CD)

Chants Soufis du Caire (Sufi Chants from Cairo) La Chadhiliyya. Insitut du Monde Arabe. (CD)

Music of the Northmen/Vikings
Edda: Myths from Medieval Iceland. Sequentia. Deutsche Harmonia Mundi. 1999. (CD)

Chapters 10–13
From Byzantium to Andalusia: Medieval Music and Poetry. Oni Wytars Ensemble. Naxos. 2006 (CD). The performance includes examples of Christian, Muslim, and Jewish (Sephardic) music of the period.

Lost Songs of a Rhineland Harper, X & XI centuries. Sequentia. RCA. 2004. (CD)

Chant Wars. Sequentia & Dialogos. Deutsche Harmonia Mundi. 2005.

Shining Light: Music from Aquitanian Monasteries (12th Century). Sequentia. RCA. 1996. (CD)

Aquitania: Christmas Music from Aquitanian Monasteries (12th Century). Sequentia. BMG. 1997. (CD)

Music for a Medieval Banquet. The Newberry Consort. HMF Classical Exp. 2001. (CD)

Music of the Gothic Era. The Early Music Consort of London. Archiv Produktion. 2002. (CD)

Beyond Plainsong: Tropes and Polyphony in the Medieval Church. Thomas Binkley. 1995. (CD)

St. Hildegard von Bingen

Canticles of Ecstasy. Cologne Sequentia for Medieval Music. RCA. 1994. (CD)

Symphoniae, Geistliche Gesange/Spiritual Songs. Sequentia. BMG Classics. 1993. (CD)

Ordo Virtutum. Cologne Sequentia Ensemble for Medieval Music. RCA. 1998. (CD)

Crusades

Music of the Crusades. The Early Music Consort of London. London. 1991. (CD)

Music from the Time of the Crusades. Thomas Binkley. Virgin Classics. 2006. (CD)

Richard Coeur-de-Lion (*Richard the Lionheart*). Alla Francesca. 1997. (CD)

Pilgrimages

On the Way to Bethlehem: Music of the Medieval Pilgrim. Ensemble Unicorn. Naxos. 1996. (CD)

Donnersöhne, Sons of Thunder: Music for St. James the Apostle, Codex Calixtinus, Santiago de Compostela, 12th Century. Deutsche Harmonia Mundi. (CD)

The Chants of Camino de Santiago. Amadis Ensemble. Jade/Bmg. 2001. (CD)

Troubadours, Trouvères, and Minnesingers

Music of the Troubadours, Ensemble Unicorn. Naxos. 1999. (CD)

Troubadours, Trouvéres, Minstrels. Thomas Binkle,, Studio der Frühen Musik. Das Alte Werk. 2008. (CD)

Chapters 14–16

Music of the 14th and 15th Centuries

Codex Faenza: Instrumental Music of the Early XVth Century. Ensemble Unicorn. 1998. (CD)

The Black Madonna: Pilgrim Songs from the Monastery of Montserrat (1400-1420). Ensemble Unicorn. 1998. (CD)

Early Music Festival. Early Music Consort. Decca. 1998. (CD)

Guillaume de Machaut: La Messe de Nostre Dame. Oxford Camerata. Naxos. 1996. (CD)

The Mirror of Narcissus—Secular Songs by Guillaume de Machaut. Hyperion. 1993. (CD)

Dufay: Missa L'homme armé, Supremum est Mortalibus Bonum. Oxford Camerata. Naxos. 1995. (CD)

Dufay: Chansons. Ensemble Unicorn. Naxos. 1996. (CD)

Josquin Desprez: Motets and Chansons. The Hilliard Ensemble. EMI Classics. 1997.

John Dunstable: Sweet Harmony—Masses and Motets. Naxos. 2005. (CD)

Obrecht: Missa Caput, Salve Regina. Naxos. 1998. (CD)

Jacob Obrecht: The Secular Works. Camerata Trajectina. Globe. 2005. (CD)

Ockeghem: Requiem; Missa Prolationum; Intemerata Dei Mater. Musica Ficta. Naxos. 1997. (CD)

Joan of Arc: Music and Chants from the 15th Century. Amadis Ensemble. Jade. 1999. (CD)

The Music at All Souls, Oxford: The Lancastrians to the Tudors. The Cardinall's Music. Gaudeamus. 2000. (CD)

Renaissance Masterpieces. Choir of New College, Oxford. Brilliant Classics. 1996. (CD)

Ars Subtilior: The Dawn of the Renaissance. Harmonia Mundi. 2005. (CD)

Songs of the Renaissance. Harmonia Mundi. 2005. (CD)

Russian Music
Russian Medieval Chant: The Divine Liturgy of St. John Chrysostom. Russian Patriarchate Choir. Opus 111. 1995. (CD) Sung in Church Slavonic.
Russian Chant for Vespers. Novapassky Monastery Choir. Naxos. (CD) Sung in Church Slavonic.
Kiev Christmas Liturgy. Moscow Liturgic Choir. Erato. 1993. (CD) Sung in Church Slavonic.

Byzantine Chant
Music of Byzantium. The Metropolitan Museum of Art. 2004. (CD) Sung in Greek.
The Fall of Constantinople. Cappella Romana. 2006. (CD) Sung in Greek.

Chapter 17–18
Catholic
Palestrina: Missa Papae Marcelli; Missa Brevis. Westminster Cathedral Choir. 1987. (CD)
Palestrina: Missa Pro Defunctis. Chanticleer. Elatus. 2006. (CD)
Heavenly Harmonies: William Byrd/Thomas Tallis. Stile Antico. Harmonia Mundi. 2008. (CD). This recording includes music by the Anglican composer, Thomas Tallis.
The Tallis Scholars Sing William Byrd. Gimell UK. 2007. (CD)
Hans Leo Hassler: Cantate Domino; Motets and Organ Works. CPO Records. 2001.CD.

Lutheran
Music of the Reformation. Himmlische Cantores. Bayern 4 Klassik. 2007 (CD). Includes music by Martin Luther.
Martin Luther: Deutsche Liedmesse (German Hymn Mass.) Westfällische Kantorei. Cantate. 1996. (CD)
Praetorius: Mass for Christmas Morning. Gabrieli Consort and Players. Musical Heritage Society. 1994 (CD)
Schütz: German Requiem; The Seven Words of Jesus Christ on the Cross. Alsfelder Vokalensemble, Himlische Cantorey. Naxos. 2004. (CD)

Dietrich Buxtehude: Sacred Cantatas. Arcadia Ensemble. Naxos. 2004. (CD)

Reformed (Calvinist)
Psaumes et Chansons de la Reforme. Ensemble Clément Janequin. Harmonia Mundi. 1998. (CD) Sung in French.
Psalms of the French Reformation. Ensemble Claude Goudimel. Naxos. 1994. (CD) Sung in French.

English
All Goodly Sports: Music of Henry VIII. Chandos Early Music. 1998 (CD)
Royal Lewters: Music of Henry VIII and Elizabeth I's Lutenists. Harmonia Mundi Fr. 2003. (CD)
Purcell: Dido and Aeneas. Tavener Choir, Tavener Players. Chandos. 1992
Purcell: Songs and Airs. Emma Kirkby. L'oiseau Lyre. 2007. (CD)

Chapter 19
Music at the Court of Louis XIV. The Concentus Musicus. Vanguard Classics. 2004. (CD)
Jean-Baptiste Lully: Ballet Music for the Sun King. Arcadia Baroque Ensemble. Naxos. 2000. (CD)
Jean Philippe Rameau: Ballet Suites. European Union Baroque Orchestra. Naxos. 2005. (CD)
Antonio Vivaldi: The Four Seasons (Le Quattro Stagioni, Op. 8 Nos 1-4). The English Concert. Archiv. 1990. (CD)
Tartini: Violin Concertos. Ariadne Daskalakis and the Cologne Chamber Orchestra. Naxos. 2007. (CD)
J.S. Bach: Actus Tragicus. Cantus Cölln. Harmonia Mundi Fr. 2000. (CD)
Bach: The Four Great Toccatas and Fugues. E. Power Biggs. Sony. 1990. (CD)

Timeline

B.C.—The World Before Christ

50,000 B.C.	Paleolithic (Old Stone) Age
10,000	Neolithic (New Stone) Age
5000–4000	The development of the World's first civilization in Mesopotamia
4000	Beginning of Egyptian civilization
4000–2000	The invention of writing
1700	Abraham, the father of Israel
1300	Exodus of Israel from Egypt
1000	David, king of Israel
961	Solomon becomes king of Israel
586	Fall of Jerusalem to Nebuchadnezzar, king of Babylon
509	Founding of the Roman Republic
323	Death of Alexander the Great
44	Assassination of Julius Caesar
37	Augustus, first Roman emperor
	Herod the Great becomes king of Judea
ca. 6–4	Birth of Jesus Christ
4	Death of Herod the Great

A.D.—Anno Domini ("In the Year of the Lord")

A.D. 6	Judea becomes a Roman province
14	Death of Augustus Caesar; Tiberius becomes emperor
ca. 28–30	Death and resurrection of Jesus Christ
	Pentecost, the birth of the Church

ca. 34–36	Death of St. Stephen, the First Martyr
	Conversion of St. Paul the Apostle
37	Caligula becomes emperor
41	Claudius becomes emperor
54	Nero becomes emperor
58	Paul the Apostle arrested in Jerusalem
68	Great Fire in Rome
	Martyrdom of Sts. Peter and Paul in Rome
	Death of Nero
71	Capture of Jerusalem by the Romans and destruction of the Jerusalem Temple
96	Nerva becomes emperor—first of the "Good Emperors"
ca. 98–100	Death of St. John the Apostle
116	Revolt of the Jews in Cyprus, Rhodes, and the cities of Egypt and North Africa
132	Bar Kochba revolt in Palestine
135	Romans crush Bar Kochba revolt, and Emperor Hadrian forbids Jews to enter Jerusalem
ca. 155	Persecution against Christians in Asia Minor; martyrdom of St. Polycarp
180	Death of Marcus Aurelius, last of the "Good Emperors"
ca. 230	Death of Tertullian
254	Death of Origen
260	Gallienus issues an edict of toleration of Christians
284	Diocletian becomes emperor
303	Beginning of the Great Persecution under Diocletian
305	Diocletian resigns as emperor
311	Emperor Galerius issues Edict of Toleration of Christians
312	Constantine defeats Maxentius at the Battle of the Milvian Bridge
313	Emperors Constantine and Licinius issued Edict of Milan
324	Constantine becomes sole ruler of the empire
	Constantine moves the imperial capital to Constantinople
325	First Ecumenical Council at Nicaea
328	St. Athanasius becomes archbishop of Alexandria

337	Death of Constantine
367	Athanasius of Alexandria compiles the canon of Sacred Scripture
373	Death of Athanasius of Alexandria
374	St. Ambrose becomes archbishop of Milan
378	The Goths destroy the Roman army at Adrianople; Emperor Valens killed
379	Theodosius I made Augustus of the eastern empire
	Death of St. Basil the Great
381	Second Ecumenical Council of Chalcedon
386	Baptism of St. Augustine of Hippo
390	Emperor Theodosius I does public penance before Ambrose at Milan
391	Theodosius I makes the Christian Faith the official religion of the empire
395	Augustine consecrated bishop of Hippo
	Death of Theodosius I
397	Synod of Carthage adopts Athanasius' canon of Sacred Scripture
	Death of Ambrose
405	St. Jerome completes the translation of Scripture into Latin
409	Vandals and Suevi invade the Iberian Peninsula
410	Alaric the Visigoth sacks Rome
	Augustine begins writing the *City of God*
419	Second Synod of Carthage ratifies canon of Scripture
429	Genseric and the Vandals invade northern Africa
430	Death of Augustine
440	St. Leo the Great becomes pope
452	Pope Leo the Great turns the Huns back from Rome
455	Genseric the Vandal sacks Rome
	Death of Pope Leo the Great
	Visigoths establish a kingdom on the Iberian peninsula
476	Odoacer deposes Romulus Augustulus, the Western Roman emperor
481	Clovis becomes king of the Franks
488	Theodoric the Ostrogoth overthrows Odoacer and becomes king of Italy
496	Baptism of Clovis
511	Death of Clovis

524	Death of Boethius
527	Justinian I, the Great, becomes Roman emperor at Constantinople
529	St. Benedict founds a monastery at Monte Cassino
529–34	Justinian's reform of Roman law
532	*Nika* Revolt in Constantinople
533	Belisarius conquers the Vandal kingdom in North Africa for Justinian
535	Belisarius opens the Gothic War against the Ostrogoths in Italy
543	Death of Benedict of Nursia
554	End of the Gothic War in Italy
565	Death of Emperor Justinian I
585	Martyrdom of St. Hermenegild
589	King Reccared and the Visigothic nobility announce their conversion from Arianism to the Catholic Faith
590	Pope St. Gregory I, the Great, becomes pope
597	St. Augustine of Canterbury lands in England
604	Death of Pope Gregory the Great
610	Beginning of Muhammad's mission
622	Muhammad's *Hejira* ("Flight") from Mecca
624	Muhammad victorious at the Battle of Bedr
628	Emperor Heraclius defeats Chosroes II of Persia
630	Mecca surrenders to Muhammad
632	Death of Muhammad
634	Arab Muslims defeat the Byzantine Roman army in Palestine
635	Damascus falls to the Muslim Arabs
636	Muslim Arabs destroy the Byzantine Roman army at Yarmouk Jerusalem falls to the Muslim Arabs
637	Antioch falls to the Muslim Arabs
639	Muslim Arabs invade Egypt
641	Death of Emperor Heraclius
642	Alexandria falls to the Arabs
644	Rise of the Ummayad caliphs
664	The Synod of Whitby in Britain forbids Celtic rites in the English Church
679	Venerable Bede enters Jarrow Abbey in Northumbria

711	Muslim Arabs conquer the Visigothic kingdom in the Iberian Peninsula
716	St. Boniface, the Apostle of Germany, begins his missionary work
717	Leo the Isaurian becomes Roman emperor and breaks the Arab siege of Constantinople
ca. 718	Battle of Covadonga, the beginning of the Spanish Reconquest
722	The pope consecrates Boniface a bishop
726	Emperor Leo III, the Isaurian begins his iconoclastic campaign
732	Charles Martel drives the Muslims from France at the Battle of Tours
737	Death of Don Pelayo, king of Asturias
741	Death of Emperor Leo III, the Isaurian
747	Rise of the Abbasid caliphs
751	Pepin the Short crowned king of the Franks
754	Martyrdom of St. Boniface
762	Founding of Baghdad in Mesopotamia as the Abbasid capital
768	Charlemagne and Carloman crowned kings of the Franks
771	Death of Carloman; Charlemagne sole ruler of the Franks
772	Charlemagne opens his long war against the Saxons
774	Charlemagne appointed Patrician of Rome
778	Charlemagne invades Spain
785	Baptism of the Saxon king, Wittekind
787	Seventh Ecumenical Council condemns iconoclasm
793	Northmen (Vikings) sack and burn the monastery of Lindesfarne
800	Pope Leo III crowns Charlemagne Roman emperor
	End of Charlemagne's Saxon war
809–10	Muslims from North Africa conquer Sardinia and Corsica
813	Rediscovery of the tomb of St. James at Compostela, Spain
814	Death of Charlemagne
817	Partition of Aachen
842	The "Triumph of Orthodoxy" over Iconoclasm
845	Vikings reach Paris, but are driven back
846	Muslims invaders plunder Rome
866	Alfonso III becomes king of Asturias

886	Viking siege of Paris lifted by the approach of Emperor Charles the Bald
	Emperor Charles the Bald gives Normandy to the Viking leader, Rollo
899	Muslims conquer Sicily
910	Duke William of Aquitaine establishes the monastery of Cluny
914	Death of Alfonso III of Asturias
919	Henry the "Fowler" elected king of Germany
936	Death of King Henry the "Fowler"; Otto I elected king of Germany
940	Birth of Gerbert of Aurillac
955	Battle of Lech—the German King Otto I defeats the Magyars
956	Birth of Vladimir of Kiev
962	Pope John XII crowns Otto I Roman emperor
967	Hroswitha writes *Deeds of Otto*
973	Death of Emperor Otto I; his son, Otto II, becomes Roman emperor
980	Vladimir becomes Grand Prince at Kiev
982	Muslims and Byzantine Greeks defeat Otto II at Crotona in Italy
983	Death of Emperor Otto II; his son, Otto III becomes emperor
987	French feudal lords elect Hugh Capet king of France
988	Baptism of Vladimir of Kiev
996	Otto III crowned Roman emperor by the pope in Rome
999	Gerbert of Aurillac becomes pope as Sylvester II
1002	Pope Sylvester II recognizes St. Stephen as king of Hungary
	Death of Otto III
	Death of Hroswitha
1003	Death of Pope Sylvester II
1015	Death of St. Vladimir of Kiev
1036	Yaroslav the Wise becomes Grand Prince of all Russia
1054	Schism between the Churches of Rome and Constantinople
1059	Pope Nicholas II establishes the College of Cardinals
1060	St. Anselm enters the monastery of Bec
1066	Battle of Hastings; William the Conqueror becomes king of England
1072	Alfonso VI becomes king of León
1073	Hildebrand elected pope as Gregory VII

1075	St. Gregory VII forbids lay investiture
1076	Emperor Henry IV declares Pope Gregory VII deposed
	Pope Gregory VII excommunicates Henry IV
1077	Emperor Henry IV does penance at Canossa
1081	Birth of Suger
	Alfonso VI banishes Rodrigo Díaz, *El Cid Campeador*
1084	St. Bruno founds the monastery of Chartreuse
1085	Death of Pope St. Gregory VII
	Toledo surrenders to King Alfonso VI
1086	The Almoravids invade Spain
1087	Death of William the Conqueror
1088	Urban II becomes pope
1090	Birth St. Bernard of Clairvaux
1094	Rodrigo Díaz (*El Cid Campeador*) reconquers Valencia
	St. Anselm becomes archbishop of Canterbury
1095	At the Council of Clermont, Pope Urban II calls the First Crusade
1096	Peasants' Crusade
1097	Anselm leaves England after a controversy with King William Rufus
1098	Founding of the Abbey of Cîteaux
	Birth of St. Hildegard of Bingen
1099	Crusaders take Jerusalem and establish the kingdom of Jerusalem
	Death of *El Cid Campeador*
1100	Death of William Rufus; Henry I becomes king of England
	Death of Godfrey of Bouillon, prince of Jerusalem
	Baldwin, count of Edessa, becomes King of Jerusalem
1107	King Henry I of England abandons lay investiture and reconciles with Anselm
1108	Death of Alfonso VI
	Louis VI becomes king of France
1109	Death of Anselm of Canterbury
1113	Bernard enters the monastery at Cîteaux
1116	Bernard founds a monastery at Clairvaux
1119	St. Norbert founds his monastery at Prémontré

1122	Concordat of Worms
	Suger becomes abbot of Saint-Denis
	Birth of Eleanor of Aquitaine
1137	Death of Louis VI of France
	Louis VII becomes king of France
1144	The crusader kingdom of Edessa falls to the Turks
1145	Bernard of Clairvaux preaches the Second Crusade
1151	Death of Suger
1152	Frederick I "Barbarossa" becomes king of Germany
	Henry Plantagenet, duke of Anjou, marries Eleanor of Aquitaine
1153	Death of Bernard of Clairvaux
1154	Henry II Plantagenet becomes king of England
1164	King Henry II issues the Constitutions of Clarendon
1169	Saladin becomes sultan in Egypt
1170	Martyrdom of St. Thomas Becket
1173	Eleanor of Aquitaine encourages her sons to rebel against their father, Henry II
1176	Frederick Barbarossa makes peace with Pope Alexander III at Legnano
1179	Death of Hildegard of Bingen
1180	Philip II "Augustus" becomes king of France
1187	Jerusalem falls to Saladin and the Turks
1189	Death of King Henry II of England
	Richard the Lion-Heart becomes king of England
	King Richard the Lion-Heart, Emperor Frederick Barbarossa, and King Philip Augustus of France set out on the Third Crusade
1190	Death of Frederick Barbarossa
1191	Richard the Lion-Heart and Philip Augustus take Acre
1192	Richard the Lion-Heart and Saladin sign a treaty, ending the Third Crusade
1195	St. Dominic ordained a priest
1198	Innocent III becomes pope
	Pope Innocent III calls on the Cistercians to re-evangelize Languedoc and preach against the Cathars

1199	Death of Richard the Lion-Heart; John "Lackland" becomes king of England
1202	Beginning of the Fourth Crusade
	Crusaders take the Christian city of Zara
1204	Death of Eleanor of Aquitaine
	The Crusaders conquer Constantinople and establish a Latin empire there
1207	Pope Innocent III's legate, Peter of Castelnau, excommunicates Count Raymond VI of Toulouse
1208	Assassination of Peter of Castelnau
1209	Beginning of the Albigensian Crusade (continues to 1218)
	Pope Innocent III approves St. Francis of Assisi's Order of Friars Minor
1212	Opening of the Iberian Crusade
	Christian Spanish kings defeat the Moors at the Battle of Las Navas de Tolosa
	St. Clare joins St. Francis of Assisi
1213	Pope Innocent III calls for a crusade to regain Jerusalem
	Simon de Montfort defeats Raymond of Toulouse at the Battle of Muret and becomes lord of southern France
1215	King John "Lackland" forced to sign the *Magna Carta*
	Emperor Frederick II vows to undertake a crusade to regain Jerusalem
	Meeting of the Fourth Lateran Council
	Genghis Khan and the Mongols invade China
	Birth of St. Louis IX
1216	Innocent III approves St. Dominic's Order of Preachers
	Death of King John of England; Henry III becomes king
	Death of Innocent III
1217	Fernando III becomes king of Castile
	Genghis Khan leads the Mongols into Samarkand and Persia
1218	Crusaders under John of Brienne take Damietta in Egypt
1219	Francis of Assisi accompanies the Fifth Crusade to Egypt
1221	Philip Augustus seizes King John of England's French lands after defeating him in battle
	John of Brienne surrenders Damietta to the Turks

	Death of St. Dominic
	Birth of St. Bonaventure
1223	Death of Philip Augustus of France
	Louis VIII becomes king of France
	The Mongols defeat the Russians at the Battle of the Kalka River and lay waste to Kiev
1224	St. Francis receives the stigmata
1225	Birth of St. Thomas Aquinas
1226	Death of St. Francis of Assisi
	St. Louis IX becomes king of France
1227	Death of Genghis Khan; Ogodei succeeds him as khan
1228	Emperor Frederick II undertakes the Sixth Crusade
1229	The sultan of Egypt gives Acre, Bethlehem, and Jerusalem to Frederick, who becomes king of Jerusalem
1231	Pope Gregory IX establishes the Inquisition
1236	Reconquest of Cordoba by King Fernando III
1237	Batu Khan leads the Mongols into Russia
1240	Mongols under Batu invade Eastern Europe
	Alexander Nevski defeats the Swedes on the Neva River
1241	Death of Ogodei Khan
	The Mongols withdraw from Eastern Europe
1242	Alexander Nevski defeats the Teutonic Knights at Lake Peipus
	Batu Khan recognizes Alexander Nevski as "Grand Prince of All Russia"
1243	Bonaventure goes to the University of Paris
	Death of Alexander Nevski
1244	The Turks retake Jerusalem
	Thomas Aquinas enters the Dominican order
1246	Reconquest of Jaén by Fernando III
1248	Louis IX leads the Seventh Crusade
	Reconquest of Seville by Fernando III
1249	Louis IX takes Damietta, but is defeated and captured by the Turks
1250	Death of Emperor Frederick II
1254	Death of Emperor Conrad IV, the last Hohenstaufen emperor

1259	Thomas Aquinas begins teaching in the papal court
1261	The Greeks drive out the last Latin-French emperor from Constantinople
1263	Muslims destroy a Christian church in Nazareth
1265	The English barons capture Henry III in battle; Simon de Montfort governs England in his place
	Birth of Dante Alighieri
ca. 1265–68	In Rome, Thomas Aquinas begins work on the *Summa Theologica*
1267	Louis IX embarks on the Eighth Crusade
1268	Christian Antioch falls to the Turks
1270	Death of St. Louis IX, on crusade in North Africa
1272	Edward I "Longshanks" becomes king of England
	Thomas Aquinas goes to Naples to open a Dominican House of Studies
1273	Thomas Aquinas receives a vision of God; stops work on the *Summa Theologica*
1274	Death of Bonaventure
	Death of Thomas Aquinas
1277	Edward Longshanks forces Llewelyn ab Gruffyd of Wales to surrender; Edward proclaims his son "Prince of Wales"
1285	Philip IV "the Fair" becomes king of France
1291	Acre, the last Christian stronghold in the Holy Land, falls to the Turks
1294	Boniface VIII becomes pope
1295	Edward I calls the "Model Parliament"
1296	Edward I invades Scotland
	Pope Boniface VIII issues the bull *Clericis Laicos*
1297	William Wallace leads a Scottish rebellion against Edward I
1302	Pope Boniface VIII issues the bull *Unam Sanctam*
	Dante Alighieri banished from Florence
1303	Execution of William Wallace
	Pope Boniface VIII assaulted at Anagni
	Death of Pope Boniface VIII
1304	Birth of Francesco Petrarca, the "Father of Humanism"
1305	Clement V elected pope in France—beginning of the "Babylonian Captivity" of the papacy

1307	Death of Edward I "Longshanks" of England
1314	Robert I "the Bruce," king of Scotland, defeats the English at Bannockburn
	Death of King Philip the Fair
1321	Death of Dante Alighieri
1324	Birth of John Wycliffe
1325	Ivan I becomes prince of Moscow
1327	Edward III becomes king of England
1328	Philip V of Valois becomes king of France, end of the Capetian line of kings
	The metropolitan archbishop of Russia moves his seat from Vladimir to Moscow
1337	The Ottoman sultan, Orkhan, captures Nicomedia
1340	Beginning of the Hundred Years' War in France
1346	The English under Edward III defeat the French at Crécy
1347	First breakout of the Black Death
1356	Edward the Black Prince defeats the French at Poitiers
	The Ottoman Turks under Orkhan invade Greece
1359	Murad, the Ottoman sultan, establishes his capital at Adrianople in Greece
1360	Edward III and Charles the Dauphin sign the Treaty of Calais
1364	The Dauphin becomes king of France as Charles V
1369	Birth of John Hus
1374	Death of Francesco Petrarca
1377	Pope Gregory XI returns to Rome, end of the Babylonian Captivity of the papacy
	Death of King Edward III of England; Richard II becomes king
1378	Urban VI becomes pope
	French cardinals elect Clement VII, who rules from Avignon. Beginning of the "Great Schism"
	Grand Prince Dmitri Donskoi of Moscow defeats the Mongols at Kulikovo Pole

1380	John Wycliffe writes a treaty denying the doctrine of transubstantiation.
	Death of Charles V of France
	Charles VI becomes French king
1381	Peasants' revolt in England
1382	The Mongols sack Moscow
1384	Death of John Wycliffe
1387	Geoffrey Chaucer begins work on the *Canterbury Tales*
1389	Ottoman Turks defeat the Serbians at the Battle of Kosovo
	Death of Dmitri Donskoi; Vasili I becomes Grand Prince of Moscow; Vasili later refuses to pay tribute to the Mongols
1399	Henry IV of Lancaster becomes king of England; execution of Richard II
1400	Death of Geoffrey Chaucer
1409	The Council of Pisa elects John XXIII pope (antipope); the pope in Rome and the anti-pope in Avignon refuse to abdicate
1410	The archbishop of Prague orders the burning of Wycliffe's books
1411	John XXIII, the Pisan antipope, places Prague under an interdict
1412	Birth of St. Joan of Arc
1413	Henry V becomes king of England
1414	Opening of the Council of Constance
1415	Henry V defeats the French at Agincourt
	The Council of Constance deposes the Pisan antipope, John XXIII
	The Council of Constance condemns John Hus as a heretic; he is burned at the stake
1417	The Council of Constance deposes the Avignon antipope, Benedict XIII, and elects Martin V pope. End of the Great Schism
1420	Henry V and Charles VI sign the Treaty of Troyes
1422	Death of Henry V of England and Charles VI of France
	Charles the Dauphin proclaims himself King Charles VII of France
1423	Death of Avignon antipope, Benedict XIII
1425	Joan of Arc begins to hear heavenly voices
	John VIII Palaiologos becomes Byzantine emperor
	Death of Vasili I, grand prince of Moscow
1429	Joan of Arc drives the English from Orléans
	Charles VII anointed king of France at Reims

1430	Joan of Arc captured by the Burgundians
1431	Martyrdom of Joan of Arc
1432	Birth of Mahomet II, Ottoman Turkish sultan
1435	Charles VII of France convinces the duke of Burgundy to break his alliance with the English
1439	The Council of Florence brings about a temporary union between the Catholic and Orthodox Churches
1444	Birth of Botticelli
1447	Beginning of the reign of Nicholas V, the first "Renaissance pope"
1448	Turks defeat John Hunyadi and the Christian forces at Kosovo
1449	Birth of Lorenzo de Medici
1451	Birth of Christopher Columbus in Genoa
1452	Birth of Leonardo da Vinci
1453	End of the Hundred Years' War
	Constantinople falls to the Ottoman sultan, Mahomet II
1454	Johannes Gutenberg prints the *Türkenkalendar*
1455	Richard, duke of York, defeats the forces of King Henry VI at St. Alban's; beginning of the Wars of the Roses
	Death of Nicholas V
	Johannes Gutenberg prints the Bible
1456	John Hunyadi and St. John Capistran break the Turkish siege of Belgrade
	A commission appointed by Pope Callistus III declares the trial of Joan of Arc and its verdict null and void
1461	Louis XI, the "Spider King," becomes king of France
	Edward IV, of York, becomes king of England
1462	Ivan III, the Great, becomes Grand Prince of Moscow
1468	Death of Mahomet II
	Death of Johannes Gutenberg
1469	Isabel of Castile wed to Fernando of Aragon
	Birth of Niccolò Machiavelli
1471	Assassination of King Henry VI
1472	Ivan the Great marries Sophia Palaiologos, niece of the last Byzantine emperor. Because of this marriage, Ivan proclaims himself tsar and autocrat of Russia, and Moscow the "Third Rome."

1474	Isabel becomes queen of Castile and León
1475	Birth of Michelangelo di Buonarroti
1478	Novgorod surrenders to Ivan the Great
1479	Fernando III becomes king of Aragon
1480	Ivan the Great refuses to pay tribute to the Mongols
1481	Botticelli stays in Rome (until 1482)
1482	Fernando and Isabel begin the reconquest of Granada
1483	Birth of Raphael Santi
	Death of Louis XI of France
	Death of Edward IV of England; Edward V becomes king
	Murder of Edward V; Richard III becomes king of England
	Birth of Martin Luther
1485	Henry Tudor (Henry VII) defeats and kills King Richard II at Bosworth Field; end of the Wars of the Roses
	Christopher Columbus seeks backing from Queen Isabel of Castile-León
1487	Ivan the Great forces the khanate of Kazan to become a vassal state of Moscow
1491	Granada surrenders to Fernando and Isabel
	Birth of St. Ignatius de Loyola
1492	Death of Lorenzo de Medici
	Christopher Columbus lands in the Americas
1498	Vasco da Gama of Portugal reaches India after sailing around Africa
1501	Marriage of Catherine of Aragon to Prince Arthur of England
1502	Death of Prince Arthur
1505	Martin Luther enters the Augustinian monastery at Erfurt, in Saxony
1506	Pope Julius II lays the cornerstone for the new basilica of St. Peter in Rome
1507	Pope Julius II proclaims a Jubilee Indulgence to fund the construction of St. Peter's basilica
	Martin Luther ordained a priest
1509	Birth of John Calvin in Noyon, France
	Henry VIII becomes king of England; marries Catherine of Aragon
1510	Death of Botticelli

1512	Opening of the Fifth Lateran Council
1513	Leo X becomes pope
1516	Charles von Habsburg becomes king of Spain
	Death of King Fernando of Aragon
	Charles von Habsburg becomes King Charles I of all Spain
	Birth of Mary, daughter of Henry VIII and Catherine
1517	End of the Fifth Lateran Council
	Martin Luther publishes his 95 Theses
	Ignatius de Loyola enters the military
1519	Death of Leonardo da Vinci
	King Charles of Spain becomes Emperor Charles V
	Martin Luther's debate with Johannes Eck
	Ulrich Zwingli of Zürich condemns the sale of indulgences
1520	Death of Raphael Santi
	Martin Luther publishes *Appeal to the German Nobility*
	Pope Leo X excommunicates Martin Luther
	The Turks under Suleiman the "Magnificent" move against Poland-Lithuania
1521	The Diet of Worms condemns Martin Luther
	Belgrade falls to the Ottoman sultan, Suleiman I, the Magnificent
	Beginning of the first war between King Francis I of France and Emperor Charles V
	Henry VIII publishes *In Defense of the Seven Sacraments*; the pope proclaims him "Defender of the Faith"
	Birth of St. Peter Canisius
	Martin Luther's associate, Karlstadt, says Mass for the first time in German
	Ignatius de Loyola injured at Pampluna, undergoes a conversion
	Death of Leo X
1522	Martin Luther translates the New Testament into German
	Martin Luther returns to Wittenberg and ends the radical reforms there
	Suleiman I conquers Rhodes
	Ignatius de Loyola leads a life of prayer at Manresa

1523	Ulrich Zwingli orders the destruction of church decorations and religious art in Zürich
	Clement VII becomes pope
1525	King Francis I captured by the forces of Charles V at Pavia
	Zürich abolishes the Mass
	Martin Luther marries Katherine von Bora
1526	The Turks defeat the Hungarians at the Battle of Mohács
	Turkish sultan Suleiman captures Buda
	Henry VIII petitions Rome to annul his marriage to Catherine
	Francis I and Charles V sign the Peace of Madrid
	Pope Clement VII joins the Holy League of Cognac against the emperor
1527	Beginning of the second war between Charles V and Francis I
	Charles V's mercenaries sack Rome
	Death of Niccolò Machiavelli
1528	Ignatius de Loyola goes to the University of Paris
1529	Protest of Speier
	Francis I surrenders to Charles V
	Suleiman besieges Vienna, but withdraws
	Henry VIII makes Thomas More chancellor of England
1530	Pope Clement VII crowns Charles V emperor
	The Lutherans present the Augsburg Confession to the Diet of Augsburg
1531	Catholic Swiss cantons defeat Protestant cantons at the battle of Kappel; death of Ulrich Zwingli
	Lutheran German princes form the Schmalkaldic League
	Clement VII tells Henry VIII he may not marry Anne Boleyn
1532	The Peace of Nuremberg
	Suleiman marches against Vienna, but withdraws
	Henry VIII makes Thomas Cranmer archbishop of Canterbury
1533	Cranmer grants Henry an annulment and blesses his marriage with Anne Boleyn
1534	Martin Luther publishes the Old and New Testaments in German
	Paul III becomes pope and calls for an ecumenical council
	The English Parliament passes the Act of Supremacy

	Martyrdom of Bishop St. John Fisher
	Ignatius de Loyola and companions take vows of poverty, chastity, and obedience
1535	Martyrdom of St. Thomas More
1536	John Calvin publishes the first edition of the *Institutes of the Christian Religion*
	John Calvin arrives in Geneva
	Beginning of third war between Francis I and Charles V
	The ecumenical council postponed
	The English parliament orders the dissolution of the monasteries
	Pilgrimage of Grace
	Beheading of Anne Boleyn
1537	Formation of the Society of Jesus
1538	John Calvin exiled from Geneva
	End of third war between Francis I and Charles V
1540	Pope Paul III approves the Society of Jesus
1541	John Calvin returns to Geneva and takes over the city's government
1542	Beginning of fourth war between Charles V and Francis I (allied with Suleiman)
	Pope Paul III establishes the Congregation of the Holy Office
	St. Francis Xavier lands in India
1544	Francis I surrenders to Charles V
1545	Opening of the first session of the Council of Trent
1546	Death of Martin Luther
	Emperor Charles V commences war against the Schmalkaldic League
1547	Charles V victorious over the Schmalkaldic League
	Death of Henry VIII; Edward VI becomes king
	Pope Paul III suspends Council of Trent
	Francis Xavier goes to Japan
	Huguenots begin organizing churches in major French cities
1549	Revolt of English peasants against imposition of the *Book of Common Prayer*
	Peter Canisius makes his Jesuit profession.

1551	Henry II of France forms league with German Lutheran princes against Charles V
	Pope Julius III opens the second session of the Council of Trent
1552	Henry II occupies territories in the western part of the empire
	Close of the second session of the Council of Trent
	Geneva proclaims John Calvin's *Institutes* "a holy doctrine which no man might speak against"
	Death of Francis Xavier
	Peter Canisius goes to Vienna
1553	Death of Edward VI; Mary becomes queen of England
1554	Charles V gives over the leadership of the empire to Ferdinand, archduke of Austria
	Queen Mary formally restores the Church of England to the Catholic Church
1555	Religious Peace of Augsburg—*cuius regio, eius religio*
	Peter Canisius publishes his "Short Catechism"
1556	Charles V abdicates; Philip II becomes king of Spain
	Death of Ignatius de Loyola
	Execution of Thomas Cranmer
1558	Death of Charles V
	Death of Queen Mary; Elizabeth I becomes queen of England
1559	St. Pius V becomes pope
	Mary, Queen of Scots, married to Francis II of France
	French Huguenots form a national church
1560	Death of King Francis II of France
	Mary, Queen of Scots, returns to Scotland from France
	Charles IX becomes king of France
1561	Huguenots slaughter Catholics at Montpellier
1562	Pope Pius V opens the third and last session of the Council of Trent
	Duke of Guise slaughters Huguenots at Vassy; beginning of first war between French Catholics and the Huguenots
1563	End of the Council of Trent
	St. Charles Borromeo consecrated archbishop of Milan
	End of first war between Catholics and Huguenots

1564	Death of Michelangelo
	Pope Pius V approves the acts of the Council of Trent
	Death of John Calvin
1565	Charles Borromeo begins his reform of the archdiocese of Milan
1566	Death of Suleiman the Magnificent
	Selim II becomes Ottoman sultan
1567	Beginning of the second war between Catholics and Huguenots in France
	Murder of Henry Stuart, Lord Darnley, husband to Mary, Queen of Scots
1568	Mary, Queen of Scots, flees to England; Elizabeth I has her arrested
1570	Pope Pius V excommunicates Elizabeth I
	Queen Catherine de Medici allows Huguenots freedom of religion; end of the second Catholic-Huguenot war
1571	The Ottoman Turks conquer Cyprus
	The Christian fleet defeats the Turks at Lepanto
1572	Henry de Bourbon becomes king of Navarre
	St. Bartholomew's Day Massacre
1576	Beginning of third war between Catholics and Huguenots in France
	Death of King Charles IX of France; Henry III becomes king of France
1580	End of the third war between French Catholics and Huguenots
1582	The English college at Douay (Reims) publishes an English translation of the Bible
1584	Death of Charles Borromeo
1585	Birth of Armand-Jean du Plessis de Richelieu
1587	Execution of Mary, Queen of Scots
1588	The destruction of the Spanish Armada
	Assassination of Henry de Guise
1589	Assassination of King Henry III, the last Valois king of France
	Henry de Bourbon becomes King Henry IV of France; beginning of the Bourbon dynasty
1593	Henry IV of France becomes Catholic
1597	Death of Peter Canisius
1598	Henry IV signs the Edict of Nantes with the Huguenots
1599	Birth of Oliver Cromwell

1603	Death of Elizabeth I
	James I Stuart (James V of Scotland) becomes king of England
1605	Richelieu becomes bishop of Luçon
1607	Founding of Jamestown in Virginia
1610	Assassination of Henry IV of France
	Louis XIII becomes king of France
1611	Publication of the Authorized (King James) Version of the Bible by King James I of England
1612	Matthias von Habsburg becomes Roman emperor and king of Bohemia
1618	Protestant Bohemians rise in revolt against Emperor Matthias and King Ferdinand of Bohemia
	The Defenestration of Prague—beginning of the Thirty Years' War
1619	Death of Emperor Matthias
	Ferdinand II elected Roman emperor
1620	English Separatists form a colony at Plymouth in Massachusetts
	Protestant Bohemian army defeated at White Mountain in Bohemia
1622	King Louis XIII of France renews the Edict of Nantes
	Tilly and the Catholic League defeat the Protestants at Höchst
	Richelieu is made a cardinal
1623	End of the Bohemian revolt
1624	Louis XIII makes Cardinal Richelieu prime minister of France
1625	King Christian IV of Denmark invades Germany
	Death of James I of England (James V of Scotland)
	Charles I becomes king of England, Scotland, and Ireland
1626	Wallenstein defeats Mansfeld at Dessau
	After two defeats at the hands of Tilly, Christian IV withdraws from Germany
1627	Richelieu and Louis XIII lay siege to Huguenot La Rochelle
1628	Charles I signs the Petition of Right
	Puritans found a colony at Salem in Massachusetts
1629	Richelieu, Louis XIII, and the Huguenots sign the Peace of Alais
	Emperor Ferdinand II issues the Edict of Restitution
	Charles I dissolves Parliament

1630	King Gustavus Adolphus of Sweden invades Germany
1631	Cardinal Richelieu agrees to fund Gustavus Adolphus's war against the empire
	Burning of Magdeburg
	Gustavus Adolphus defeats Tilly at Breitenfeld
1632	The Swedes defeat Tilly on the Lech River; death of Tilly
	Battle of Lützen; Gustavus Adolphus killed
1634	Assassination of Wallenstein
	Imperial troops destroy the Swedes at Nördlingen
	King Charles I of England forces seaport towns to pay "ship money"
1635	France declares war on the empire and Spain
1636	Spanish forces nearly take Paris and invade southern France
1637	Death of Emperor Ferdinand II
	Ferdinand III elected Roman emperor
	Charles I forces Scottish churches to use the English *Book of Common Prayer*
1638	Scottish Covenanters rebel against Charles I
	Birth of Louis XIV of France
1639	The Pacification of Benwick ends first Covenanters war
	Charles I summons the "Short Parliament"
1640	Portugal rebels against Philip IV of Spain
	Charles I dissolves Parliament
	Covenanters defeat Charles I's army in northern England
	Charles I summons the "Long Parliament"
1641	Charles I orders the execution of Lord Stafford
	Parliament issues the Grand Remonstrance against Charles I; beginning of the Great Rebellion
1642	Royalists defeat the Parliamentarian army at Edgehill
	Death of Cardinal Richelieu
	Cardinal Mazarin becomes French prime minister
1643	The French defeat the Spanish at Rocroi
	Opening of peace talks between the empire and France and Sweden
	Death of Louis XIII of France

	Louis XIV becomes king of France
	Parliament signs "solemn league and covenant" with the Covenanters
1644	Parliamentarians and Covenanters defeat Royalists at Marston Moor
1645	Oliver Cromwell given command of the "New Model" army
	Oliver Cromwell's Ironsides defeat Royalists at Naseby
1646	Swedes and French occupy Bavaria
	Charles I surrenders to Parliament
1647	Charles I escapes from Parliament's custody
1648	The Peace of Westphalia ends the Thirty Years' War
	Royalist Scottish army invades England; defeated by Oliver Cromwell
	Charles I surrenders to Parliament
1649	Execution of Charles I
	Oliver Cromwell invades Ireland
1651	Oliver Cromwell's army defeats Charles II's Scottish forces at Worcester
1653	Oliver Cromwell dissolves the Rump and Barebone's Parliaments
	Oliver Cromwell proclaimed Lord Protector of England, Scotland, and Ireland
1658	Death of Oliver Cromwell
1659	End of the war between France and Spain
1661	Charles II crowned king of England and Ireland
	Parliament enacts the Clarendon Code
	Death of Cardinal Jules Mazarin
1662	Charles II marries Catherine of Braganza
1665	Death of Philip IV of Spain
	Charles II becomes king of Spain
	Beginning of Louis XIV's war to seize the Spanish Netherlands (the "War of Devolution")
1668	End of the War of Devolution
1671	James Stuart becomes Catholic
1672	Charles II issues, and rescinds, the Declaration of Indulgence
	Beginning of Louis XIV's war against Holland (the "Franco-Dutch War")
1673	Parliament enacts the Test Act
1678	End of the Franco-Dutch War

1679	Charles II vetoes the Exclusion Act
1681	Charles II dissolves Parliament
1682	Founding of Louisiana by La Salle
1685	Death of Charles II of England, Scotland, and Ireland
	James II becomes king of England, Scotland, and Ireland
1686	Formation of the League of Augsburg
1687	James II issues the Declaration of Indulgence
1688	The "Glorious Revolution" drives James II from England
	Louis XIV invades the Rhenish Palatinate—beginning of the War of the League of Augsburg
1689	The "Glorious Revolution"—Parliament crowns William III and Mary II king and queen of England, Scotland, and Ireland
	James II goes into exile in France
1694	Death of Queen Mary II of England, Scotland, and Ireland
1697	The Treaty of Ryswick ends the War of the League of Augsburg
1700	Death of King Charles II; end of Spain's Habsburg dynasty
	Philip of Anjou (the first Bourbon in Spain) becomes king of Spain
1701	Death of James II
	Beginning of the War of the Spanish Succession (Queen Anne's War)
1702	Death of King William III of England, Scotland, and Ireland
	Anne becomes queen of England, Scotland, and Ireland
1704	The Duke of Marlborough defeats the French at Blenheim
	Death of Bishop Jacques-Bénigne Bossuet
1706	The French driven out of Italy
1707	Articles of Union form the United Kingdom of Great Britain
1709	The French driven from the Netherlands
1711	Archduke Charles von Habsburg becomes German emperor
1713	The Peace of Utrecht ends the War of the Spanish Succession
1714	Death of Queen Anne of Great Britain
	George I becomes king of Great Britain; beginning of the House of Hanover
1715	Death of Louis XIV; Louis XV becomes king of France
1726	Cardinal Fleury becomes prime minister of France

1727	Death of George I of Great Britain
	George II becomes king of Great Britain
1733	France begins a war with Austria in Poland (the "War of the Polish Succession")
1738	End of the War of the Polish Succession
1743	Death of Cardinal Fleury
1760	Death of George II of Great Britain
	George III becomes king of Great Britain
1774	Death of King Louis XV of France
	Louis XVI becomes king of France

Pronunciation Guide

Please note: the pronunciation of italicized words is the pronunciation of the word as it occurs in the original language.

Introduction

Assyria	ah-SEER-ree-ah
Babylon	BA-bih-lohn
Dacia	DAY-she-ah *or* DAY-sha
Dardanelles	DAR-dah-nells *or* dard-n-ELLS
Euphrates	yu-FRAYT-ees
Illyricum	il-ir-EYE-kum
Mesopotamia	meh-so-po-TAY-mee-ah

Chapter 1

Caiaphas	KAI-ah-fuhs
Herod Archelaus	HAIR-ehd ar-keh-LAY-ehs
Pharisees	FAYR-eh-sees
Sadducees	SAD-dyeh-sees

Chapter 2

Aelia Capitolina	AY-lee-ah Cah-pee-toh-LEE-nah
Aeneas	ay-NEE-ehs
Aeneid	ay-NEE-id
Agrippina	ag-reh-PEE-neh
Arbiter Elegantiae	AR-bee-tayr eh-leh-GAHN-tsee-ay
Boadicea	boh-AD-eh-see-eh
Commodus	cah-MOHD-duhs
caligae	CAH-lee-gay
Diocletian	dye-eh-KLEE-shen
Domitian	doh-MISH-en
Flavius Vespasian	FLAY-vee-ehs veh-SPAY-zhen
Gaius Julius Caesar Octavianus	GAI-oos YOO-lee-oos CHAY-sahr ohk-tah-vee-AH-noos
Kniva	KNEE-vah
Marcus Cocceius Nerva	MAR-koos koh-CHAY-oos NAYR-vah
Marcus Lepidus	MAR-kehs LEH-pi-dehs
Marcus Ulpius Trajanus	MAR-koos OOL-pee-oos trah-YAH-noos
Nicomedia	ni-ko-MAY-dee-ah
Niš	nish
Petronius Arbiter	peh-TROH-ni-ehs AR-bi-ter
Poppaea Sabina	pop-PAY-ah sah-BEE-nah
Praetorian	preh-TOR-i-ehn
Ptolomy	TAH-leh-mee
Publius Aelius Hadrianus	POO-blee-oos AY-lee-oos hah-dree-AH-noos
Sassanids	SAH-sah-nids
Severii	seh-VAYR-ee-ee
Suetonius	swe-TOH-ni-ehs
Tiberius Claudius Nero	tee-BAYR-ee-oos KLOW-dee-oos NAYR-oh
Titus Aurelius Antoninus	TEE-toos ow-RAY-lee-noos ahn-TOH-nee-noos
Trajan	TRAY-jehn
Vindabona	vin-dah-BOH-nah

Chapter 3

Adversus Haereses	ahd-VAYR-soos HAIR-eh-says
Constantius	con-STAHN-tsi-ehs
Danube	DAN-yube
Decius	DEE-shee-ehs
en toutoi nika	en TOO-toy NEE-kah
Gallienus	gahl-lee-EHN-ehs
gnosis	NOH-sis
Gnosticism	NAHS-ti-sih-sem
in hoc signo vinces	in hoke SEE-nyo VIHN-ches
Irenaeus	ir-eh-NAY-ehs
Marcion	MAHR-see-on
Origen	OR-ih-jen
Plato	PLAY-toh

Chapter 4

Adeodatus	ah-DAY-oh-DAH-tehs
Alaric	AHL-eh-rik
Caesarea	sehs-ah-REE-ah
Constantius	con-STAN-tsi-ehs
De Civitate Dei	day chi-vi-TAH-tay DAY-ee
Gratian	GRAY-shee-ehn *or* GRAY-shen
Hispania	hi-SPAH-nee-ah
homoousios	hoe-moe-OO-see-ohs
Manicheanism	ma-ni-KEE-an-ism
Nicomedia	ni-koh-MAY-dee-eh
Pelagianism	peh-LAY-jee-an-ism
Pelagius	peh-LAY-jee-ehs
Stilicho	STIL-ih-koh
Tagaste	tah-GAH-steh
traditores	trah-dee-TOR-ays
vulgaris	vool-GAR-ees
Wulfilas	wool-FEE-lahs

Chapter 5

Amalasuntha	ah-mah-lah-SOON-ta
Austrasia	ah-STRAY-zha
Avitus	ah-VEE-tehs
Baëtica	bah-EH-ti-keh
Boethius	boh-EE-thee-ehs
Byrhtwold	BEERGHT-wohld
Cartagena	kar-tah-GAYN-eh
Clodovech	KLOH-doe-vekh
Clotilde	kloh-TIL-deh
Ecija	eh-SEE-ha
Freia	FRY-ah
Fulgentius	ful-JEN-tsi-oos
Genseric	GEN-seh-rik
Hermanreich	HAIR-mahn-reykh
Merovech	MAYR-oh-vekh
Neustria	NOO-stree-eh
Odoacer	OHD-eh-way-sehr
Reccared	REHK-kar-ehd
Severianus	seh-VAYR-ee-AHN-oos
Tiw	tyoo
Willebrord	VIL-leh-brohrd
Wodin	VOH-dihn

Chapter 6

Anicii	ah-NIH-see-ee
Athalaric	ah-thal-AR-ik
Codex Justinianus	COH-deks YOO-stih-nee-AHN-oos
Hagia Sophia	HA-gee-ah soh-FEE-ah
Leoghaire	Leary
Missale Romanum	mih-SAHL-ay roh-MAH-noom
Nika	NEE-kah
servus servorum Dei	SAYR-voos sayr-VOHR-oom DAY-ee
Symmachus	SIM-mah-kehs

Chapter 7

Abu Bakr	AH-boo BAHK-ehr
Abu Obeida	AH-boo oh-BAY-deh
Amr ibn al-As	AH-mir ihb-uhn al-AHS
Chosroes	khaws-ROH-ehs
Ctesiphon	TES-eh-fahn
djinn	jin
emir	eh-MEER
hajj	hajh
Hasan	ha-SAHN

Hejra	HEH-jra
Hegira	heh-JEER-ah
Kaaba	KAH-bah
Khalid ibn al-Walid	KAH-lihd ihb-uhn al-wah-LIHD
Khazar	KAH-zar
Jibr al-Tarik	JIH-ber al-tah-REEK
jihad	jih-HAD
Mu'awiya	moo-AH-wee-uh
Omar ibn al-Khattab	OH-mahr IHB-ehn al-KHAT-tahb
Quraish	koo-RAYSH
Quran	koo-RAHN
salat	seh-LAHT
Scipio	SIP-pi-oh
Sharia	shah-REE-ah
shehada	sheh-HAH-dah
Shiite	SHEE-ite
sura	SUR-eh
Ummayyad	oo-MY-yahd
Yarmouk	YAR-muk

Chapter 8

Aachen	AH-khen
Abd-ar-Rahman	AB-dar RAH-mehn
Al-Andalus	al-AHN-dah-loos
Alcuin	AL-kwehn
Bede	beed
Boniface	BON-ih-fehs
Bordeaux	BOR-doh
Ceolfrith	CHOL-frid
Childerich	khil-DEHR-ikh
Cova Dominica	COH-vah doh-MIHN-ih-cah
Eudo	YU-doh
iconodule	eye-CON-oh-dyul
Isauria	i-SOR-ee-ah
La Janda	la HAN-dah
Loire	leh-WAH
Maslama	mahs-LAH-mah
missi dominici	MIS-see doh-mih-NEE-chee
Mozarabes	moh-ZAHR-ah-behs
Pelayo	peh-LYE-oh
reconquista	ray-cohn-KEES-tah
Suleiman	su-LAY-mahn
Toulouse	too-LOOZ
Weser	VEH-sehr
Wittekind	WIHT-teh-kint

Chapter 9

dux	dooks
feod	FEH-ohd
fief	feef
jarl	yarl
Garonne	geh-ROHN
Homme	ohm
Lige	LEE-geh
Nantes	nahnt

Chapter 10

Aurillac	aw-ree-(Y)AK
Benefice	BEH-neh-fis
Cluny	KLOO-nee
Cîteaux	SIH-toe
Gerbert	jer-BAIR
Hroswitha	hrohs-VIHT-ah
Kunigunde	koo-nih-GOON-deh
Legnano	leh-YNA-noh
Mainz	meynts
Prémontré	preh-MOHN-tray
Reims	rinz
Regula	REH-goo-lah
Worms	vohrms

Chapter 11

Aragon	ahr-eh-GOHN
Al-Quadir	al KAH-dehr
Anjou	AHN-joo
Asturias	ah-STOOR-ee-ahs
Bayeux	BAY-yoo
Caen	kahn
Capet	kah-PAY *or* KAH-pet
Chrétiens de Troyes	KRAY-tyen deh trwah
Clairvaux	KLAIR-voh

Clara Vallis	KLAH-rah VAHL-lees
Coeur de Lion	KEHRD-ehl-EE-ohn
Conquistador	kohn-KEES-tah-dohr
Cur Deus Homo	coor DAY-oos (H)OH-moh
El Cid Campeador	el SID cahm-peh-ah-DOHR
Fontevrault	FOHN-teh-vroh
Galicia	gah-LEE-see-ah
Guienne	gwee-YEN
Iberia	ee-BAYR-ee-ah *or* eye-BIR-ih-yeh
Lanfranc	LAHN-frahnk
León	leh-OHN
Navarre	NAH-vahr
Notre Dame	NOH-treh DAHM
Oviedo	oh-vee-AY-tho
Pallium	PAH-lee-oom
Parlement de Paris	PAHR-leh-mahnt day PAH-ree
Parzival	PAHR-tsi-fal
Plantagenet	plahn-TAH-jeh-net *or* plahn-tah-jeh-NAY
Poitiers	PWAH-tyay
Poitou	pwah-TOO
Provençal	PRAHV-ehn-sehl
Saint-Denis	sahnt DEH-nee
Sainte-Chapelle	sahnt SHAH-pel
Santiago Matamoros	SAHN-tee-AH-goh mah-tah-MOH-rohs
Sephardim	seh-FAHRD-ehm
Suger	SOO-zhay
Toledo	toh-LAY-doh
Walter von der Vogelweide	VAHL-tehr fohn dehr FOH-gehl-VYE-deh
Wolfram von Eschenbach	VOHL-frahm fohn ESH-ehn-bakh

Chapter 12

Acre	AHK-reh
Adhemar of Le Puy	AHD-heh-mahr of leh PWEE
Béziers	BAYZ-yay
Brienne	BREE-en
Carcassonne	kar-keh-SOHN
Cathari	kah-TAR-ee
Cerro de los Olivares	SAYR-oh day lohs oh-lee-VAHR-es
Godfrey of Bouillon	GAHD-free of boo-YOHN
Guy	gee
Guzman	goo-ZMAHN
Kerullarios	kehr-ool-LAHR-ee-ohs
Krak de Chevalliers	krahk deh sheh-VAHL-lee-ay
Languedoc	LAHN-geh-dohk
Languedoui	LAHN-geh-dway *or* LAHN-geh-dwee
Lusignan	LOO-see-ynan
marquis	mahr-KEE
Miramammolin	mir-ah-MAHM-moh-lin
Outremer	OO-tray-mehr
Saladin	SAL-eh-den

Chapter 13

Albertus Magnus	ahl-BAYR-toos MAH-ynoos *or* MAHG-noos
Bologna	boh-LOHN-yah
Benavente	beh-neh-VEN-tay
Chartres	shart-rah
Diego d'Azevado	dee-AY-goh dah-zeh-VAH-doh
Doctor Angelicus	DOHK-tohr ahn-JEH-lee-koos
Domini canes	DOH-mee-nee KAH-nehs
Domingo Muñoz	doh-MEEN-goh MOO-nyohz
Fratres Minores	FRAH-trehs mee-NOHR-ays
Genghis Khan	jen-geh-SKAHN *or* gen-geh-SKAHN
Laon	lahn
Montpellier	MOHN-peh-lyay
Ogodei Khan	ah-geh-DIE kahn
Orvieto	or-vee-AYT-oh
polyphony	peh-LIF-eh-nee
quadrivium	kwa-DRIH-vee-oom
schola	SKOH-lah
Subedei	suh-beh-DIE
Teano	tay-AH-noh
Summa Theologica	SOO-mah tay-oh-LOH-jee-kah
trivium	trih-vee-oom
Ubeda	oo-BAY-dah

Yangtze	YAN-see

Chapter 14

Anagni	ah-NAH-nyee
Avignon	AH-veen-yon
Clericis Laicos	CLAIR-ee-chees LAH-ee-kohs
Dante Alighieri	DAHN-tay al-eg-YEHR-ee
Ghibelline	GIB-eh-leen
Guelf	gwelf
Guillaume de Nogaret	GEE-yohm deh NOH-gah-ray
Hohenstaufen	hoh-hen-SHTOW-fen
Opus Evangelicum	OH-poos eh-vahn-JHEL-ee-coom
Prague	prahg
Prignano	pree-YNAN-oh
Trialogus	tree-ah-LOH-goos

Chapter 15

Armagnacs	AHR-mehn-yak
Bayonne	BAY-ohn
Bertrand du Guesclin	BAYR-trahn doo GEH-klahn
Bordeaux	BOHR-doh
Calais	KAH-lay
Cauchon	COH-shon
Crécy	KREH-see
D'Alençon	DAHL-ahn-sohn
Dauphin	DAW-fen
Dnieper	NEE-pehr
duma	DOO-mah
fleur-de-lis	FLUHRD-ehl-ees
Gloucester	GLOS-tehr
Guienne	GWEE-yen
Jehanne	zhahn
Khazar	KAH-zar
Lancaster	LAN-cehs-tehr
Pechenegs	PECH-eh-negs
Polovsty	poh-LOHV-stee
Ponthieu	POHN-tyoo
Ravnoapostol	RAH-vnoh-ah-post-tol
Riazan	ree-eh-ZAHN
Rostov	ros-TOF
Sluys	sloys
Tver	teh-VEHR
Valois	VAL-wah
veche	VEH-keh

Chapter 16

Aquinas	ah-KWY-nehs
Botticelli	baht-eh-CHEL-lee
Enrique	ehn-REE-kay
Filippo Bruneschelli	fih-LEE-poh bruh-neh-SKEL-lee
Gutenberg	GOO-ten-bayrg
Machiavelli	mah-kee-ah-VEL-lee
Michelangelo di Buonarroti	mih-kehl-AHN-jeh-loh dee bwon-eh-ROH-tee
Medici	MED-ih-chee
Palaiologos	pah-lay-oh-LOH-gohs
Parentucelli	pahr-ehn-too-CHEL-lee
Rannuccio Farnese	rahn-NOO-chee-oh fahr-NAY-say

Chapter 17

(*Note:* the ü in German words has no exact equivalent in English. In pronouncing ü, the tongue should be so placed as to make a long *e* sound, with the lips rounded as if one were pronouncing a long *u*.)

benefice	BEH-neh-fiss
Boleyn	buh-LIN
Curia	KUHR-ee-ah
Douai-Reims	DOO-ay REEMS or DOO-ay RINZ
Exsurge Domine	eks-SOOR-jay DOH-mee-nay
Francisco Jiménez	frahn-SIS-coh hih-MEH-nez
Fribourg	FREE-boorg
Jagiello	yah-GAY-woh
Karlstadt	KARL-shtadt
Pico della Mirandola	PEE-koh DEHL-lah meer-AHN-doh-lah

Schmalkald	SHMAL-kalt
Schwyz	shveitz
sola fide	SOH-lah FEE-day
sola gratia	SOH-lah GRAH-tsee-ay
sola scriptura	SOH-lah skrip-TOO-rah
Speier	SHPIE-ehr
Tridente	trih-DEHN-tay
Ulrich Zwingli	OOL-rikh TSVEEN-glee
Unterwalden	OON-tehr-VAHL-den
Uri	OO-ree
Wartburg	VAHRT-boorg
Wittenberg	VIT-ten-bayrg
Zug	tsoog
Zürich	ZÜR-eekh
Zwickau	TSVIHK-ow

Chapter 18

(Note: the ö in German words has no exact equivalent in English. In pronouncing ö, the tongue should be so placed as to make a short *i* sound, with the lips rounded as if one were pronouncing a long *o* sound.)

Alais	AH-lays
Alcalá	ahl-kah-LAH
Antoine de Bourbon	AHN-twahn deh BUHR-bohn
Benedictus Deus	beh-nay-DEEK-toos DAY-oos
Borromeo	bohr-oh-MAY-oh
Bourges	buhrzh
Ciudad Real	SEE-oo-dahd RAY-ahl
Guise	GEE-zeh
Höchst	hökhst
Huguenot	HYOO-geh-not
Iñigo	IH-nyeh-goh
Jeanne d'Albret	zhehn DAHL-bray
Laetare Jerusalem	LAY-tah-ray yeh-ROO-sah-lem
Lech	lekh
Montauban	MAHNT-oh-bahn
Nantes	nahnt
Nijmegen	NEYE-may-vehn
Nördlingen	NÖRD-leen-gehn
Richelieu	RISH-ehl-yoo
Rocroi	roh-KRWA
Tserclaes	TSAYR-klays
Ultramontane	UHL-trah-mahn-TAYN
Wallenstein	VAHL-ehn-shteyn
Xavier	ZAH-vee-ehr

Chapter 19

André-Hercule de Fleury	ahn-DRAY-EHR-cool deh FLEH-ree
Après moi, le deluge	ah-preh mwa, leh DEL-yoozh
château	SHAH-toh
châteaux	SHAH-tohz
Connaught	KAHN-oht
Drogheda	DROI-eh-dah
Durham	DUHR-em
Franche-Comté	fransh-COHM-tay
Jean-Baptiste Colbert	zhahn-bah-TEEST KOHL-behr
Le Roi Soleil	leh rwah soh-LEY
L'etat c'est moi	LAY-tah seh mwa
Jacques-Bénigne Bossuet	zhak BEH-neen BOH-sway
Killiekrankie	kil-ee-KRAN-kee
René-Robert Cavelier	reh-NAY-ROH-behr cah-VEHL-lee-ay
Ryswick	RIZ-wik
Strasbourg	STRAHS-boorg
Utrecht	OO-trekht
Versailles	vehr-SYE
Whig	hwig
Worcester	WUS-ter

California Social Studies Standards Correlation Chart

Note: All California Standards not met in this National Edition are to be offered as Supplemental Studies Units at no charge.

Course	Standard No.	Standard Text	Page Correlation	Notes/Supplements	Supplement Page Correlation
Light to the Nations: Part 1					
World History and Geography: Medieval and Early Modern Times	7.1.1	Study the early strengths and lasting contributions of Rome (e.g., significance of Roman citizenship; rights under Roman law; Roman art, architecture, engineering, and philosophy; preservation and transmission of Christianity) and its ultimate internal weaknesses (e.g., rise of autonomous military powers within the empire, undermining of citizenship by the growth of corruption and slavery, lack of education, and distribution of news).	29, 39-41, 42-43, 47-67, 69 87, 89-97, 103-113, 123-128, 130-136, 139-146, 150-165		
World History and Geography: Medieval and Early Modern Times	7.1.2	Discuss the geographic borders of the empire at its height and the factors that threatened its territorial cohesion.	22, 47-48, 84, 103-109, 115 116, 130-133, 139, 143-145		
World History and Geography: Medieval and Early Modern Times	7.1.3	Describe the establishment by Constantine of the new capital in Constantinople and the development of the Byzantine Empire, with an emphasis on the consequences of the development of two distinct European civilizations, Eastern Orthodox and Roman Catholic, and their two distinct views on church-state relations.	81-87, 89-95, 123-126, 128, 139-146		
World History and Geography: Medieval and Early Modern Times	7.2.1	Identify the physical features and describe the climate of the Arabian peninsula, its relationship to surrounding bodies of land and water, and nomadic and sedentary ways of life.	170-171, 180		
World History and Geography: Medieval and Early Modern Times	7.2.2	Trace the origins of Islam and the life and teachings of Muhammad, including Islamic teachings on the connection with Judaism and Christianity.	172-176		
World History and Geography: Medieval and Early Modern Times	7.2.3	Explain the significance of the Qur'an and the Sunnah as the primary sources of Islamic beliefs, practice, and law, and their influence in Muslims' daily life.	173	Explain that Sunnah refers the social, religious, and legal customs practiced by the Muslims. Second only to the Koran, it is a source of Shariah, or Muslim law.	
World History and Geography: Medieval and Early Modern Times	7.2.4	Discuss the expansion of Muslim rule through military conquests and treaties, emphasizing the cultural blending within Muslim civilization and the spread and acceptance of Islam and the Arabic language.	173-174, 178-191, 197		
World History and Geography: Medieval and Early Modern Times	7.2.5	Describe the growth of cities and the establishment of trade routes among Asia, Africa, and Europe, the products and inventions that traveled along these routes (e.g., spices, textiles, paper, steel, new crops), and the role of merchants in Arab society.	170-171, 181-189, 203-204	Confirm product knowledge by asking students what they know about e.g., spices, textiles, paper, steel, new crops, products traveled along these routes.	
World History and Geography: Medieval and Early Modern Times	7.2.6	Understand the intellectual exchanges among Muslim scholars of Eurasia and Africa and the contributions Muslim scholars made to later civilizations in the areas of science, geography, mathematics, philosophy, medicine, art, and literature.	185, 203-204, 348-349		
World History and Geography: Medieval and Early Modern Times	7.3.1	Describe the reunification of China under the Tang Dynasty and reasons for the spread of Buddhism in Tang China, Korea, and Japan.		China Supplement	5, 8-9
World History and Geography: Medieval and Early Modern Times	7.3.2	Describe agricultural, technological, and commercial developments during the Tang and Sung periods.		China Supplement	9, 10-11
World History and Geography: Medieval and Early Modern Times	7.3.3	Analyze the influences of Confucianism and changes in Confucian thought during the Sung and Mongol periods.		China Supplement	11-12, 13-14
World History and Geography: Medieval and Early Modern Times	7.3.4	Understand the importance of both overland trade and maritime expeditions between China and other civilizations in the Mongol Ascendancy and Ming Dynasty.	342-344	China Supplement	13-17
World History and Geography: Medieval and Early Modern Times	7.3.5	Trace the historic influence of such discoveries as tea, the manufacture of paper, woodblock printing, the compass, and gunpowder.	344	China Supplement	11
World History and Geography: Medieval and Early Modern Times	7.3.6	Describe the development of the imperial state and the scholar-official class.		China Supplement	2, 3-5, 10, 14

California Social Studies Standards Correlation Chart

Note: All California Standards not met in this National Edition are to be offered as Supplemental Studies Units at no charge.

Course	Standard No.	Standard Text	Page Correlation	Notes/Supplements	Supplement Page Correlation
World History and Geography: Medieval and Early Modern Times	7.4.1	Study the Niger River and the relationship of vegetation zones of forest, savannah, and desert to trade in gold, salt, food, and slaves; and the growth of the Ghana and Mali empires.		Africa Supplement	2-3, 4, 8-13
World History and Geography: Medieval and Early Modern Times	7.4.2	Analyze the importance of family, labor specialization, and regional commerce in the development of states and cities in West Africa.		Africa Supplement	4-5, 8-12
World History and Geography: Medieval and Early Modern Times	7.4.3	Describe the role of the trans-Saharan caravan trade in the changing religious and cultural characteristics of West Africa and the influence of Islamic beliefs, ethics, and law.		Africa Supplement	4-5, 9-11
World History and Geography: Medieval and Early Modern Times	7.4.4	Trace the growth of the Arabic language in government, trade, and Islamic scholarship in West Africa.		Africa Supplement	9, 10-11
World History and Geography: Medieval and Early Modern Times	7.4.5	Describe the importance of written and oral traditions in the transmission of African history and culture.		Africa Supplement	9, 10
World History and Geography: Medieval and Early Modern Times	7.5.1	Describe the significance of Japan's proximity to China and Korea and the intellectual, linguistic, religious, and philosophical influence of those countries on Japan.		Japan Supplement	1, 3-4
World History and Geography: Medieval and Early Modern Times	7.5.2	Discuss the reign of Prince Shotoku of Japan and the characteristics of Japanese society and family life during his reign.		Japan Supplement	3, 4
World History and Geography: Medieval and Early Modern Times	7.5.3	Describe the values, social customs, and traditions prescribed by the lord-vassal system consisting of shogun, daimyo, and samurai and the lasting influence of the warrior code in the twentieth century.		Japan Supplement	5 – 7
World History and Geography: Medieval and Early Modern Times	7.5.4	Trace the development of distinctive forms of Japanese Buddhism.		Japan Supplement	3-4, 7
World History and Geography: Medieval and Early Modern Times	7.5.5	Study the ninth and tenth centuries' golden age of literature, art, and drama and its lasting effects on culture today, including Murasaki Shikibu's Tale of Genji.		Japan Supplement	4-5, 8-9
World History and Geography: Medieval and Early Modern Times	7.5.6	Analyze the rise of a military society in the late twelfth century and the role of the samurai in that society.		Japan Supplement	2, 5-7
World History and Geography: Medieval and Early Modern Times	7.6.1	Study the geography of the Europe and the Eurasian land mass, including its location, topography, waterways, vegetation, and climate and their relationship to ways of life in Medieval Europe.	117, 221, 230-231, 269, 285, 299, 316		
World History and Geography: Medieval and Early Modern Times	7.6.2	Describe the spread of Christianity north of the Alps and the roles played by the early church and by monasteries in its diffusion after the fall of the western half of the Roman Empire.	117-129, 146-150, 159-162, 198-202, 243-264		
World History and Geography: Medieval and Early Modern Times	7.6.3	Understand the development of feudalism, its role in the medieval European economy, the way in which it was influenced by physical geography (the role of the manor and the growth of towns), and how feudal relationships provided the foundation of political order.	219-240, 243, 246, 248		
World History and Geography: Medieval and Early Modern Times	7.6.4	Demonstrate an understanding of the conflict and cooperation between the Papacy and European monarchs (e.g., Charlemagne, Gregory VII, Emperor Henry IV).	204-216, 222-223, 251-263, 301-302, 305-307, 309-310, 317-321, 359-361, 364-372, 389-407		
World History and Geography: Medieval and Early Modern Times	7.6.5	Know the significance of developments in medieval English legal and constitutional practices and their importance in the rise of modern democratic thought and representative institutions (e.g., Magna Carta, parliament, development of habeas corpus, an independent judiciary in England).	273-278, 280-291, 315, 335		
World History and Geography: Medieval and Early Modern Times	7.6.6	Discuss the causes and course of the religious Crusades and their effects on the Christian, Muslim, and Jewish populations in Europe, with emphasis on the increasing contact by Europeans with cultures of the Eastern Mediterranean world.	295-323		
World History and Geography: Medieval and Early Modern Times	7.6.7	Map the spread of the bubonic plague from Central Asia to China, the Middle East, and Europe and describe its impact on global population.	374, 377		

California Social Studies Standards Correlation Chart

Course	Standard No.	Standard Text	Page Correlation	Notes/Supplements	Supplement Page Correlation
Light to the Nations: Part 1		Note: All California Standards not met in this National Edition are to be offered as Supplemental Studies Units at no charge.			
World History and Geography: Medieval and Early Modern Times	7.6.8	Understand the importance of the Catholic church as a political, intellectual, and aesthetic institution (e.g., founding of universities, political and spiritual roles of the clergy, creation of monastic and mendicant religious orders, preservation of the Latin language and religious texts, St. Thomas Aquinas's synthesis of classical philosophy with Christian theology, and the concept of "natural law").	123-129, 206-216, 228, 243-263, 275-276, 330, 332-342, 349-355, 359-377		
World History and Geography: Medieval and Early Modern Times	7.6.9	Know the history of the decline of Muslim rule in the Iberian Peninsula that culminated in the Reconquista and the rise of Spanish and Portuguese kingdoms.	197-198, 200-202, 268-272, 290, 309-312, 432-434		
World History and Geography: Medieval and Early Modern Times	7.7.1	Study the locations, landforms, and climates of Mexico, Central America, and South America and their effects on Mayan, Aztec, and Incan economies, trade, and development of urban societies.		Latin America Supplement	1-2, 2-6
World History and Geography: Medieval and Early Modern Times	7.7.2	Study the roles of people in each society, including class structures, family life, warfare, religious beliefs and practices, and slavery.		Latin America Supplement	3-6, 8-9
World History and Geography: Medieval and Early Modern Times	7.7.3	Explain how and where each empire arose and how the Aztec and Incan empires were defeated by the Spanish.		Latin America Supplement	3-6, 8-9, 7-10, 13-14
World History and Geography: Medieval and Early Modern Times	7.7.4	Describe the artistic and oral traditions and architecture in the three civilizations.		Latin America Supplement	3-6, 8-9
World History and Geography: Medieval and Early Modern Times	7.7.5	Describe the Meso-American achievements in astronomy and mathematics, including the development of the calendar and the Meso-American knowledge of seasonal changes to the civilizations' agricultural systems.		9-10 Latin America Supplement	
World History and Geography: Medieval and Early Modern Times	7.8.1	Describe the way in which the revival of classical learning and the arts fostered a new interest in humanism (i.e., a balance between intellect and religious faith).	414-418, 438-439		
World History and Geography: Medieval and Early Modern Times	7.8.2	Explain the importance of Florence in the early stages of the Renaissance and the growth of independent trading cities (e.g., Venice), with emphasis on the cities' importance in the spread of Renaissance ideas.	419, 439		
World History and Geography: Medieval and Early Modern Times	7.8.3	Understand the effects of the reopening of the ancient "Silk Road" between Europe and China, including Marco Polo's travels and the location of his routes.	344		
World History and Geography: Medieval and Early Modern Times	7.8.4	Describe the growth and effects of new ways of disseminating information (e.g., the ability to manufacture paper, translation of the Bible into the vernacular, printing).	431		
World History and Geography: Medieval and Early Modern Times	7.8.5	Detail advances made in literature, the arts, science, mathematics, cartography, engineering, and the understanding of human anatomy and astronomy (e.g., by Dante Alighieri, Leonardo da Vinci, Michelangelo di Buonarroti Simoni, Johann Gutenberg, William Shakespeare).	417, 420-422		
World History and Geography: Medieval and Early Modern Times	7.9.1	List the causes for the internal turmoil in and weakening of the Catholic church (e.g., tax policies, selling of indulgences).	443-447, 477, 479		
World History and Geography: Medieval and Early Modern Times	7.9.2	Describe the theological, political, and economic ideas of the major figures during the Reformation (e.g., Desiderius Erasmus, Martin Luther, John Calvin, William Tyndale).	446-452, 454-457, 463-464, 477-478		
World History and Geography: Medieval and Early Modern Times	7.9.3	Explain Protestants' new practices of church self-government and the influence of those practices on the development of democratic practices and ideas of federalism.	453-457, 477-478, 529-531		
World History and Geography: Medieval and Early Modern Times	7.9.4	Identify and locate the European regions that remained Catholic and those that became Protestant and explain how the division affected the distribution of religions in the New World.	465-466, 471-477		
World History and Geography: Medieval and Early Modern Times	7.9.5	Analyze how the Counter-Reformation revitalized the Catholic church and the forces that fostered the movement (e.g., St. Ignatius of Loyola and the Jesuits, the Council of Trent).	483-494, 514-517		

California Social Studies Standards Correlation Chart

Note: All California Standards not met in this National Edition are to be offered as Supplemental Studies Units at no charge.

Course	Standard No.	Standard Text	Page Correlation	Notes/Supplements	Supplement Page Correlation
Light to the Nations: Part 1					
World History and Geography: Medieval and Early Modern Times	7.9.6	Understand the institution and impact of missionaries on Christianity and the diffusion of Christianity from Europe to other parts of the world in the medieval and early modern periods; locate missions on a world map.		China, Japan, Africa, and Latin America Supplements	
World History and Geography: Medieval and Early Modern Times	7.9.7	Describe the Golden Age of cooperation between Jews and Muslims in medieval Spain that promoted creativity in art, literature, and science, including how that cooperation was terminated by the religious persecution of individuals and groups (e.g., the Spanish Inquisition and the expulsion of Jews and Muslims from Spain in 1492).	203-4, 268-72, 347	We do not deal with the Spanish Inquisition, but we treat the Medieval Inquisition—the inquisition established by the Church and the paradigm for all subsequent European inquisitions, including the Spanish. As it is the paradigm, students can best understand the nature of the Inquisition as an institution through the Medieval Inquisition. The chief difference between the Medieval and Spanish Inquisitions is that the former was an ecclesiastical institution while the latter was a state institution which the Church approved (at times reluctantly) and in which Spanish churchmen participated.	
World History and Geography: Medieval and Early Modern Times	7.10.1	Discuss the roots of the Scientific Revolution (e.g., Greek rationalism; Jewish, Christian, and Muslim science; Renaissance humanism; new knowledge from global exploration).	414-418, 438-439	Scientific Revolution Supplement	
World History and Geography: Medieval and Early Modern Times	7.10.2	Understand the significance of the new scientific theories (e.g., those of Copernicus, Galileo, Kepler, Newton) and the significance of new inventions (e.g., the telescope, microscope, thermometer, barometer).	519-520	Scientific Revolution Supplement	
World History and Geography: Medieval and Early Modern Times	7.10.3	Understand the scientific method advanced by Bacon and Descartes, the influence of new scientific rationalism on the growth of democratic ideas, and the coexistence of science with traditional religious beliefs.		Scientific Revolution and Age of Enlightenment Supplements	
World History and Geography: Medieval and Early Modern Times	7.11.1	Know the great voyages of discovery, the locations of the routes, and the influence of cartography in the development of a new European worldview.	434-438	China, Japan, Africa, and Latin America Supplements	
World History and Geography: Medieval and Early Modern Times	7.11.2	Discuss the exchanges of plants, animals, technology, culture, and ideas among Europe, Africa, Asia, and the Americas in the fifteenth and sixteenth centuries and the major economic and social effects on each continent.		China, Japan, Africa, and Latin America Supplements	China: 5, 8-10, 13-15; Japan: 9-10; Africa: 11-12, 13-15;
World History and Geography: Medieval and Early Modern Times	7.11.3	Examine the origins of modern capitalism; the influence of mercantilism and cottage industry; the elements and importance of a market economy in seventeenth-century Europe; the changing international trading and marketing patterns, including their locations on a world map; and the influence of explorers and map makers.		Capitalism Supplement	1-4, 7
World History and Geography: Medieval and Early Modern Times	7.11.4	Explain how the main ideas of the Enlightenment can be traced back to such movements as the Renaissance, the Reformation, and the Scientific Revolution and to the Greeks, Romans, and Christianity.		Scientific Revolution and Age of Enlightenment Supplements	1-6, 12-13, 15-18, 21-24, 31-34
World History and Geography: Medieval and Early Modern Times	7.11.5	Describe how democratic thought and institutions were influenced by Enlightenment thinkers (e.g., John Locke, Charles-Louis Montesquieu, American founders).		Age of Enlightenment Supplement	26-30, 34-37
World History and Geography: Medieval and Early Modern Times	7.11.6	Discuss how the principles in the Magna Carta were embodied in such documents as the English Bill of Rights and the American Declaration of Independence.	522, 533-537		